Strategic Marketing Decisions
2006–2007

The Chartered
Institute of Marketing

Strategic Marketing Decisions

2006–2007

Isobel Doole and Robin Lowe

ELSEVIER

AMSTERDAM • BOSTON • HEIDELBERG • LONDON • NEW YORK • OXFORD
PARIS • SAN DIEGO • SAN FRANCISCO • SINGAPORE • SYDNEY • TOKYO

Butterworth-Heinemann is an imprint of Elsevier

Butterworth-Heinemann is an imprint of Elsevier
Linacre House, Jordan Hill, Oxford OX2 8DP, UK
30 Corporate Drive, Suite 400, Burlington, MA 01803, USA

First edition 2006

British Library Cataloguing in Publication Data
A catalogue record for this book is available from the British Library

Library of Congress Cataloging-in-Publication Data
A catalog record for this book is available from the Library of Congress

ISBN-13: 978-0-7506-8013-4
ISBN-10: 0-7506-8013-X

For information on all Butterworth-Heinemann publications
visit our website at books.elsevier.com

Typeset by Integra Software Services Pvt. Ltd, Pondicherry, India
www.integra-india.com
Printed and bound in Italy
06 07 08 09 10   10 9 8 7 6 5 4 3 2 1

Working together to grow
libraries in developing countries

www.elsevier.com | www.bookaid.org | www.sabre.org

ELSEVIER   BOOK AID
            International   Sabre Foundation

Contents

Appendices

Index

Preface
welcome to the CIM coursebooks

An introduction from the academic development advisor

The authoring team, Elsevier Butterworth-Heinemann and I have all aimed to rigorously revise and update the coursebook series to make sure that every title is the best possible study aid and accurately reflects the latest CIM syllabus. This has been further enhanced through independent reviews carried out by CIM.

We have aimed to develop the assessment support to include some additional support for the assignment route as well as the examination, so we hope you will find this helpful.

The authors and indeed Senior Examiners in the series are commissioned for their CIM course teaching and examining experience, as well as their research into specific curriculum-related areas and their wide general knowledge of the latest thinking in marketing.

We are certain that you will find these coursebooks highly beneficial in terms of the content and assessment opportunities and a study tool that will prepare you for both CIM examinations and continuous/integrative assessment opportunities. They will guide you in a logical and structured way through the details of the syllabus, providing you with the required underpinning knowledge, understanding and application of theory.

The editorial team and the authors wish you every success as you embark upon your studies.

Karen Beamish
Academic Development Advisor

How to use these coursebooks

Everyone who has contributed to this series has been careful to structure the books with the exams in mind. Each unit, therefore, covers an essential part of the syllabus. You need to work through the complete coursebook systematically to ensure that you have covered everything you need to know.

Each unit of this coursebook contains a selection of the following standard elements:

- o *Learning objectives* tell you what you will be excepted to know, having read the unit.
- o *Syllabus references* outline what part of the syllabus is covered in the module.
- o *Study guides* tell you how long the unit is and how long its activities take to do.

- ○ *Questions* are designed to give you practice – they will be similar to those you get in the exam.
- ○ *Answers* (at the end of the book) give you a suggested format for answering exam questions. *Remember* there is no such thing as a model answer – you should use these examples only as guidelines.
- ○ *Activities* give you a chance to put what you have learned into practice.
- ○ *Debriefings* (at the end of the book) shed light on the methodologies involved in the activities.
- ○ *Hints and tips* are tips from the Senior Examiner, examiner or author, and are designed to help you avoid common mistakes made by previous candidates and give you guidance on improving your knowledge base.
- ○ *Insights* encourage you to contextualize your academic knowledge by reference to real-life experience.
- ○ *Key definitions* highlight and explain the key points relevant to that module.
- ○ *Definitions* may be used for words you must know to pass the exam.
- ○ *Summaries* cover what you should have picked up from reading the unit.
- ○ *Further study* provides details of recommended reading in addition to the coursebook.

While you will find that each section of the syllabus has been covered within this text, you might find that the order of some of the topics has been changed. This is because it sometimes makes more sense to put certain topics together when you are studying, even though they might appear in different sections of the syllabus itself. If you are following the reading and other activities, your coverage of the syllabus will be just fine, but don't forget to follow up with trade press reading!

About MarketingOnline

Elsevier Butterworth-Heinemann offers purchasers of the coursebooks free access to MarketingOnline (www.marketingonline.co.uk), our online support engine for the CIM marketing courses. On this site you can benefit from:

- ○ Fully customizable electronic versions of the coursebooks enabling you to annotate, cut and paste sections of text to create your own tailored learning notes.
- ○ The capacity to search the coursebook online for instant access to definitions and key concepts.
- ○ Useful links to e-marketing articles, provided by Dave Chaffey, Director of Marketing Insights Ltd and a leading UK e-marketing consultant, trainer and author.
- ○ A glossary providing a comprehensive dictionary of marketing terms.
- ○ A frequently asked questions (FAQs) section providing guidance and advice on common problems or queries.

Using MarketingOnline

Logging on

Before you can access MarketingOnline you will first need to get a password. Please go to www.marketingonline.co.uk and click on the registration button where you will then find registration instructions for coursebook purchase. Once you have got your password, you will need to log on using the onscreen instructions. This will give you access to the various functions of the site.

If you have specific queries about using MarketingOnline then you should consult our fully searchable FAQs section, accessible through the appropriate link in the top right hand corner of any page of the site. Please also note that a *full user guide* can be downloaded by clicking on the link on the opening page of the website.

unit 1
introduction to strategic marketing decisions

Learning objectives

Strategic marketing decisions need to be made throughout the marketing planning process as well as at critical times in response to the competitive challenges facing the company. At these times, strategic marketing decision-making may not necessarily be within the formal planning or budgeting cycle, but as part of the iterative process of strategy development. In this module, the development of a sustainable competitive advantage is viewed as a continual process requiring a constant stream of strategic marketing decisions that are individually sound and that collectively contribute to the marketing planning process and add value for shareholders as well as other stakeholders.

In this unit you will:

1.1   Examine the role of life cycles in strategic decisions to manage competitive advantage across global, international and domestic markets.

1.2   Examine the influence of market position on strategy and performance.

1.3   Critically appraise the changing dimensions of strategic decisions made to sustain competitive advantage in today's global markets.

1.4   Assess how product/market/brand/customer life cycles can be managed strategically across markets.

1.5   Examine the role of competitive relationships and how organizations compete to achieve customer preference.

Having completed this unit, you will be able to:

○ Appraise a range of corporate and business visions, missions and objectives and the processes by which they are formulated, in the light of the changing bases of competitive advantage across geographically diverse markets.

○ Demonstrate the ability to develop innovative and creative marketing solutions to enhance an organization's global competitive position in the context of changing product, market, brand and customer life cycles.

This unit relates to the statements of practice

Bd.1 Promote a strong market orientation and influence/contribute to strategy formulation and investment decisions.

Gd.1 Select and monitor channel criteria to meet the organization's needs in a changing environment.

Key definitions

A stakeholder – is anyone who has an interest in or an impact on an organization's activities.

Strategic marketing decisions – are the decisions made as part of the iterative process of strategy development. A company makes these decisions in response to the changing dimensions of the marketing environment in order to ensure a sustainable competitive advantage. Strategic marketing decisions are part of the problem-solving process and are required throughout the process of analysis, strategic choice and implementation.

A sustainable competitive advantage – is the achievement of a company to develop a superior, differentiated position in the marketplace which creates superior value for customers, shareholders and stakeholders and which they are able to maintain over a period of time.

Hard-edged marketing – is the process by which marketing managers ensure they make decisions that create superior value for all stakeholders, especially customers and shareholders and prove the value of marketing's contribution to business by the use of meaningful marketing metrics.

Market/competitive life cycles – describe the cyclical nature of the demand and competitive activity in markets. Life cycles are based on the notion that during the lifetime of a market, it passes through a number of distinct phases, each of which has particular characteristics with regard to the nature of competitor activity, the demand for a product and the type of strategies that are appropriate to meet the distinct characteristics of the phase.

Study Guide

This coursebook is critical to the overall understanding of the Strategic Marketing Decisions syllabus. It will help you to develop the knowledge and skills necessary to contribute to strategic marketing decisions in the formulation of a competitive marketing strategy. The end point of the module is a set of strategic decisions for the organization that may be built into a marketing or business plan. The module builds on the skills you have developed in the Marketing Planning module at Professional Diploma in Marketing and the Analysis & Evaluation module at Professional Postgraduate Diploma in Marketing. The knowledge and skills you develop in studying this module will be then taken forward into implementation in the Managing Marketing Performance module. This study guide incorporates an examination of the relevant knowledge and understanding of strategic decisions within domestic, international and global contexts. The knowledge and skills you acquire can then be applied in the Strategic Marketing in Practice module.

The Strategic Marketing Decisions module examines how, in this dynamic environment, competitive advantage might be developed through strongly differentiated positioning, which is exploited in a cost-effective manner. Its emphasis is on where and how the organization competes, and in doing this, it highlights the strategic marketing significance of brands, innovation, alliances and relationships and e-marketing. Whilst the syllabus is divided into five elements, as a whole it incorporates two important building blocks:

1. The development of the capabilities within an organization to make effective strategic marketing decisions.
2. The development of innovative marketing solutions that enhance an organization's competitive position in its chosen markets whilst delivering superior value to the customers and to the shareholders of the company.

This study guide focuses on the key components of the syllabus that will enhance your ability to develop a more innovative approach to the strategic development of an organization, which is committed to building a competitive advantage which in turn will create added value for customers, shareholders and other stakeholders. Table 1.1 gives you an indication of the learning outcomes and the units in which they are covered. However, it is necessary for participants to study the guide in an integrated way and view the complete strategic decision process of identifying new marketing opportunities, areas for innovation and value creation in an organization as an iterative and continuous process. As you go through the guide, we will help you apply the lessons of good practice discussed through the activities and questions which you should try to apply to your own organizations as well as others that operate in different contexts from your own.

In each unit, we have tried to direct the reader to the main components of the syllabus and incorporated questions and activities to help develop your learning. The core textbook for the syllabus, which accompanies this workbook, is

Doole and Lowe (2005) *Strategic Marketing Decisions in Global Markets*, Thomson Learning, 184480 142 x.

To fully study the concepts and material of the syllabus, you do need to read this textbook, to ensure you have the necessary in-depth knowledge you will require for the examination.

The CIM examination for the Strategic Marketing Decisions is 50 per cent case study based and integrative in nature. In this coursebook, we have included exam-type questions to help you progress through the book. We have also included a full, specimen examination paper at the end of the coursebook.

Table 1.1 Learning outcomes/unit guide

Learning outcomes	Study units/syllabus reference
Appraise a range of corporate and business visions, missions and objectives and the processes by which they are formulated, in the light of the changing bases of competitive advantage across geographically diverse markets	Units 1, 2, 3, 5, 6, 7
Identify, compare and contrast strategic options and critically evaluate the implications of strategic marketing decisions in relation to the concept of 'shareholder value'	Units 2, 5, 7, 10, 11, 12
Evaluate the role of brands, innovation, integrated marketing communications, alliances, customer relationships and service in decisions for developing a differentiated positioning to create exceptional value for the customer	Units 3, 4, 8, 9, 10, 12
Demonstrate the ability to develop innovative and creative marketing solutions to enhance an organization's global competitive position in the context of changing product, market and brand and customer life cycles	Units 1, 2, 4, 6, 7, 8, 9, 10
Define and contribute to investment decisions concerning the marketing assets of an organization	Units 4, 6, 8, 9, 11
Demonstrate the ability to re-orientate the formulation and control of cost-effective competitive strategies, appropriate for the objectives and context of an organization operating in a dynamic global environment	Units 5, 6, 10, 11, 12

The above is meant only to be indicative. It is important that students understand that the learning outcomes at the Postgraduate Professional Diploma and particularly for Strategic Marketing Decisions are integrative in nature and are developed by building skills across the units of this coursebook. They are not necessarily outcomes of any individual units. The module requires the student to develop the ability to synthesize material from across the units and apply it to the context given in the examination question.

Introduction

To develop the capabilities within an organization to make effective strategic marketing decisions, a company needs to have the ability to understand the changing dimensions of the market in which it operates and the impact this has on its competitive advantage (syllabus element 1). It needs to be able to challenge traditional thinking and develop an innovative culture through learning and knowledge management in order to re-orientate and re-formulate competitive strategies, in order to sustain its advantage in the market (syllabus element 2). Finally, it must have the ability to appraise strategic marketing decisions and assess strategic options with regard to the potential return on any investments made (syllabus element 5).

To sustain a competitive advantage over time, companies need to develop innovative marketing solutions that enhance an organization's competitive position whilst delivering superior value to the customers and to the shareholders. In order to achieve, this a company must build its knowledge and understanding of the strategic issues involved in leveraging competitive capability across global markets (syllabus element 3) and it needs the skills and the capabilities necessary to manage a marketing portfolio across global markets (syllabus element 4). In creating innovative marketing solutions, a firm must also ensure it has the necessary budgetary and planning control systems and appropriate performance measurement systems to ensure that in the execution of strategies a positive contribution is made to shareholder value (syllabus element 5).

The development of strategies that build upon and leverage an organization's competitive position globally is fundamental to the achievement of a sustainable competitive advantage. The challenges of doing this across a spectrum of fast moving and, geographically and culturally varied markets in an effective manner represent a significant intellectual challenge and require the development and refinement of decision-making skills. In this unit, we examine how strategic marketing decisions need to be taken at critical times in response to the competitive challenges facing companies and not necessarily only within the formal planning or budgeting cycle. As said earlier, in this syllabus, it is recognized that the development of a marketing strategy is a continuous process, requiring a constant stream of strategic decisions to be made that are individually sound and that collectively contribute to the marketing strategy planning process of an organization.

Question 1.1

What capabilities do you think a company needs to make effective strategic decisions?

Changing dimensions of competitive advantage

The emergence of a more open world economy, the globalization of consumer tastes and the unabated construction of global electronic highways all increase the interdependency and interconnections of nations' economies across the globe. The marketplace is becoming increasingly complex, as some markets become more saturated and fragmented, the competitive pressures increase and survival and growth become more difficult to sustain. The need for managers to develop the skills to respond to these pressures affects companies of all sizes.

The global marketing environment is becoming increasingly complex. Global wealth overall is increasing and this is again reflected in changing demand structures across markets. Increasing affluence and demand means that consumers are now actively seeking choices across the globe with the result that the competitive landscape is changing as companies compete to win the battle for disposable income. Commercial dynamism has seen nations across Asia; South America and Eastern Europe emerge as high growth economies and their companies increasingly seek new markets globally and so they themselves are emerging as powerful competitors in today's global markets.

The global marketplace is simultaneously becoming economically, culturally and technically interdependent through the consistent thrust in technological innovation. The Internet, in particular, is helping to level the playing field among large and small firms in business-to-business (B2B) and business-to-consumer (B2C) e-commerce. Information moves anywhere in the world at the speed of light and, what is becoming known as the global civilization is being facilitated by the convergence of long distance telecommunications, cuts in the cost of electronic processing and the growth of Internet business.

Question 1.2

What are the main environmental factors impacting on the way companies are now seeking a sustainable competitive advantage?

On the supply side, there is a trend towards globalization, seeking world standards for efficiency and productivity. This in itself has led to companies reconfiguring as they endeavour to realign themselves to better position themselves globally. In many industries, we have seen the rationalization and consolidation of global competitors. This means that in order to sustain a competitive advantage, companies cannot rely on historical data and simply extrapolate it to forecast the trends of the future. Nor can they simply assume that their competitors will behave in the way they have done so in the past. Changes in the environment and in the structure of competitor activity mean the basis on which companies compete has also changed and the competitive game has become harder to win. The performance of a company is determined by not only its own actions but also the actions and reactions of competitors, customers, governments and other stakeholders. As the environment becomes more complex, these have become much harder to predict and more difficult in themselves to manage.

The dimensions on which marketing managers achieved their competitive advantage used to be very much focused on the transaction itself. However, if companies are to sustain a competitive advantage in today's market, the focus has to be on the total integrated marketing effort delivering superior customer value in the market. Marketing, over the past decades, has evolved through several stages from the early days of transaction marketing through to the concept of value-based marketing. According to Doyle (2000) in doing this, marketing thinking has travelled through four stages:

1. *Transactional marketing* – Where the focus was on the actual exchange and building short-term profits for the company. The main performance indicator was sales volume and so marketing decisions were primarily concerned with enhancing the efficiency and effectiveness of that sale.
2. *Brand marketing* – In this stage, the focus was on building of the augmented product where value was built through the brand image and related product benefits. In brand marketing, customer loyalty is built by building an emotional relationship between the customer's lifestyle and the lifestyle built around the brand.
3. *Relationship marketing* – In relationship marketing, customer retention is the key strategic objective. It is based on the notion that profitability is sustained by building customer loyalty and so achieving customer retention. The focus is on getting existing customers to buy more and to keep them in the habit of buying the companies' products through loyalty schemes such as store cards and rewards for loyal customers.
4. *Value-based marketing (VBM)* – Recognizes the need for a totally integrated marketing effort that manages the whole of the marketing process to deliver customer value and so builds value for the shareholders of the company. Proponents of value-based marketing argue that to compete effectively a company needs to do more than build a brand, or build relationships – it has to build value. Thus, whilst relationships and brands are important, markets are changing the basis for competition and new types of competition are emerging which means that to achieve a sustainable competitive advantage companies need to offer a total value proposition to their customers.

Activity 1.1

What approach to achieving competitive advantage predominates in your company? What do you see as the strengths and weaknesses of the approach taken by your company in the way it has built its competitive advantage?

The concept of Value-based marketing (VBM) is examined in some depth in Unit 2 of this coursebook. In this unit what is important for you to understand in studying for this module is that, because of the changing dimensions of competitive advantage, in order to be successful, organizations need to put a great deal of effort into learning not just about their customers and competitors, but also into developing a detailed understanding of environmental factors. These will impact on their markets and the perceptions and expectations of their partners in their supply chain and other relationships they may need to form, to help them build a strategy which will deliver competitive advantage. In achieving this, strategic marketing decision-makers have now to deal with certain priorities which, according to Wilson and Gilligan (2004), are

- ○ The pace of change and the need for marketing managers to rapidly respond with innovative solutions with regard to products, services and marketing processes
- ○ Fragmented markets and the increasing need for customization to smaller targeted niches
- ○ The delivery of superior customer value as a basic ingredient of competitiveness
- ○ Information, market knowledge and the ability to learn as the premier source of competitive advantage
- ○ The strategic significance of new types of partnerships and new networks of relationships in the supply chain.

Insight

The county of Kent is often referred to as 'the garden of England', but as farming and the economics of energy production change, it could become the leaders in the creation of fuel from crops as an alternative to fossil fuels.

After discussions with Countess Sondes of the Lees Court Estate in Kent, a long-time champion of non-food crops, the leader of the county council, Sir Sandy Bruce-Lockhart, is championing a proposal for a 'Global Centre for Non-Food Crops'. It has already been approved by the UK government and is being considered by the UN in New York, the Food and Agricultural Organization in Rome and the World Bank.

Worldwide, there are many initiatives to develop bio-fuels but Kent claims it has a strong agricultural base with research facilities and industrial links too. It will have to develop new partnerships and alliances if it wishes to progress this strategy.

Source: Adapted from D Sapsted, Garden of England may become global hothouse for fuel crops, *The Daily Telegraph*, 26 September 2005.

Firms, therefore, need to devote significant resources to building their knowledge capability on all these aspects to ensure a sustainable competitive advantage can then be based upon a genuine understanding. They also need to make sure these capabilities are then fed into the strategic marketing decision process of the company. You can read in some detail in Chapter 2 of the core textbook for this syllabus (Doole and Lowe [2005] *Strategic Marketing Decisions in Global Markets*): how the development of a learning organization underpins the development of these capabilities within an organization. In the following section, we will discuss the implications of the changing dimensions of competitive advantage on strategic marketing decision-making.

The changing dimensions of strategic marketing decisions

The challenges outlined mean it is now vital that marketing within companies takes on a much more strategic role and has a more prominent influence in the corporate strategic direction the company takes. The boundary lines between marketing and other function areas such as operations, finance and human resources are much more blurred as marketing takes this more strategic role within an organization. Anthony Brown of IBM (*Marketing Business*, December 2003) suggests there are two types of corporations, those with marketing departments and those with marketing souls.

> If companies are to have a marketing soul then strategic marketing decisions need to involve everyone in the company not just the marketing department and should be concerned with bringing together all the business processes that contribute to the design and development of the marketing offering to deliver superior value in the market. All of this has implications for a company's approach to strategic marketing decision making.

The need for innovative thinking

Senior marketing managers need not only the ability to develop problem-solving strategies but also the mindset that enables them to reinvent periodically the basis on which an organization can compete in response to changes in their markets. The challenges of the new competitive environment cannot be met if marketing decision-makers follow the same linear rational planning procedures that have been propagated in the last decades. The challenges in today's marketing environment require managers to be innovative and creative in their thinking if they are to build a sustainable competitive advantage.

Question 1.3

Explain what is meant by innovative and creative thinking? Why is such thinking important in strategic marketing decision-making?

The need to take a more strategic role

If marketing decision-makers are to take on a more strategic role, then they have a responsibility to show how the marketing decisions taken can deliver better revenue growth, more profit and increased customer satisfaction. In today's highly competitive marketplace, marketing managers are required to be much more accountable for their actions, show the cost-effectiveness of marketing tactics and show how marketing strategies add to the shareholder value of an organization. The concept of shareholder value will be examined in Unit 2.

The CIM firmly believes if marketing is to take on a more strategic role, it has to become 'hard edged'. This means marketing has to help companies make better decisions and become more influential in driving a business forward. 'Hard-edged marketing' is the process by which marketing managers ensure they make decisions that create superior value for all stakeholders, especially customers and shareholders, and prove the value of marketing's contribution to business by the use of meaningful marketing metrics. CIM research found that out of the top 20 companies in Fortune 500, only one, General Electric, had a chief marketing officer representing marketing at board level. One of the reasons for this, they feel, is the perception that the benefits of marketing activities are not measured in terms of profitability. Marketing managers, they argue, have a responsibility to make a demonstrable contribution to the success of the business. Thus, it is important for students of the Postgraduate CIM Diploma to show they understand that marketing does not operate in either a commercial or a creative vacuum. Strategic marketing decisions have to be related to organizational goals and the impact of marketing activities has to be judged against the organizations' key performance indicators.

The need to take a more strategic role at the board level of organizations has therefore focused the dimensions of strategic marketing decisions. Hard-edged marketing requires the application of robust marketing metrics to marketing decisions (see Units 11 and 12 of this coursebook) and it requires marketing decisions which deliver an effective strategy and a performance which in turn will create demonstrable superior value for all stakeholders. This theme is the focus of all the units examining the design, development and implementation of strategic marketing decisions throughout this coursebook. However, central to the theme of hard-edged marketing is that if strategic marketing decisions are to drive business success, then the executives making those decisions must undergo a fundamental change in attitude and direction. It is important then that you, the reader, as a student of the CIM Postgraduate Diploma, are able to understand and overcome the obstacles faced in marketing, achieving influence at a board level and show how, in the strategic marketing decisions you make, you have embraced marketing metrics as an integral part of the decision-making process.

Activity 1.2

Consider the manner in which your organization makes strategic marketing decisions. How *hard edged* do you think your organization is in making such decisions?

The role of life cycles

One of the first requirements in making optimal strategic marketing decisions that focus creativity in the right places and drive the business forward is understanding the nature of the market/competitive life cycle in which the products/services of a company are competing. Thus, to make appropriate decisions, managers need to have an understanding of the role of life cycles in managing competitive advantage across global, international and domestic markets.

The reader of this coursebook will be well acquainted with the concept of the product/market life cycle for the Professional Diploma of the CIM syllabus. However, in making strategic decisions with regard to a company's marketing strategy, it is important not just to understand the product life cycle but how all life cycles, be it the market life cycle, the competitive life cycle or the brand and customer life cycles, affect the company's strategic position in the marketplace.

Market/industry life cycle

There are four distinct stages to the market/industry life cycle.

Stage 1 – There is little or no market concentration. Newly deregulated firms, start-ups and industries spun off from others are all present at this stage.

Stage 2 – Leading companies start to emerge, and concentration of competitive activity increases.

Stage 3 – Companies extend their core businesses, eliminate secondary operations or swap them with other companies for assets closer to their core activity.

Stage 4 – There has been a process of rationalization, as weaker competitors have withdrawn from the market and the leading companies have consolidated to dominate the market.

Wilson and Gilligan (2004) suggest that it is the market/industry life cycle which should be the focus of attention of strategic marketing decision-makers and not so much the product life cycle. It is this cycle that helps decision-makers identify how the market is likely to evolve and how it will be affected by changing needs, new technology, developments in the channels of distribution and so on.

Activity 1.3

Consider the life cycle of an industry or market known to you. Can you identify the stages as outlined in the section above? What characteristics were most predominant at each stage? What shape do you think the life cycle took?

Demand/technology life cycles

The stage of industry/market life cycle is the starting point for understanding the inter-relationships of the other life cycles such as the demand life cycle and the technology life cycle. It is the demand life cycle which is concerned with the underlying need within a market. The technology life cycle, by contrast, is concerned with the particular ways in which this need is satisfied. Doole and Lowe (2005) in Chapter 3 illustrate this by looking at the need for a data processing capability. The demand life cycle for this has been there for many long years and is still growing. Whilst the actual growth rate itself has slackened in recent years, the overall demand for faster data processing capability still continues on its upward trend. However, the way that need has been satisfied over the years and the technology used to process data has changed substantially and itself gone through several life cycles from paper-based technology to mechanical aids, to large computers and then to smaller and smaller but faster and faster computers. Each of these phases had a technology life cycle in itself within the overall framework of the demand life cycle. The demand cycle, therefore, is concerned with the evolution of the need itself, the technology life cycle is concerned with the detail of how the need is met.

Case study

Sainsbury's fight back

Sainsbury supermarkets have been suffering competitively to the other major supermarkets over latter years and losing market share to the other major players such as TESCO. Now Sainsbury's is fighting back by rebranding its value product range as 'Basics' in an attempt to re-establish its pricing credentials with consumers. Using Sainsbury's orange and white brand colours, they are planning to reinforce Sainsbury's promise of 'bringing food to life'.

Tim Lennox, Sainsbury's Basics brand manager, said: 'Value ranges are an important part of the retail landscape today – they appeal to people from different walks of life who decide to be pragmatic about some of the products they buy.'

By offering low price basics, we can cut the cost of their shopping, while still guaranteeing them the Sainsbury's quality that our customers have come to expect.

Source: Adapted from *The Retail Bulletin*, 28 January 2005.

Question 1.4

Identify the strengths and weaknesses of the strategic marketing decision taken by Sainsbury's.

The competitive life cycle

The pattern of the market, demand and technology life cycles will also impact on the competitive life cycle within a market. In the beginning of the competitive life cycle, the company, which is the pioneer in the market, may have achieved a first mover advantage and so may be, if only for a short time, the sole supplier and so have no direct competitors. As the market progresses, as we discussed previously, competitors move in and the market share of the first mover may be affected. As more competition penetrates the market price, competition tends to increase with the result that the scope for premium pricing on the part of the pioneer declines. As the market develops yet further and more firms enter the market, the perceived value of the product tends to decline, with the result that there is a gradual shift towards what Wilson and Gilligan (2004) refer to as commodity competition.

Question 1.5

Far from providing a useful insight, it is thought by many that the life cycle concept is misleading and not helpful to managers making strategic marketing decisions for future time horizons. Fully discuss this statement using examples from your own experience.

Managing life cycles across the globe

Companies competing globally will have a plethora of such life cycles to manage simultaneously as life cycles across the globe may well be at differing stages. This makes managing life cycles across global markets extremely challenging in some markets. Competition today in many markets is global rather than domestic for many products and services. Consequently, there is a reduced time lag between product research, development and production, leading to the simultaneous appearance of a standardized product in major world markets. Whilst many companies simultaneously launch new products across the globe, the shape and patterns of the life cycles that emerge as markets develop can vary enormously. Firms operating globally still need to develop an understanding of how to manage such life cycles across their markets.

Activity 1.4

Look at a product life cycle for a product or service that is known to you, which is sold across a number of international markets. In what ways does the life cycle vary across the key markets? Looking at the product from a market perspective, draw the shape of the life cycle and plot the positions of the various countries at the different stages they have reached.

How organizations compete to achieve customer preference

In order for companies to compete effectively to achieve customer preferences, according to Treacy and Wieresma (1995), they need to focus on achieving operational excellence, product leadership, customer intimacy and brand leadership.

Operational excellence – Companies which pursue this may well offer middle market products at the best price with the least inconvenience. Thus, they do not seek to be the technological innovators in the market, but compete by targeting a customer preference for value for money. It is this no-frills approach which characterizes many of the retailers such as Wal-Mart, Matalan and Gap and airline companies such as Ryanair and EasyJet. In highly competitive and largely mature markets, for example, an ever greater number of organizations have to compete directly against competitors who offer almost identical products across 70–80 per cent of the range.

Product leadership – Involves focusing upon developing and offering products, which consistently push at the boundaries of innovation; both Intel and Nike are examples of this. Offering innovative solutions with the latest product developments requires a high investment in research and development (R&D) and a strong innovation capability. This means employing the leading researchers in the field and building an organizational culture where creativity can flourish. Examples of such companies are Microsoft, Glaxo, SmithKline Beecham, Procter & Gamble, and 3M.

Customer intimacy – In a time when technology has allowed marketers to move from mass marketing to mass customized marketing, companies now have the technical capability to target on an individual basis and so create customer value through the illusion of having an individual personal relationship with their customers. Lastminute.com, Amazon.com and a number of other Internet suppliers are able to offer individual buying solutions through the information built from purchasing profiles. However, customer intimacy is much more prevalent in B2B marketing when customers often require high value bespoke solutions to technical problems.

Brand leadership – The global brands of Nike, Sony and McDonald's have become world-wide phenomena by pursuing such a policy. However, brand leadership is only sustainable if it offers superior value to the customer. Companies basing their strategic positioning on brand leadership need to work actively to deliver an extra value proposition, which is valued by the customer in order to sustain brand leadership over a period of time.

Insight

Telewest B2B rise to government challenge

The UK government commitment that all public sector services be online by 2005 has proved to be a huge marketing opportunity for Telewest B2B division. The company has grown phenomenally within a year from £39 to £80 million, much of this growth being fuelled by the growing demand for broadband from the public sector. The fact that government procurement has been centralized to maximize buying power and ensure the different authorities do not buy incompatible networks has only served to help Telewest further.

Source: Adapted from Crush, P., 'Government Diagnosis', *Marketing Direct*, March 2004.

Question 1.6

In the above section, it is suggested that in order to compete for customer preference, companies should aim to achieve operational excellence, brand leadership or customer intimacy. Identify the strengths and weaknesses of using each of these to achieve a customer preference.

The role of competitive relationships

The question facing many companies in today's global market is whether they can effectively compete for customer preference alone or whether some kind of relationship with competitors is required in order to sustain a competitive advantage over time. Companies such as General Motors, General Electric and Glaxo Smith-Kline Beecham have maintained their market leadership, but an integral part of their strategy to do so has been either the acquisition of companies or the formation of strategic alliances they perceived that they needed to help them compete more effectively in the marketplace. In today's marketing environment, when competing for customer preference, companies (as will discuss further in Unit 10 of this coursebook) not only have to identify who it is they are competing against but they need to also identify which competitors they may conceivably compete with, in order to deliver superior value to their customers.

There are a number of driving forces for this trend:

o Companies do not have sufficient resources alone to realize their full global potential and so may form a relationship to achieve better operational excellence or perhaps greater customer intimacy.
o The pace of innovation and market diffusion is ever more rapid and so to achieve global brand leadership, relationships may be formed so that new products and services can be exploited quickly by effective diffusion into the global market.
o High R&D costs mean it is increasingly difficult, costly and risky for companies to develop breakthrough innovations alone. Thus to achieve product leadership, relationships may be formed in R&D as in the Sony/Philips alliance, which produced the new mini disc player.
o In mature markets such as the car and airline industries, operational excellence has been achieved by the formation of alliances, mergers and takeovers to rationalize competition, achieve economies of scale and so achieve cost leadership in the industry.
o Some companies use relationships to acquire the capability to access new markets where they have little expertise or experience so they are better positioned to compete for customer preference in those markets.

The formation of customer and supply-chain relationships is examined in some depth in Unit 10. However, the important concept for the reader to familiarize themselves with at this stage is that in strategic marketing decisions, to compete for customer preference, the manager needs to question the assumption that this is something the company will achieve alone. It may be that in many markets today, it is the company that understands the strategic significance of partnerships and has a network of relationships that is most able to effectively compete for customer preference.

Case study

Fujitsu computers and Siemens engineering joint venture

One may think it strange for a Japanese computer giant and a German engineering giant to form a successful and cooperative relationship through a joint venture, but that is just what Siemens and Fujitsu have achieved. In their high-tech world, innovation is critical in the race to build a global and sustainable competitive advantage. Fujitsu brought a high level of successful technical innovation and expertise in consumer electronic to the relationship and Siemens brought a high level of engineering quality and expertise in mobile technology. The synergies have built a joint-venture company with an impressive R&D muscle backed up by an impressive investment by both companies, which is now allowing the firm to win a number of technological races. For instance, the first e-mails sent from an aeroplane were from a Fujitsu Siemens notebook from nearly 40 000 feet up!

Source: Adapted from Stern, S., 'Cultures with a feather in their cap', *Financial Times*, 13 January 2005.

Question 1.7

Explain the reasons behind the success of the Fujitsu/Siemens joint venture? Why are such relationships so important in the high-tech market?

Activity 1.5

What approach to developing potential relationships with your competitors does your company take?

See CIM SMD Examination December 2004, Question 2

In preparing for the SMD examination, it is necessary for you to tackle questions, which expose you to a number of different contexts. The senior examiner will always try to ensure that candidates are presented with a number of varying contextual situations in the examination. This question looks at a B2B service provider making strategic marketing decisions in a fast-moving, uncertain environment and so a good one to help you prepare for such questions.

Summary

- The development of a sustainable competitive advantage is viewed as a continual process requiring strategic marketing decisions to be made that are individually sound and collectively add value for shareholders as well as other stakeholders.
- It is necessary for participants to study this coursebook in an integrated way and view the complete strategic decision process of identifying new marketing opportunities, areas for innovation and value creation in an organization as an iterative and continuous process.
- Strategic marketing is about the development of innovative marketing solutions that enhance an organization's competitive position in its chosen markets whilst delivering superior value to the customers and to the shareholders of the company.
- It is now vital that marketing within companies takes on a much more strategic role and has a more prominent influence in the corporate strategic direction the company takes.
- In making strategic decisions, it is important to understand how all life cycles, be it the market life cycle, the competitive life cycle or the brand and customer life cycles, affect the company's strategic position in the marketplace.
- In competing for customer preference, companies not only have to identify who it is they are competing against but they need to also identify which competitors they may conceivably co-operate with, in order to deliver superior value to their customers.

Further study

For a more detailed treatment of what strategic marketing decisions making is about, you should read:

Doole, I. and Lowe, R. (2005) *Strategic Marketing Decisions in Global Markets*, Thomson Learning, Chapters 1 and 3.

Doyle, P. (2000) *Value Based Marketing: Marketing Strategies for Corporate Growth and Shareholder Value*, Wiley & Sons Ltd, Chapter 1.

Wilson, R.M.S. and Gilligan, C.T. (2004) *Strategic Marketing Management: Planning Implementation and Control*, 3rd edition, Butterworth-Heinemann, Chapters 1 and 2.

Hints and tips

The concept of 'hard-edged marketing' is central to the whole of the CIM Chartered Diploma. In this module, this means that you need to show that you understand that if strategic marketing decisions are to drive business success, then marketing has to take a strategic role in the organization. This means in the examinations, you will need to show that for the case study/scenario provided, you can make marketing decisions of the calibre required by a company at board level. It is important, therefore, that you can show how the decisions you make help deliver superior customer value, and that you understand that the application of marketing metrics is an integral part of the strategic marketing decision-making process

Bibliography

Doole, I. and Lowe, R. (2005) *Strategic Marketing Decisions in Global Markets*, Thomson Learning.

Doyle, P. (2000) *Value Based Marketing: Marketing Strategies for Corporate Growth and Shareholder Value*, Wiley & Sons Ltd.

Treacy, M. and Wieresma, F. (1995) *The Discipline of Market Leaders*, London: Harper.

Wilson, R.M.S. and Gilligan, C.T. (2003) *Strategic Marketing Planning*, Butterworth-Heinemann.

Wilson, R.M.S. and Gilligan, C.T. (2004) *Strategic Marketing Management: Planning Implementation and Control*, 3rd edition, Butterworth-Heinemann.

Sample exam questions and answers for the Strategic Marketing Decisions module as a whole can be found in Appendix 3 at the back of the book

unit 2
challenging traditional strategic thinking

Learning objectives

The CIM syllabus for Strategic Marketing Decisions emphasizes the need for candidates to show that they can do more than simply go through the traditional marketing planning process. You need to be able to demonstrate that you can rethink market boundaries and product/service boundaries that prevail within the market and create innovative strategies that change the basis on which a company can compete.

In this unit you will:

2.1   Examine the significance and application of new marketing thinking to strategic decisions.

2.5   Determine drivers for realignment in strategic thinking.

2.6   Explore the alternative approaches to strategic marketing decisions (e.g. formal/analytical approach v transformation approaches).

2.10   Examine issues in strategic marketing decision-making in SMEs.

4.1   Explain and evaluate the contribution of value-based marketing.

Having completed this unit you will be able to:

o   Appraise a range of corporate and business visions, missions and objectives and the processes by which they are formulated, in the light of the changing bases of competitive advantage across geographically diverse markets.

o   Identify, compare and contrast strategic options and critically evaluate the implications of strategic marketing decisions in relation to the concept of 'shareholder value'.

o   Demonstrate the ability to develop innovative and creative marketing solutions to enhance an organization's global competitive position in the context of changing product, market, and brand and customer life cycles.

This unit relates to the statements of practice

Bd.2   Specify and direct the strategic planning process.

Gd.1   Select and monitor channel criteria to meet the organization's needs in a changing environment.

Gd.2   Select and monitor channel criteria to meet organization needs in a changing environment.

Key definitions

Breakpoints – Occur in markets as a consequence of a major change in the environment or the competitive nature of the market, which results in a previously successful strategy being made obsolete.

Value-based marketing – A marketing strategy that is based on a totally integrated marketing effort, which delivers superior value to customers and so in turn delivers superior value to shareholders.

Shareholder value principle – The shareholder value principle asserts that marketing strategies should be judged by the economic returns they generate for shareholders, the returns being measured by dividends and increases in the company share price.

Emergent Strategies – A strategy that has been developed through an iterative learning process so that the resultant strategy is the one that has emerged through the creative and iterative process of crafting a strategy of proactively seeking new opportunities whilst reacting to the challenges faced in the market.

Study Guide

By reading and completing the questions and activities in this unit you should start to build the skills to develop innovative and creative strategies that deliver added value to customers. Most of the concepts introduced in this unit will be revisited in some depth in later units of the coursebook. At Professional Diploma of the CIM syllabus, you developed the skills and knowledge to undertake a rigorous marketing plan. These skills are still important, but in this module, you need to build on this knowledge and develop the ability to apply the skills to difficult competitive situations, which may need added flair and creativity, whilst at the same time, ensuring any strategic decisions made are viable in terms of adding value to the customers and shareholders of a company. Using the driving analogy, at Professional Diploma you learnt the mechanics of driving a car and have successfully passed your test. At this stage, it is akin to taking an advanced driving test and so you need to show that you can apply those skills to adverse weather conditions and in complex situations where you have to be able to anticipate difficult situations ahead and respond quickly and appropriately to maintain the safety and well-being of your company.

Drivers for realignment in strategic thinking

 ## Activity 2.1

Before you start to read the next section, consider the environmental factors in a market or industry known to you that are requiring a company to realign their strategic thinking.

The drivers for strategic alignment centre on four emergent needs:

1. Rising customer expectations
2. The drive for increased revenue and growth from the marketplace
3. The intensification of global competition
4. The need for innovation and creativity.

In the global marketing place there are a number of environmental factors giving rise to the drivers outlined above:

The increasing globalization of the marketplace – means all companies, even if they operate in one national market, are subject to international competitive pressures. As trade barriers reduce, markets become increasingly open to international competitors. In the European Union (EU), the accession of Central and Eastern European countries, whilst increasing market opportunity, also means companies in the high-cost countries of Western Europe will be increasingly subject to the competitive pressure from competitors with a high level of technical capability and much lower labour costs. The accession of China to the World Trade Organization (WTO) signals China's intention to further develop as a serious international competitor.

The emergence of the global village – is a culmination of the visible trends that social and cultural differences between countries become much less of a barrier and global needs that transcend political and national boundaries are satisfied by an increasing number of global brands such as Microsoft, Intel, Coca-Cola, McDonald's, Nike and so on.

The growth and movement in populations across the globe – Whilst the world population is growing dramatically, the growth patterns are not consistent around the world. The significant variations in changing populations are heralding social changes across the globe. Eighty per cent of the world's population live in developing countries; by 2005 this is likely to reach 85 per cent. There are also visible moves in the population within many countries leading to the formation of huge urban areas where consumers have a growing similarity of needs across the globe. The population of Greater Tokyo is just under 30 million and Mexico 20 million. Cities such as Lagos, Buenos Aires and Jakarta will soon outstrip cities such as Paris, London and Rome.

The growing body of international law – affects the marketing strategies developed by companies. International conventions, agreements from world institutions such as the IMF, the World Bank and WTO increasingly impact on how companies compete globally. The harmonization of legal systems within regional economic groupings such as the EU is increasingly impacting on how companies operate in such markets.

Piracy – in markets with limited trademark and patent protection is a serious challenge for global competitors. Increasingly, international laws are being developed to cover things such as piracy, patents and trademarks legislation. For many companies in the high-tech industries this is vital if they are to compete effectively in the growth markets around the world. Bootlegged software constitutes 87 per cent of all personal computer software in use in India, 92 per cent in Thailand and 98 per cent in China, resulting in a loss of US$8 billion for software makers a year.

Shrinking communications – means, increasingly, that in the global marketplace information is power. At the touch of a button we can access information on the key factors that determine our business. Manufacturers wanting to know the price of components around the globe or the relevant position of competitors in terms of their share price or in terms of new product activity have it at their immediate disposal.

The Internet and the access gained to the World Wide Web – is revolutionizing international marketing practices. An estimated 765 million people now have access to the Internet. The United Nations estimates that global e-business is now worth US$10 trillion. Most of this is B2B marketing as opposed to B2C marketing.

Case study

Proctor & Gamble join forces with Gillette

Two of America's biggest consumer-goods firms, P&G and Gillette, have agreed to team up. A big factor behind the mammoth deal rests on the good fit between the two firms' product lines. P&G, best known for making such things as Pampers disposable nappies, Tide washing powder and Crest toothpaste, has gone further into grooming since the year 2000. They have also recently acquired Wella and Clairol, two makers of hairdressing products. The addition of Gillette's razors and other, mainly male products, gives a greater breadth to P&G's product line.

P&G spends some $5.5 billion a year on advertising and boasts a particular expertise in marketing to women, while Gillette's forte is in selling to men. Combining the two firms' marketing spend – Gillette's is $1 billion – will also give them more power to negotiate advantageous deals with media companies.

P&G's quest for size is also a response to the growing power of retailers. P&G's biggest customer is Wal-Mart, the world's largest retailer. Such is its dominance in America, where it accounts for about 8 per cent of total retail sales, and its increasing presence in the rest of the world, that it wields huge power over its suppliers. Wal-Mart is notoriously tough in bargaining down the price it pays suppliers. As consolidation among retailers around the world gathers pace, this pressure is sure to grow. P&G may reckon that bulking-up will help redress the balance. It may also be betting that only the vastest companies will take full advantage of the opportunities offered by globalization and the rise of big new consumer markets (e.g. China).

Source: Adapted from 'Marriage made in heaven – and in the bathroom', *The Economist*, 28 January 2005.

Question 2.1

What do you see as the main drivers for the strategic realignment that P&G hopes to achieve in the creation of this new mega global company? How do you think the competition will respond?

Question 2.2

How far do you think the growing access to the Internet has been a driver for strategic alignment?

Significance and application of new marketing thinking to strategic decisions

The changes in the marketing environment discussed above and the changes brought by the growth of e-business have all contributed to a global environment where the competitive landscape is much more complex: product, market and brand life cycles are shorter; and the search for competitive advantage by companies is more difficult to sustain over time. This has led to the changing dimensions in competitive advantage and the changing dimensions in strategic marketing decision-making we discussed in Unit 1 of this coursebook. Consequently, marketing managers have had to rethink the way they approach marketing decisions and incorporate new values into the marketing strategy process.

Insight

According to a global Web-based survey by Interbrand, the Google brand had the most impact on people's lives. Google beat established brands such as Coke and Apple. Some commentators believe the success of such brands has huge lessons for marketing managers, as the tools and approaches used off-line often do not work on the Web. Catch phrases are of little use as most Internet users are searching for information.

Many companies use websites to boast of their achievements which are of no interest to potential consumers surfing the net for instant accessing to the simple and functional information they are searching for.

Equally a new generation is now growing up, skilled in accessing the world though their computer screens. Their motivations, the way they seek information and the stimuli they react to are of a completely different character to that of the previous generation. This in turn is impacting on how such consumers should be targeted off-line and requiring marketing managers to rethink their traditional marketing tools.

Question 2.3

Critically evaluate the implications of the Internet on the off-line strategic marketing decisions of the future. Do you think this will require a total realignment of off-line marketing strategies?

The need for innovative thinking

To respond to the environmental challenges, strategic marketing decision-makers have had to rethink the market boundaries in which they operate and base their market definition in terms of the customers they serve, rather than the product market they are in. This has meant they have to break free of the notion that they have a localized customer base and so seek new customers globally, and they have to break free of their thinking in terms of the product/service boundaries that prevail within the market so that they can create innovative strategies that change the basis on which they compete.

In this, of the drivers for strategic realignment discussed above, it is almost inevitable that at some stage, marketing managers will face the problems of breakpoints. According to Wilson and Gilligan (2004), these could arise for a number of reasons:

- Changes in the demographics or social structure of a market which herald changes in customer needs, their values and/or expectations of the product and services they seek.
- Technological breakthroughs which provide the innovative organization with a major competitive advantage but which in turn put competitors at a disadvantage.
- The identification of new business opportunities by companies, which redefine the market boundaries, cause a rethink amongst competitors as to how they should now compete.
- Shifts within the distribution network, which lead to changes in the balance of power between manufacturers and retailers and very different sets of expectations – this could sometimes mean changes in the supply chain, which offer scope for major reductions in cost.
- Indirect competitors developing a new resource capability and so becoming direct competitors bringing into the competitive landscape a different set of skills as well as a different perspective on the market.
- A mature market, where companies are facing increasing price competition and so declining returns, which force a radical rethink of how the company is operating and how it should develop in the future.

 Activity 2.2

In the company in which you work or for a company known to you, what breakpoints can you identify that rendered the company's strategy obsolete? What strategic decisions did the company make to overcome the breakpoints?

It also means, as discussed in Unit 1, that in order to compete effectively in today's marketing environment, marketing decision-makers need to take on a more strategic role and ensure they are able to show how the marketing decisions taken can deliver better revenue growth, more profit and increased customer satisfaction. As said previously, in today's highly competitive marketplace, marketing managers are required to be much more accountable for their actions, be able to show the cost-effectiveness of marketing tactics and show how marketing strategies add to the shareholder value of an organization.

According to Piercy (2002), if strategic marketing decisions made by marketing managers are to clearly show how they contribute to shareholder value, this means companies have to develop customer focused strategies based on offering value to customers which in turn enhances company performance and so increases shareholder value. This means strategic marketing decisions need to be concerned with:

How to create value – Piercy views this as the key issue in achieving and sustaining competitive success, particularly in relation to branding and customer relationship management given the increasing demands made by customers.

How to harness the power and impact of the Internet – Particularly in relation to the need to develop an integrated and multi-channel routes to a company's markets.

How to achieve a totally integrated marketing effort – The need to ensure the strategic decisions made exploit all the company's resources and capabilities to deliver value to the customer.

How to engender creativity in the strategy of a company – Piercy argues that the focus of strategic decision-making should be on *strategizing and creativity* and not on the bureaucracy and structures of formal planning.

Question 2.4

Explain what is meant by a totally integrated marketing effort? How can a company achieve this?

The need to deliver shareholder value

According to Doyle (2000), by delivering shareholder value, marketing is more able to influence strategic decisions in the boardroom at a corporate level. Shareholder value marketing offers a way for managers to show how marketing strategies increase the value of the firm as well as provide a framework and language for integrating marketing more effectively with other functions of the business. Doyle suggests the need to deliver shareholder value redefines the marketing concept as:

> The marketing concept states that the key to creating shareholder value is building relationships with target customers based on satisfying their needs more effectively than competitors. (Doyle, 2000, p. 75)

The traditional marketing objectives of increasing market share and building customer loyalty, he argues, are not enough in themselves, unless they can be linked to the increasing of shareholder value and higher financial performance. The techniques and tools for assessing the viability of strategic marketing decisions and measuring shareholder value are examined more thoroughly in Unit 11 of this coursebook. In this unit, we are simply concerned with introducing the concept of the shareholder value principle and discussing the implication for strategic marketing decision-makers.

The shareholder value principle asserts that marketing strategies should be judged by the economic added value they generate for the company, be it owned by shareholders or owned privately: the returns being measured by dividends and increases in the company value. This is based on two principles:

1. The primary obligation of managers is to maximize returns for shareholders and owners.
2. The stock market value of a company is based on the investors' expectations of the cash-generating abilities of the company.

Question 2.5

What do you understand by the term 'shareholder value' (i.e. shareholder value/economic value added)? Why is such a principle important to strategic marketing decisions?

This of course means that the role of marketing managers therefore is to deliver marketing strategies that maximize the cash flow of a company over time and so create value. The essence of the shareholder value principle is that managers create economic added value which in turn generates greater return than their cost of capital. If marketing managers are to make decisions that deliver economic added value they need to harness the thinking of Value-Based Marketing.

Case study

The added value of technological innovation

The need for innovation is critical to success, but how long is anything innovative and leading edge? The colour television in 1954 was heralded as a breakthrough, high-tech innovation and yet today it is seen as little more than a commodity – unless it has a plasma flat screen. Today the cost of a new flat screen TV is not dissimilar to the price of a colour TV in 1954 – about £750. Over the years, the standard colour TV has plummeted in price and now can be purchased for less than £50.

DVD players, only a few years ago, were the fastest ever selling technological innovation and yet today the price of these has plummeted to such an extent that they are seen almost as a commodity where any brand will do and more than not they can be picked free through promotional offers, something that the consumer picks up as a bonus for buying another product. Thus, the commoditization process that took place over 50 years of the life cycle of the colour TV has taken less than 5 years for the DVD player.

Question 2.6

How does a company continue to maximize shareholder/stakeholder value in a market of tumbling prices?

Activity 2.3

Look at your own organization and identify the potential obstacles to applying the economic value-added principle to your company? What are the reasons for this and what are the implications for strategic marketing decisions?

The concept of Value-based marketing

Value-based marketing recognizes the need for a totally integrated marketing effort that manages the whole of the marketing process to deliver customer value and so build value for the company. Proponents of value-based marketing argue that to compete effectively, a company needs to do more than building a brand or build relationships, it has to build value. Thus, whilst relationships and brands are important, markets are changing the basis for competition and new types of competition are emerging which mean that to achieve a sustainable competitive advantage companies need to offer a total value proposition to its customers. As Doyle (2000) says, it is 'by delivering superior value to customers that management can in turn deliver superior value to shareholders'.

According to Doyle (2000), delivering value-based marketing takes four major steps:

1. The development of a deep understanding of customer needs, operating procedures and decision-making processes.
2. The formulation of value propositions that meet the needs of customers and create a differential advantage.
3. Building long-term relationships with customers so that a level of loyalty and trust is built based on satisfaction and confidence in the supplier.
4. An understanding that the delivery of superior value to customers requires superior knowledge, skills, systems and marketing assets.

Incorporating this concept redefines marketing as being

the management process that seeks to maximise returns to shareholders by developing and implementing strategies to build relationships of trust with high value customers and create a sustainable differential advantage. (Doyle, 2000, p. 70)

Question 2.7

What are the main components of value-based marketing?

According to Treacy and Wieresma (1995), if managers are to harness the thinking of value-based marketing, they need to come to terms with making three key strategic marketing decisions:

What is its value proposition? – The implicit promise the company is going to make to customers to deliver its particular combination of values.

What is its value-driven operating model? – The combination of operating processes, management systems, structure and culture the company feels it needs to have if it is to have the ability to deliver on its value proposition.

What are its value disciplines? – In other words what is the way the company is going to combine its operating models and value propositions to achieve a differential competitive advantage in their markets?

 Activity 2.4

Does your company hold core values? If so, identify three or four value disciplines that you think are considered important in making strategic marketing decisions within your company?

If you think your company does not have any core values then consider the implications of this to their strategic marketing decision-making.

Value disciplines are an important element of the work carried out by Collins and Porras (1997) and Collins (2000), in their 6-year longitudinal study of high performing companies in the USA. They found that businesses with long-standing reputations for business excellence had a strong core ideology. The ideology, they suggest, consists of three components: core values, core purpose and an envisioned future.

1. *Core values* – are sets of guiding principles that have intrinsic value and importance to those inside the organization.
2. *Core purpose* – is seen to be the fundamental reason for being a company, the reason the firm exists. Collins and Porras view an effective purpose as reflecting the importance people attach to the company's work.
3. *Envisioned future* – is viewed as the defining direction of the firm's strategy, a view of the future that comprises BHAGs (big hairy audacious goals).

The core ideology, therefore, has implications for how strategic marketing decisions should be led by the executive and it will also determine the orientation of the company to its strategic decision-making processes.

Insight

Space tourism

Is Space tourism the ultimate in market niches? Richard Branson is already gearing up for this market in the UK. In the USA market analysts suggest that there are at least 10 000 potential space tourists willing to spend $1 million for the two-hour trip into space. NASA has explicitly stated it has no interest in this market. A number of smaller firms see this as the ultimate market niche, if they can build the capability to design a reusable launch system that is not too expensive and has guaranteed safety. Could there be huge rewards for the first into the market?

Alternative approaches to strategic marketing decisions

Whilst there are many different approaches to the making of strategic decisions to formulate and develop a strategy, the two we will discuss in this unit are the rational formal approach and the emergent strategy approach.

The key component of the rational planning approach is that it is a highly formal linear sequence, which requires a highly formalized approach to strategic marketing decision-making and a mechanical programming approach to the implementation of those decisions. Underlying the rational approach is the assumption that the process of strategy development is like a machine, if each of the component parts are executed as specified, then the end product, that is the resultant strategy, will be effective and efficient. In terms of strategic decision-making, there will be a strict hierarchy of decisions which need to be made in a particular sequence. The implementation of those decisions whilst important is perceived as being something that is considered as a consequence of the strategic decisions and not necessarily as part of the decision-making process. This means that the rational formal approach has certain characteristics such as:

- ○ Strategies result from a controlled conscious process of formal planning which incorporates a sequence of distinct steps in the decision-making process.
- ○ Responsibility for the whole process rests with the chief executive but the implementation is the responsibility of operational managers and the two are seen as separate.
- ○ Strategies are comprehensive and highly detailed and quite explicit in nature. This means they can then be implemented through detailed operational plans specifying objectives, action plans, budgets and control measures.

The emergent school of strategy development on the other hand believes strategies are formed and not necessarily formulated. In other words strategies are built from a number of little actions and decisions made by different managers in an organization, sometimes with little thought to the strategic consequences. Taken together over time these small changes produce a major shift in direction. Thus the strategy emerges from the various corners of an organization and forms itself, as over time these small changes crystallize and take shape until they reach a form when they can be clearly articulated as a strategy.

In making strategic marketing decisions to meet the challenges of today's markets, firms in many ways need to make strategic decisions as to how they will proactively develop new markets and new strategies, whilst at the same time making decisions as to how they should react to changes and developments in the marketplace. This is much akin to the emergent strategy development process proposed by Mintzberg (1973). He distinguishes between deliberate strategy (rigid plans set from above) and emergent strategy that changes as new market insights arise. Mintzberg sees strategy development as something that emerges through the creative and iterative process of crafting a strategy of proactively seeking new opportunities whilst reacting to the challenges faced in the marketplace stating that strategy '. . . is developed through long experience and commitment. Formulation and implementation merge into the fluid process of learning through which creative strategies emerge.'

Strategy development, therefore, is a multidimensional iterative process which can be built from any aspect of the marketing process and transcend up an organization rather than being dictated from above. There has to be a thorough systematic analysis, but it also requires intuition and experience, innovation and creativity from all the persons involved in the company's operations.

Question 2.8

Evaluate the two approaches to strategic marketing decision-making outlined in the section above. Making reference to examples show how each of the approaches can be used by marketing decision-makers.

See CIM SMD Examination December 2004, Question 4

As we have seen in the study text, a major criticism of marketing teaching has been the focus on simply the rational planning approach which is viewed as a highly formal linear sequence. In the SMD syllabus, you need to think about alternative approaches and show an appreciation of the implications of different approaches to strategy formulation on strategic marketing decisions. This question allows you to prepare for questions on this subject.

Issues of strategic marketing decision-making in small- and medium-sized Enterprises

Small- and medium-sized enterprises (SMEs) face particular problems in decision-making in that they have limited resources of time, finance and professional expertise. This means they often do not have the capacity to set up the formal knowledge management systems of many larger organizations. In many SMEs, the managing director may have the sole responsibility for all marketing decisions. This means such persons should have the capacity within themselves to generate ideas, assess options and clarify the best route forward. They do not have the luxury of bringing together teams of experts and professionals within the organization to help them analyse information and share the responsibility of decision-making. Thus the responsibility of making strategic decisions can be a lonely and onerous one. Consequently, they take a much more emergent approach to decision-making. Many commentators would argue this is a much healthier approach to strategic marketing decisions and gives SMEs an inbuilt flexibility to quickly respond to challenges in the marketing environment.

In order to overcome their limited resources, many SMEs create a *virtual organization* by developing a network of lateral partnerships through which they can access information, clarify their assessment of strategic options and can seek assurance that the decisions being made are appropriate. Partnerships are formed by SMEs with an array of organizations such as consultants, universities, government agencies, banks, professional bodies and contacts in the market they perceive as being valuable to their business.

Thus, in developing long-term relationships, firms develop an extended flexible organization, almost a virtual structure. They build a network of partnerships of varying degrees of intensity and use these relationships to enhance their capability to compete in their markets. The added value created through these relationships is derived from the ability it gives SMEs to gain access to both markets and to information, and to build barriers to competition as well as to ensure they can effectively service their markets.

If used effectively such relationships can play a huge part not only in advising SMEs in decision-making but also in the provision of information on which to base decisions and helping to validate any decisions made as appropriate to the market conditions. These relationships therefore play an important role in strategic marketing decisions as part of the iterative strategy development process. Relationships both *inform* the strategy development process and *add form* to the strategy.

Insight

Not such a Red Letter Day for stakeholders

Red Letter Days was set up by Rachel Elnaugh to sell memorable experiences, such as driving a Formula 1 car or climbing a mountain. The gifts are sold in major retail stores such as Boots and Debenhams. The experiences are provided by a network of suppliers to Red Letter Days. In May 2005, it planned to float on the Alternative Investment Market and was valued at £20–25 million. Only two months later, however, suppliers were reported to have lost patience with Red Letter Days over late payments and had begun legal action. Racing track operators were reported to be owed £300 000 and a charity that provided whale and dolphin watching trips in Cornwall claimed it had not been paid for four months.

The £20 million per annum turnover business went into administration in July 2005. This was rather embarrassing for Rachel Elnaugh, who was a judge on Dragons' Den, a TV show in which would-be entrepreneurs made a pitch to successful entrepreneurs for investment in their idea.

Red Letter Days and the jobs of its 150 employees were saved when another Dragons' Den judge Peter Jones and a partners bought the company. However it seemed unlikely that Red Letter Days' network of suppliers would see any money.

Source: Adapted from 'A Osbourne Red Letter sails close to the wind as suppliers play safe', *The Daily Telegraph*, 30 July 2005 and 'Gift firm thrown dragon lifeline', BBC News Online, 2 August 2005.

Activity 2.5

Interview the managing director of an SME. Discuss with them the process of strategic marketing decision-making within the firm and the issues and problems they face in making such decisions.

Summary

- o In the global marketing place, there are a number of environmental factors driving the realignment of strategic thinking. Consequently, marketing managers have had to rethink the way they approach marketing decisions and incorporate new values into the marketing strategy process.
- o The drivers for strategic realignment mean it is almost inevitable that at some stage marketing managers will be faced with a breakpoint that renders their current strategy obsolete.
- o Marketing managers have to show how they contribute to shareholder value through customer-focused strategies based on offering value to customers, which enhances company performance and so increasing economic added value. By delivering enhanced value, marketing is more able to influence strategic decisions in the boardroom at a corporate level.

- Value-based marketing recognizes the need for a totally integrated marketing effort that manages the whole of the marketing process to deliver customer value and so build value for the shareholders and owners of the company.
- There are two principal views as to how strategic decisions are formulated, the rational linear approach and the iterative emergent approach. Mintzberg suggests strategy development is something that emerges through the creative and iterative process of crafting a strategy.
- SMEs face particular issues in making strategic marketing decisions, as they generally do not have formal procedures and so need to form external relationships to contribute to validate the decision-making process.

Further study

For a more detailed treatment of the issues discussed in this unit you should read

Doole, I. and Lowe, R. (2005) *Strategic Marketing Decisions in Global Markets*, Thomson Learning, Chapters 1 and 3.

Doyle, P. (2000) Value-Based Marketing: Marketing Strategies for Corporate Growth and Shareholder Value, Wiley & Sons Ltd.

Wilson, R.M.S. and Gilligan, C.T. (2004) *Strategic Marketing Management: Planning Implementation & Control*, 3rd edition, Butterworth-Heinemann.

Hints and tips

The Strategic Marketing Decision examination paper requires candidates to apply their learning to a specific case study or industry scenario. In discussing the concepts examined in this unit, it is important that candidates recognize that not all organizations are the same. You should therefore make sure that your answers reflect the size and competitive position of the companies specified in the scenario or case study provided in the examination. To build your skills in this, it is a good idea to contextualize your learning as much as possible by applying the concepts learnt to different organizations in varying competitive situations. Reading marketing journals and the quality press can help you to build a portfolio of situations to which the concepts can be applied. In the examination, if you are able to provide examples to illustrate your points, you can ensure that you make your answers applicable to the situation specifics.

Bibliography

Collins, J. (2000) *Good to Great: Why Some Companies Make the Leap … and Others Don't*, Century.

Collins, J.C. and Porras, J.I. (1997) *Built to Last: Successful Habits of Visionary Companies*, Century.

Doyle, P. (2000) *Value-Based Marketing: Marketing Strategies for Corporate Growth and Shareholder Value*, Wiley & Sons Ltd.

Hamel, G. and Prahalad, C.K. (1994) *Competing for the Future*, Boston: Harvard Business School Press.

Mintzberg, H. (1973) *The Nature of Managerial Work*, New York: Harper & Row.

Piercy, N.F. (2002) *Market Led Strategic Change: A Guide to Transforming the Process of Going to Market*, 4th edition, Oxford: Butterworth-Heinemann.

Porter, M.E. (1985) *Competitive Advantage: Creating and Sustaining Superior Performance*, New York: The Free Press.

Treacy, M. and Wieresma, F. (1995) *The Discipline of Market Leaders*, London: Harper.

Wilson, R.M.S. and Gilligan, C.T. (2004) *Strategic Marketing Management: Planning Implementation & Control*, 3rd edition, Butterworth-Heinemann.

Sample exam questions and answers for the Strategic Marketing Decisions module as a whole can be found in Appendix 3 at the back of the book, for this unit you may want to try the December 2004 paper, Question 4.

unit 3
competitive strategy as a learning process

Learning objectives

As we have discussed in previous units the accelerated pace of change in the marketing environment means that if companies are to sustain a competitive advantage over time there has to be a process of continuous learning. To compete effectively companies must learn to both adapt and be flexible in their approach to the strategic marketing decisions made.

In this unit you will:

2.7   Explore competitive marketing strategy as an emergent/learning process.

2.8   Examine the role of knowledge management in sustaining competitive advantage.

2.9   Evaluate the incorporation of customer-led Internet marketing into marketing strategies.

3.9   Appreciate the value of effective knowledge management in creating competitive advantage.

Having completed this unit you will be able to:

○ Appraise a range of corporate and business visions, missions and objectives and the processes by which they are formulated, in the light of the changing bases of competitive advantage across geographically diverse markets.

○ Evaluate the role of brands, innovation, integrated marketing communications, alliances, customer relationships and service in decisions for developing a differentiated positioning to create exceptional value for the customer.

This unit relates to the statements of practice

Bd.1   Promote a strong market orientation and influence/contribute to strategy formulation and investment decisions.

Bd.2   Specify and direct the strategic marketing planning process.

Key definitions

Market orientation – The presence of a culture within an organization, which is focused towards the understanding of customer and competitors and so can create superior value for consumers.

Learning organization – An organization that has an effective learning capability and is able to efficiently manage its knowledge base to re-orient strategies and respond to competitive challenges and so reshape themselves to sustain their competitiveness.

Signal learning – Signal learning is concerned with monitoring the environment and the signalling of challenges and changes in a firm's markets and its performance in that market.

3R learning – The 3Rs stand for reflect, re-evaluate and respond. 3R learning occurs in anticipation of, and in response to, critical events occurring in a firm's markets. It is this type of learning that firms that successfully reinvent themselves undergo in reflecting on the demise of their traditional basis for competitive advantage.

Knowledge management – The systematic management of the knowledge gained through rigorous approach to the research and analysis undertaken. To make effective strategic decisions it is of paramount importance that the knowledge built is trustworthy, credible and verifiable and that it is accessible to all the managers involved in the decision-making process.

Study Guide

The concepts studied in this unit underpin the strategic marketing decision process in any successful company. Without a strong learning capability and an effective knowledge management system it is difficult for a company to build a sustainable competitive advantage. In the analysis and evaluation module of the Postgraduate Diploma of the CIM syllabus you will have studied in some depth the techniques and processes of carrying out an external analysis of the marketing environment and an internal audit of a company's capabilities. This unit builds on the skills and knowledge you have developed in that particular module and examines the issues of how that analysis should be incorporated into the strategic marketing decision process through the development of a learning capability and the management of the knowledge gained through rigorous analysis.

This unit signifies a fundamental shift in emphasis in the CIM syllabus away from a preoccupation from teaching the marketing planning process as a unidimensional linear process, which assumes a predetermined sequence of steps and recognizes that competitive strategy in a large number of organizations is an emergent process of iterative development of learning. This means in studying this unit the CIM candidate has to learn how to apply their learning in a more flexible manner and move away from the idea that the CIM syllabus is simply a matter of getting the process right. A learning outcome of this unit is the ability to appraise competitive strategies and mission statements in the light of the learning capability of an organization. To do that you will need to develop the ability to question assumptions you may have previously held and critically evaluate the competitive strategies of companies.

Competitive strategy as an emergent learning process

In order to build superior performance over time, a firm must be able to deliver superior customer value that is unique and difficult to imitate. To do this, firms need to develop the capability to adapt and develop competencies in a changing environment. The strategic marketing decisions made by managers in the process of developing their strategy have their roots in the perceptions of the senior management of their competitive situation. Understanding the relationship between how those perceptions underlie the strategic decisions made is critical to understanding effective strategy implementation. The process that links the two is the company's orientation towards the market and towards learning. It is the skills developed by the learning in an organization that drive the strategic decisions, which in turn generate competitive advantage. According to Wilson and Gilligan (2004), the three key elements of a customer value-based philosophy, which will deliver this capability, are a strong market orientation, a process of continuous learning and a commitment to innovation.

 ## Activity 3.1

Identify five companies that you consider to be successful. For each company evaluate to what extent they have developed a customer-based philosophy.

Question 3.1

Identify what characteristics have to be present in an organization in order to create a learning environment.

The importance of learning in strategy development

Over time whatever the industry and whatever the market they may compete in, all firms at some point will go through a period of substantial change, whether driven by customers, competitors or technology suppliers. There is a continuous pressure therefore on businesses to reshape themselves as well as to augment their products and services to maintain or increase their value to customers. It can be argued that firms are only able to sustain their competitiveness by understanding customer needs in a manner that allows superior value to be provided and by being aware of both existing and potential competitor activities that firms are in a position to take appropriate actions to respond to identified opportunities and threats. It is the firms that develop the learning capability to achieve this that are able to reshape themselves and so sustain their competitiveness.

Four organizational values are necessary for a firm to have effective learning capability:

1. A commitment to learning
2. Open mindedness
3. A shared vision
4. Organizational knowledge sharing.

For a more detailed discussion of these values read Chapter 2 of the Doole and Lowe (2005) *Strategic Marketing Decisions in Global Markets* textbook which accompanies this unit.

The learning capability required to overcome barriers and develop solutions to deal with the ambiguities and challenges encountered is an important part of the strategy development process itself. Firms need to be proactive in the building of knowledge of the marketplace so they are better able to react to environmental changes and defend their competitive positions in their markets. The focus of the strategy then is proactive in developing the knowledge base and building the resources to react and respond to the learning derived from the knowledge gained. According to Hamel and Prahalad (1994), it is the companies that are not able to transfer their learning to the strategy development process that fail to maintain their competitiveness, as depicted in Figure 3.1.

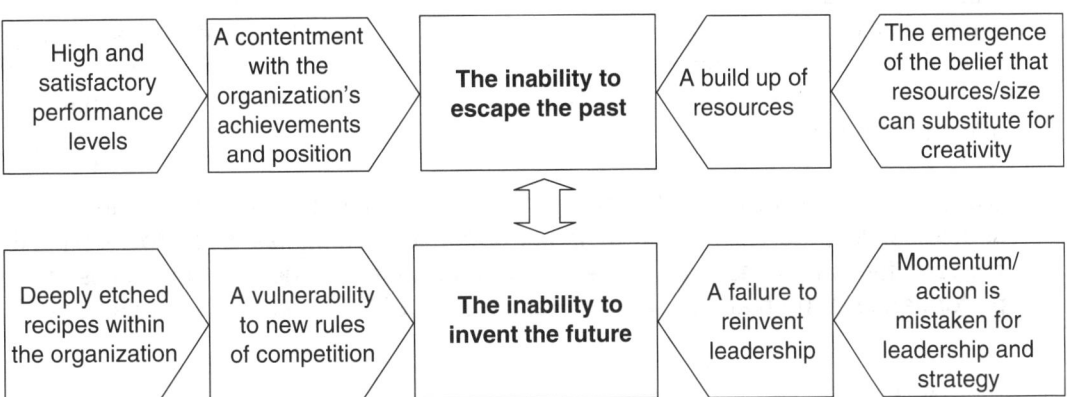

Figure 3.1 Barriers to escaping from the past and building for the future
Source: Adapted from Hamel and Prahalad (1994) *Competing for the Future*, Harvard Business Press

To avoid failure therefore in the making of strategic marketing decisions there needs to be a process of reflection and examination so that the strategy development process can be developed and clarified over a period of time. The strategy development process itself is an iterative learning process from which the resultant strategy gradually emerges. A firm's long-term strategy tends to be incrementally built as a firm undergoes the process of reflecting on their experiences and responding to the challenges faced.

Insight

Granville Technology

At its peak Granville Technology, the UK's largest computer manufacturer and maker of Time and Tiny computers, was manufacturing 500 000 computers a year and selling them through 150 stores in UK high streets. It also supplied supermarkets including ASDA, TESCO and Woolworths. It collapsed in July 2005, with a loss of 1500 jobs.

The problem for Granville was that it was impossible to compete by making products in a higher labour cost country when the cost of computers fell. PCs from India were being sold for as little as $225. Furthermore, the low retail margins that were constantly being eroded by Internet sellers, such as Dell, made Time's high overhead retailing operation unsustainable.

Source: Adapted from Tiny PCs goes into administration, 27 July 2005 BBC News Online, Guardian Online, 27 July 2005 and other public sources.

Types of learning in strategy development

Two types of learning are important in the strategy development process: *signal learning* and *3R learning*.

Signal learning

Signal learning is concerned with monitoring the environment. A company will carry out learning activities that enable it to generate the knowledge to *signal* the likely challenges and ambiguities in a firm's markets and so ensure that the firm is able to adapt and ensure the appropriateness of the strategic decisions they make. This type of learning is concerned with the traditional activities of the operations of a company. It means a company needs to have an understanding of the key indicators relevant to their products and services so they can monitor their markets and pick the right signals. Hendrix (2003) uses the term *limited visibility* for a situation when companies cannot see their market clearly because they are using the wrong type of indicators. In signal learning therefore it is important for companies to clearly articulate the factors they need to monitor in order to determine critical changes in the market, which may affect their products and services.

Signal learning is also a central component to the firms' ability to control the delivery of their strategies. In order to assess their performance, companies need to identify their critical success factors to monitor and evaluate how they are performing against the criteria to performance in the markets and the maintenance of their competitive advantage.

Activity 3.2

For your own organization or an organization of your choice identify six key indicators that would help your company identify potential opportunities and threats in the market in which they operate.

3R learning

3R learning (reflect, re-evaluate and respond) occurs in anticipation of, and in response to, critical events occurring in a firm's markets. It is this type of learning that firms that successfully reinvent themselves undergo in reflecting on the demise of traditional markets. Both Dell Computers and Ryanair are good examples of companies that have undergone such a process. They were able to question long-held assumptions about themselves, their customer base and the strategic focus of their competitors and so developed a new way of competing in their industries. Thus, it is not merely about adaptation, but challenging traditional assumptions, reflecting, evaluating the new learning and responding with newly developed strategic thinking.

Important to this learning process is the ability to acquire knowledge, reflect and then generalize those experiences in the new competitive situation. 3R learning, it is suggested, is the type of learning required by the firm to help it move forward and reduce the frequency and magnitude of the impact of events in a turbulent environment. This type of capability enables firms to develop *advance knowledge* of key events in markets, build the *flexibility* to quickly reconfigure operations and reallocate resources to focus on an emergent opportunity or threat identified, and so achieve a *rapid response* to it.

The 3R learning occurs largely through a firm's interaction with, and its observation of, the environment. Customer demand uncertainty; technological turbulence and competitive uncertainty are crucial environmental factors which demand an innovative capability from a company if they are to survive in such environments. A company that is committed to 3R learning can enhance its innovative capability in a number of ways:

o It is more likely to have developed the internal competence to build and market a technological breakthrough.
o It has the knowledge and the ability to understand and anticipate latent needs in potential customers and so has the ability to spot opportunities created by emerging market demand.
o An organization committed to 3R learning is likely to have a greater innovation capability than its competitors and be much more prepared to learn from its failures as well as its successes.

Both 3R learning and signal learning require a well-managed knowledge capability within an organization. The development of this will be examined in the following sections.

Question 3.2

Critically evaluate the role of 3R learning in the strategic marketing decision-making process.

The role of knowledge management

The task involved in developing a market intelligence system sufficient to provide the knowledge capability necessary to make sound global marketing decisions is enormous. Such a knowledge management system would not only have to identify and analyse potential markets but also should have the capacity to generate an understanding of the many environmental variables. As such, the role of the market researcher is to provide an assessment of market demand globally, an evaluation of potential markets and of the risks and costs involved in market entries, as well as detailed information on which to base effective marketing strategies.

Insight

Canon: The knowledge management company

In Western Europe, Canon is the number one brand in digital cameras. They put down their success to their ability to pioneer new technologies and their ability to move faster than their competitors in this ever-changing sector. Canon has an impressive commitment to R&D. It is committed to spending 8.1 per cent of its global revenues in R&D each year. However, market analysts see one of the core strengths of Canon is its ability to transfer technology developed for the professional market and filter it down into consumer products. To achieve this they need to have a strong empathy with the consumer markets and an understanding of how technology interfaces with consumers.

Such knowledge capability will incorporate three levels of analysis:

1. Analysis of the macro environment
2. Analysis at an industry/market level
3. Analysis of customers and competitors.

The macro environment

In examining the macro environment a manager needs to evaluate which variables will be the key market drivers in the future. In other words, to evaluate which factors are likely to exert the greatest influence on the market over the next 1–2 years as well as in the longer term. Once these variables have been identified it will be necessary to assess the impact of those factors on the marketing process. The company will need to make an evaluation of what difference the drivers will make (favourable/unfavourable) to their markets/products/brands/customers life cycles over the next few years and what strategic marketing decisions need to be made if the company is to maintain their ability to sustain a competitive advantage. Readers of this coursebook will be familiar with the SLEPT/PEST environmental model used for such an analysis. In Unit 2 we highlighted some of the key drivers in the macro environment that are impacting on the strategic marketing decisions made by companies; it is the drivers that are relevant to the products and services being offered by companies that managers need to build a knowledge capability of. To do this, managers will monitor changes in the political and legal environments, which may impact on their markets. Developments in the economic environment and the changing trends in the sociocultural environment will also need to be analysed, as will the impact of technological changes influencing change in the marketing environment.

Industry/market analysis

The second stage of the external analysis is that of the industry or market. When carrying out such an analysis the starting point is to formulate a wide definition of a company's market in terms of both the industry and the geographical boundaries. In defining markets by geography a firm needs to ask itself whether it holds the view that the firm is competing in a single global market or a series of separate and national or regional markets, and if so how wide a geographical area would they define their markets as being.

Industry market boundaries are defined by the potential to substitute products and services. An industry is a group of firms, which supplies any given market. Thus in defining its market a firm needs to consider also the boundaries of its industry. On the demand side, a market will be defined by the ability of customers to substitute a firm's product or service for another. Mobile phones can now do many wondrous things including taking pictures, thus redefining the traditional market boundaries of the camera market. On the supply side, the industry boundaries are defined by the ease of which a firm can transfer the products and services to new market segments.

Case study

NHS Direct – good health a phone call away

In 1997, NHS Direct was established to provide 'easier and faster advice and information for people about health, illness' and the NHS so that they could manage many of their problems at home or know where to turn to for appropriate care.

The intention was also to increase cost-effectiveness and reduce unnecessary demand on other NHS services. The services were provided by telephone, online and text. In the UK, there is constant criticism of the delays in getting to see a doctor, in the length of time taken to have an operation and the often-inadequate facilities, from patients. Despite increases in funding NHS staff complain of shortages of staff and equipment.

The question is whether these aims are in reality being delivered. A survey of user needs in 2001 showed the website had been set up too quickly without really understanding of user needs in detail. Later research questioned the real impact of the new service and suggested that the service was being used by the same people who already make use of existing health services, the white, healthy middle class and was underused by older people. It was shown that improving access in this way could be expensive without resulting in significant reductions in the use of other primary care services.

Source: Adapted from Nicholas, D., Huntington, P., Williams, P. and Jordan, M. (2002) NHS Direct Online: its users and their concerns, *Journal of Information Science*, 28(4), 305–319 and Chapman, J., Zechel, A., Carter, Y. and Abbott, S. (2004) 'Systematic review of recent innovations in service provision to improve access to primary care'. *Br. J. Gen. Pract.*, 54, 374–381 and NHS Direct Online at www.nhsdirect.nhs.uk

Question 3.3

Are these simply early problems that are to be expected as the organization grows or is there a more fundamental difficulty with politically driven innovation?

Question 3.4

What factors should be taken into account in conducting a detailed analysis of our competitors?

Competitor analysis

A primary objective of competitor analysis is to understand and predict the rivalry or interactive market behaviour between firms competing in the same market arena.

However, in order to assess the relative strengths and weaknesses of rivals or track their moves, a firm must be able to identify who their competitors are and from which direction their future competitors are likely to emerge. Managers who simply focus their competitor analysis on their current product/market arena may fail to notice threats that are developing due to the resources and latent capabilities of indirect and potential competitors. How a firm therefore decides to define its market boundaries is a critical decision in how the company then chooses to identify and analyse the competition.

The analysis should, therefore, include potential suppliers of products/services that consumers view as substitutes as well as those suppliers of related products and services in the arena the company has defined as its potential market. Competitor identification also needs to include an analysis of the degree to which products and services fulfil similar functions and address similar needs in the eyes of the consumer as well as an analysis of the degree to which firms have similar capabilities and benefits.

Having identified competitors, it is of course necessary to evaluate their relative capabilities and compare their relative strengths and weaknesses. In order to predict who in the future is the likely stronger competitor, it is necessary to assess how their capabilities differ and which competitor has the capabilities best suited to the market needs being served. Bergen and P'eteraf (2002) suggest that competitors should be mapped against two criteria as can be seen in Figure 3.2. First is the degree to which the competitors are direct competitors, that is the degree to which they are competing in common markets; this they term as 'market commonality'. Secondly, competitors should be mapped as to the degree they are similar in their strengths in serving the needs of the defined market; this they term as 'resource similarity'. A firm that scores high on both axes will be identified as a direct competitor, whilst a firm with similar strategic capabilities but not operating in the same market arena will be identified as a potential competitor. Firms scoring low on both axes are viewed as incipient competitors. These firms perhaps need to be monitored to spot any changes in resource capability of market activity which could give them the capability to become direct competitors.

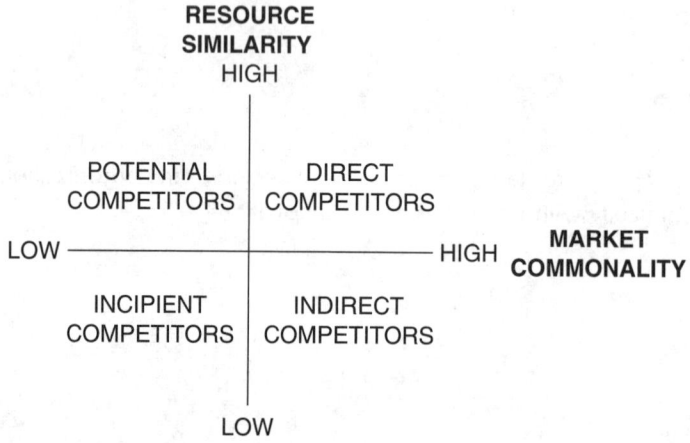

Figure 3.2 Identification of competitors
Source: Adapted from Bergen and P'eteraf (2002)

An outcome of the competitor analysis is to try and predict the strategic marketing decision a competitor will initiate and how the competitor may respond to the marketing decisions made by the firm carrying out the analysis as well as other competitors in the market.

Case study

From brick to video clips: The mobile phone a changing

Ten years ago the mobile phone was a brick sized contraption used just for talking to people. Now it is a miniaturised fashion accessory that you can use to e-mail, take videos and photographs, access the Internet and use as a computer.

Worth US$70 billion globally the market is now being fuelled by the growth in such markets as China and India.

Competitively, the mobile phone industry is interesting, in that it operates at the intersection of three major industries – communication devices, computers and consumer electronics. In the past, the barriers to entry have been high and the global market has been dominated by large vertically integrated firms such as Nokia, Motorola and Ericsson who had a wealth of expertise in high technology, mass production, managing complex supply chains as well as understanding mass consumer markets.

However, now these firms are being challenged. The hardware and software are being commoditized as the giants increasingly outsource manufacturing. Now the original design manufacturers, mainly in China and Taiwan as well as smaller specialist firms in handset design, chip design and software specialists are starting to chip away and cherry-pick at the market shares of the giants.

Source: Adapted from 'Battling for the palm of your hand', *Economist*, 1 May 2004.

Question 3.5

Assess the implications of the changing competitive structure of the mobile phone market to either Nokia or Motorola.

 Activity 3.3

For your own organization, identify the key competitors and assess the degree to which they are direct, potential or indirect competitors.

Customer analysis

Central to the success of any commercial enterprise is the organization's relationship with its customer. If an organization is to be truly consumer oriented then the analysis and understanding of their customers is of paramount importance. Without customers, businesses cannot operate. In order to meet the needs of the customer, a company needs to know who their existing and potential customers are and understand their current and emergent needs. Thus, the company needs to know:

- o Who are its customers and what do they buy?
- o Who is involved in the decision-making unit in making the purchase?
- o Why and how do they make their purchases?
- o When, where and how often do they make their purchase?

It is also important to assess the factors that influence customers. These influences tend to fall into three groups:

1. *Social/cultural influences* – such as the culture/sub-culture of the society in which the customer lives, their social status as well as the peer groups and family grouping with which they interact.
2. *Personal influences* – the personal wealth of the customer, their age, occupation and personal circumstances.
3. *Psychological influence* – their attitudes, perceptions and motivations towards the purchase they are making.

41

Likewise is it important to have an understanding of the process a company's customers go through in making a purchase. Consumers may go through the stages of the buying process at varying speeds and not necessarily through all the stages in a linear fashion. The start of the buying process is when it is recognized by a potential customer that there is a buying problem to be solved, thus when the customer senses there is a difference between their actual state and desired state. Once a purchasing problem is recognized, it sometimes may stay unsatisfied, in which case it will remain a latent need. However, a consumer may go on from that position to either actively searching for information or simply have a heightened awareness and so be more receptive to external stimuli. In searching for information, particularly on the Internet, the consumer may be faced with a huge number of potential alternative solutions to their buying problem.

Most consumers will not have the time or the energy to make an exhaustive evaluation of these alternatives and so will try to identify specific criteria, either subconsciously or consciously, to help them decide amongst the alternatives on offer. The result of the evaluation stage is the ranking of the alternatives. Potential customers will develop a final shortlist for a more in-depth evaluation to help the formation of the purchase intention. The choice made and the actual decision to purchase is the outcome of the evaluation stage. Sometimes the choice is easy to make if there is a clear alternative or perhaps if it is a simple purchase and so the risk of making a wrong decision is not costly. Customers having made a purchasing decision will seek reassurance after the purchase that the decision made was the correct one and so will make a post-purchase evaluation. Obviously this process will vary enormously depending on the level of risk attached to the purchase, the value of the purchase and the frequency of which the purchase is made. What is important is that managers understand the buying process of their customers and make appropriate strategic marketing decisions that minimize the risks and uncertainties at each stage and so facilitate the smooth passage from problem recognition to a positive purchase decision.

 ## Activity 3.4

For a product or service purchase you have recently made, explain how you completed the different stages of the decision-making process.

B2B vs B2C customers

As readers studying this coursebook will be aware, in principle, there are two main types of customers, the individual/family customers, often referred to as Business to Consumer (B2C), and organizational customers. However, there are several different types of organizational customers, principally business-to-business (B2B), business-to-government (B2G), not-for-profit organizations and internal customers. (For a more detailed examination of all these types of customers see Chapter 3 of the Doole and Lowe, 2005.) In the context of this coursebook, what is important is that in carrying out a customer analysis to identify who customers are, how and why they buy, the reader needs to be aware that a customer operating in an organizational environment can differ from the individual customer.

Building a knowledge management system

To build the learning capability discussed in the previous sections, marketing managers need to ensure they systematically manage the knowledge gained in all the analysis as well as a planned and rigorous approach to the research undertaken. To make effective strategic decisions, it is of paramount importance that the knowledge built is trustworthy, credible and verifiable and that it is accessible to all the managers involved in the decision-making process. Earlier in this unit we referred to two types of learning, signal learning and 3R learning. In this section we will examine the type of data gathering techniques used in the external marketing environment that are useful in building these learning capabilities and in the following section we will discuss the requirement of an effective learning organization.

Knowledge gathering activities for signal learning

According to Slater (2001), the type of information gathering tools that could help develop the capability to recognize the signals of potential problems and opportunities and be responsive are:

- Use of focus groups, customer surveys to understand customer wants and perceptions of current products and services
- Concept testing, conjoint analysis to guide the development of new products and services
- Relationships with customers to gain insights into customer desires
- Customer information files to improve segmentation and targeting efforts
- Customer satisfaction surveys to improve ways of keeping and maintaining customers.

As said previously, another important role of signal learning is monitoring a company's performance in the marketplace. This topic will be dealt with some depth in Units 11 and 12 of this coursebook.

Knowledge gathering activities for 3R learning

For 3R learning, companies need to acquire and evaluate market information in a systematic and anticipatory manner so they are able to understand the unexpressed needs of customers and the capabilities and plans of their competitors. To do this firms need to:

- Scan the market broadly
- Have a long-term focus to their information gathering activities
- Share knowledge throughout the organization in a coordinated and focused manner.

In this type of learning, companies would combine traditional marketing research techniques with other techniques to uncover customers' unarticulated needs. For 3R learning therefore companies would make use of qualitative research to observe customers and to build a picture of how they behave as consumers. They would work closely with lead users in the market and build up a number of different types of knowledge-based relationships to develop an effective flow of information from all the stakeholders in the market. The objective of these relationships would be to gain access to specialist knowledge, either to understand better the most efficient route to market, or to obtain advance information of imminent occurrences in the market as well as potential long-term trends. Such relationships enhance the quality of decision-making and help a company to validate the appropriateness of the decisions made to meet the changing dimensions of the market.

An effective learning organization

Garvin (1993, p. 80) considered effective learning organizations as those that become skilled at '*creating, acquiring and transferring knowledge, and at modifying behaviour to reflect new knowledge and insights*'. Senge (1992, p. 1), more poetically, described such organizations as:

> *organisations where people continually expand their capacity to create the results they truly desire, where new and expansive patterns of thinking are nurtured, where collective aspiration is set free, and where people are continually learning how to learn together.*

However, an organization may well effectively learn, but the learning outcome may itself be misguided and not contribute to the making of strategic marketing decisions that are effective in building customer value. There has to be a link therefore between effective learning and performance improvements. A company can only make such a link if it uses its knowledge management and its learning to build an efficient organizational memory which can be accessed through an effective knowledge management system. Without an effective organizational memory, firms can be caught in a trap where ongoing learning efforts breed long-term dynamism in their marketing programmes but fail to produce long-term market performance improvements.

In creating an effective learning organization, a company needs to develop a comprehensive learning strategy for the company, which integrates knowledge management and learning. Integrating learning activities with an effective knowledge management is not easy, and requires good dialogue and understanding from all parties. Collaboration amongst functional departments is therefore important. The IT department may be responsible for building the architecture but it is important in the marketing context that the decision of what is meaningful information and, the management of that information is the responsibility of the marketing executives who will be using the information.

Question 3.6

What do you see as the major barriers to the integration of knowledge management and learning activities for strategic marketing decisions? How can these be overcome?

The role of Internet-based strategies in developing a sustainable competitive advantage

Insight

Online shopping

According to the Hitwise report, Online shopping continues to excite the imagination of more and more consumers, but what are the sorts of sites we like to shop. Hitwise market report shows that auctions such as eBay now have a 34 per cent market share followed by department store sites such as John Lewis and

Argos achieving 12 per cent, Books, once the main player, now accounts for only 6 per cent of the online market.

And what sort of people are now shopping online? In Mosaic segmentation language it used to be predominantly the *urban intelligence* set, nowadays, however, the growth is coming from such segments as the *suburban comfort* and the *ties of the community*.

Source: Adapted from Hitwise; Online Retails Report, November 2004.

An estimated 765 million people now have access to the Internet. The United Nations estimates that global e-business is now worth US$10 trillion. Most of this is B2B not B2C purchases. The Internet has meant huge opportunities for companies of all sizes and played an important role in helping companies develop a sustainable competitive advantage. It has enabled them to substantially reduce the costs of reaching customers and because of the low entry costs of the Internet, it has permitted firms with low capital resources to become global marketers, in some cases overnight.

 ## Activity 3.5

Consider your own company. In what ways has the company embraced the Internet in developing its competitive marketing strategies? How has this changed the ways in which it approaches its strategic marketing decision-making?

The implications of being able to market goods and services online have been far-reaching. The Internet has led to an explosion of information to the consumer, giving them the potential to source products from the cheapest supplier in the world. This has impacted on the way firms compete globally. The increasing standardization of prices across borders, or at least, to the narrowing of price differentials as consumers become more aware of prices in different countries by using the Internet, has meant that in order to build a sustainable competitive advantage companies have had to rethink the way they compete in the market, the way they segment their markets and the way they build their routes to market.

The Internet, by connecting end-users and producers directly, has reduced the importance of traditional intermediaries (i.e. agents and distributors) as more companies have built the online capability to deal directly with their customers, particularly in B2B marketing. To survive, such intermediaries have begun offering a whole range of new services. The value added of their offering no longer being principally in the physical distribution of goods but rather in the collection, collation, interpretation and dissemination of vast amounts of information. The critical resource possessed by this new breed of 'cybermediary' is information rather than inventory. The Internet has also become a powerful tool for supporting networks both internal and external to the firm. Many global firms have developed supplier intranets through which they source products and services from preferred suppliers who have met the criteria to gain access to their supplier intranets. It has also become the efficient new medium for building knowledge on the customer base and ensuring an effective learning strategy for the company in the way the Internet enables companies to monitor everything from hits on a website to building detailed profiles of customers and so helping companies build mass customization strategies.

45

Thus Internet-based strategies play an important role in helping companies build a sustainable competitive advantage. It has created a fundamental shift in the marketing environment and requires a radically different strategic approach affecting all aspects of the strategic marketing decision process.

Question 3.7

How has the growth of Internet-based strategies by companies impacted on the services offered by intermediaries in the supply chain?

Case study

Changing the business model with The Officers' Club

After qualifying as an accountant David Charlton worked in the clothing industry for Jackson's the Tailor, now part of Arcadia Group. When parts of the business closed down several of the factory managers set up their own business, sourcing material, manufacturing in the UK and retailing through their own shops. Charlton worked for the operation but was envious of the money the bosses made.

The trigger to Charlton becoming an entrepreneur was his brother's redundancy. In 1979 Charlton persuaded him to put his £4500 redundancy cheque into setting up an upmarket clothing business, Fiori. In 1987 Charlton bought out his brother and a venture capitalist took a 13 per cent stake in the firm.

As the recession of the 1990s took hold the company went into receivership. But in true entrepreneurial spirit Charlton tried again. A visit to the US convinced him that discount retailers, with their fast stock turnover were busiest, so he made the decision to go to the opposite end of the spectrum from luxury fashion and set up a discount clothing retailing business.

His suppliers were confident in his business model and were prepared to provide stock, and his landlord allowed him to pay rent one month in arrears. With only a small loan secured on his house he started up the business. He realised that he had to make money from day one, as he had no financial cushion for security but deep discounting brought in the customers. The Officer's Club now have 180 stores in the UK.

Source: Adapted from 'The Officers' Club at www.startups.co.uk accessed on 29 September 2005.

Question 3.8

What are the key lessons from this for strategic marketing decisions?

Question 3.9

Having taken a decision to opt for a discount retailing approach, how would you use a 'learning approach' to maintain competitive advantage?

Summary

- The values that underlie strategic marketing decisions need to include a strong company orientation towards learning about the market competitors, as the strategy development process itself is an iterative learning one.
- Firms need to be proactive in the building of knowledge of the marketplace so they are better able to react to environmental changes and defend their competitive positions in their markets.
- Such knowledge capability of a company should incorporate three levels of analysis: analysis of the macro environment, analysis at an industry/market level and an analysis of customers and competitors.
- A primary objective of competitor analysis is to understand and predict the rivalry or interactive market behaviour between firms competing in the same market arena.
- In an effective learning organization, a company will link the knowledge it has built and the learning it has gained to build an efficient organizational memory which can be accessed through an effective knowledge management system.
- For some companies the growth of Internet-based strategies has played a significant role in the way they compete in the marketplace and has impacted on all aspects of the marketing process and the way in which decisions are made. Other companies simply view the Internet as a medium for them to advertise their products and service, in which case the impact of the Internet has been far less.

Further study

Doole, I. and Lowe, R. (2004) *International Marketing Strategy: Analysis, Development & Implementation*, 4th edition, Thomson Learning, Chapters 2 and 3 (ISBN 1-86152-772-1).

Doole, I. and Lowe, R. (2005) *Strategic Marketing Decisions in Global Markets*, Thomson Learning, Chapter 2.

Wilson, R.M.S. and Gilligan, C.T. (2004) *Strategic Marketing Management: Planning Implementation & Control*, 3rd edition, Butterworth-Heinemann.

Hints and tips

Candidates of the Strategic Marketing Decision syllabus need to be aware of the scope of this module. International Marketing Strategy is no longer taught as a separate module but has been subsumed across all modules. All modules therefore take a global perspective in their scope and orientation. In this module it is expected that the candidate is able to think, analyse and make strategic marketing decisions on a global scale. It is important therefore that you understand the global dimensions of marketing and you collect information on companies that operate globally as well as nationally.

Likewise it is expected that there will be increasing emphasis on the importance of the Internet in competing globally. References to the Internet and to global markets are incorporated into many of the units of this coursebook. Whilst Internet-based strategies and international marketing are not taught explicitly at Postgraduate Diploma of the CIM syllabus they are both deeply entrenched into the syllabus and so candidates need to be prepared to answer examination questions where an understanding of the issues involved in these areas is required.

Bibliography

Bergen, M. and P'eteraf, M.A. (2002) 'Competitor identification & competitor analysis: A broad based managerial approach', *Managerial & Decision Economics*, **23**, p. 160.

Doole, I. and Lowe, R. (2005) *Strategic Marketing Decisions in Global Markets*, Thomson Learning.

Garvin, D.A. (1993) 'Building a learning organization', *Harvard Business Review*, July–August, pp. 78–90.

Hamel, G. and Prahalad, C.K. (1994) *Competing for the Future*, Boston: Harvard Business School Press.

Hendrix, P.E. (2003) 'Limited visibility', *Marketing Management*, pp. 41–47.

Senge, P.M. (1992) *The Fifth Discipline*: The Art and Practice of The Learning Organisation, Century Press.

Slater, S.F. (2001) 'Developing a customer value based theory of the firm', *Journal of the Academy of Marketing Science*, **25**(2).

Wilson, R.M.S. and Gilligan, C.T. (2004) *Strategic Marketing Management: Planning Implementation & Control*, 3rd edition, Butterworth-Heinemann.

Sample exam questions and answers for the Strategic Marketing Decisions module as a whole can be found in Appendix 3 at the back of the book.

unit 4

developing corporate-wide marketing innovation

Learning objectives

The CIM syllabus for Strategic Marketing Decisions requires you to demonstrate an understanding of the impact of innovation throughout the organization's marketing activities.

In studying this unit you will:

2.2 Explain the nature of innovation in marketing and the factors affecting its development in decisions to create competitive advantage and customer preference.

2.3 Evaluate the role of innovation management and risk-taking in achieving competitive advantage.

2.4 Examine the issues in creating an innovative marketing culture within an organization.

2.9 Evaluate the incorporation of customer-led Internet marketing into marketing strategies.

Having completed the unit, you will be able to:

○ Evaluate the role of brands, innovation, integrated marketing communications, alliances, customer relationships and service in decisions for developing a differentiated positioning to create exceptional value for the customer.

○ Demonstrate the ability to develop innovative and creative marketing solutions to enhance an organization's global competitive position in the context of changing product, market, brand and customer life cycles.

○ Define and contribute to investment decisions concerning the marketing assets of an organization.

This unit relates to the statements of practice

Bd.1   Promote a strong market orientation and influence/contribute to strategy formulation and investment decisions.

Cd.1   Promote organization-wide innovation and co-operation in the development of brands.

Ed.1   Promote corporate-wide innovation and co-operation in the development of products and services.

Key definitions

Diffusion curve – is the model of the spread of a new product into the markets, split into customer response segments (innovators, early adopters, early majority, late majority and laggards).

Industry breakpoints – are defined (Strebel, 1996) as a new offering to the market that is so superior in terms of customer value that it disrupts the rules of the competitive game. Two types of breakpoints are discussed. *Divergent breakpoints* are associated with the sharply increasing variety in the competitive offerings and consequently higher value for the customer. *Convergent breakpoints* are the result of improvements in the system and processes resulting in lower delivered costs.

Continuous innovations – cause negligible or slightly disruptive effects upon the purchase and consumption of the product.

Dynamically continuous innovations – have a more disruptive effect on the way that the products and services are used.

Discontinuous innovations – have a highly disruptive effect upon usage and purchasing patterns and these innovations require a high level of marketing to explain the benefits and to educate consumers about how the product should be used.

Study Guide

This unit is concerned with making strategic marketing decisions that are innovative and, therefore, might challenge the often highly planned, conventional marketing strategies of many organizations. This unit is concerned with examining the ways in which organizations can promote corporate-wide innovation. In doing this, it is useful to identify the nature and sources of innovation, and the implications of pursuing innovation for marketing management. We examine how technological innovation, such as the Internet, has provided both a threat and an opportunity for firms. Smaller entrepreneurial firms are often at the forefront of innovation and it is useful to learn from them. Larger firms need to accept that risk is associated with innovation and create a supportive environment that will protect and encourage innovators.

In order to better understand entrepreneurial marketing and motivate themselves to be more innovative, students should read how entrepreneurs have successfully identified and exploited new opportunities. Students should also familiarize themselves with Internet marketing and e-business. Suggestions for further reading are included in the 'Further study' section at the end of this unit.

The nature and impact of innovation

Innovation is characterized by occasional 'great leaps forward' interspersed with continuous small-scale improvements. Although the most obvious impact of innovation is the launch of an entirely new product or service into a market, in practice it is possible for organizations to gain improved performance and increase competitive advantage through continual innovation in every aspect of the marketing activity. At the outset, it is important to recognize that innovation is not the same as invention. Inventions drive the major technological breakthroughs but the majority of innovations involves creativity in many different areas such as design, brand imagery, service development, process improvement, new routes to market and so on.

Continual small-scale innovation throughout the organization is essential. Customers are becoming more demanding and have higher expectations of products, services and process as they are exposed to a greater variety of competitive products. Organizations must respond by continually seeking to improve every aspect of their offerings in order to retain customer interest and loyalty, whilst they wait for the next great breakthrough.

It is important to recognize too that to be successful in innovation it is not enough to simply have good ideas. It is vital to have an effective process that will lead to commercial success. An innovation is not a success until it is profitably satisfying customer demands.

Technology life cycle

Technology has a major impact on innovation and there is a technology life cycle. Figure 4.1 shows the nature of the relationship between investment in R&D and the impact on performance in a particular technology. At the top of the S-curve, little further improvement in performance is possible, no matter how much further investment is made, as the product (e.g. black and white television technology) has reached the limits of development. At this point, a new technology derived from an earlier invention will provide a product (e.g. colour televisions) to satisfy the emerging customer needs. Initially, the new technology will provide a basic product with limited performance, but it will be improved over time with further R&D investment.

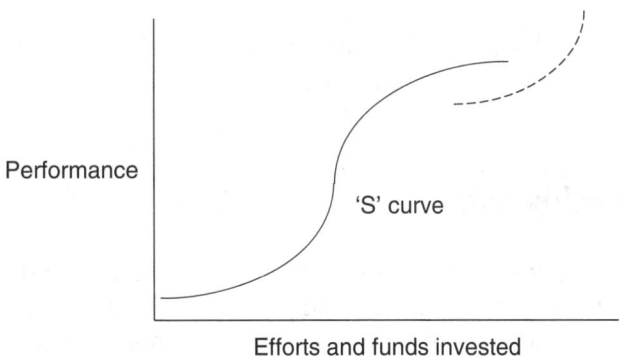

Figure 4.1 R&D investment, performance and discontinuity

Technology both drives change in many market sectors and provides a means of responding to change. As illustrated in Figure 4.2, those firms that are the first to embrace a new technology and find a practical application, for example creating a new product, service or a new route to market, will gain a new source of competitive advantage. However, this might well set new standards for the industry sector, and competitors will have to also achieve those standards if they wish to compete in the future. Therefore, all competitors in the sector catch up by embracing the new technology. Consequently, the innovative firm again has to find a new technological advance that allows them to get ahead again.

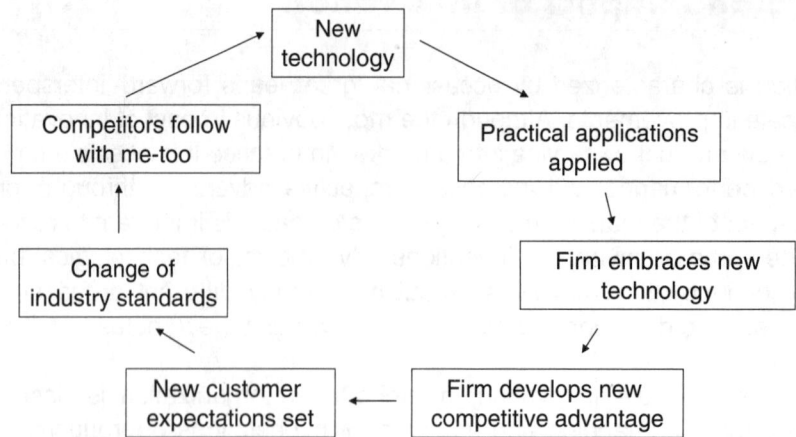

Figure 4.2 Technology and competitive advantage
Source: Doole and Lowe (2005) *Strategic Marketing Decisions in Global Markets*

Insight

Kodak switching their strategies to digital

The rate of changeover by consumers to digital cameras from traditional film formats has led to a major opportunity and a massive problem for Kodak, one of the leading players in the field. The industry has clearly reached a breakpoint in the S-curve, with sales of film, single-use cameras and other traditional products falling by 20 per cent in 2004. However, Kodak was still able to report higher quarterly profits because digital camera sales increased by 41 per cent in the year. The company expected growth to continue at the rate of 37 per cent per year up to 2007.

The major management challenge for Kodak is to restructure its business to cope with the change. It had to cut costs in its film manufacturing and processing business and this has meant a cut in its workforce worldwide of 12 000 jobs (20 per cent of its workforce).

Source: Adapted from 'Kodak eyes faster digital growth', 20 October 2004, BBC News Online.

Industry breakpoints

Major structural changes occur in markets from time to time and it is essential that companies are able to anticipate and respond rapidly to them. Breakpoints can be the result of not only technological breakthrough but also other factors such as an economic downturn, a new source of supply, changes of government policy or legislation, shifts in customer expectations, changes in distribution channels, declining revenues, new entrants and the identification of new opportunities by one company leading to new responses from competitors.

See CIM SMD Examination June 2005, Question 3

The SMD syllabus deals frequently with companies having to take a new direction due to their being in the mature phase of the life cycle. This question takes one such company and requires the candidate to discuss the different levels of innovation, *incremental and radical* and evaluate how each may be used in the context given.

The impact of information and communications technology

The developments in information and communications technology, particularly the development of the Internet, illustrate this. The Internet and other associated technologies do not just provide new products and services but also provide the solutions to old marketing process problems, such as how customers in remote locations around the world can contribute to the design of a new global product as much as the customer next door, and how a ten-person business can market its products or services to its potential customers in forty or fifty countries.

Question 4.1

Explain the concepts of technical discontinuities and industry breakpoints. Using examples describe the marketing activity that can be used to successfully exploit the opportunities that result.

New technologies facilitate innovation in many other marketing processes. Technology does not change the elements, challenges and dilemmas associated with the marketing decision-making process, but do have a major impact on the nature of the marketing strategy that is used and the solutions that are developed. Most importantly, these technologies have speeded up many of the marketing processes and have integrated internal processes with external processes. For example, internal data on sales of an individual product in an individual supermarket can be made available through an Extranet to suppliers, who can arrange a delivery to the supermarket against an open order in order to keep the shelves filled.

Categories of innovation and the marketing implications

There are a number of ways of categorising innovations. At a fundamental level, the types are shown in the insight.

Insight

The types of innovation

Product innovation: Changes in the product and services the organisation offers.

Process innovation: Changes in the way products and services are created and delivered for example, on-line banking.

Position innovation: Changes in the context in which products and services are introduced. For example, simplified mobile phones to appeal to older users, who just want to make a phone call

Paradigm innovation: Changes in the underlying mental models, which frame what, the organisation does.

Source: Utterback, J. (1994) *Mastering the Dynamics of Innovation*, Harvard Business School Press, Boston Mass, 256.

Innovations can also be placed into one of three categories – continuous, dynamically continuous and discontinuous innovations – according to the disruption they cause to customer buying and usage patterns. The significance of this is in the nature and cost of marketing activity that is needed to educate customers about the new product and service, explain how it is different from existing products and services and persuade customers to buy the new one.

Flat screen monitors for computers are continuous innovations and have not changed how customers use them, and so marketing activity focuses on the aesthetics rather than the need to re-educate consumers. As consumers become more knowledgeable, however, there is no guarantee that continuous innovations will be accepted without question. Products that are going to be consumed in the same way but with substantially changed ingredients (e.g. genetically modified (GM) ingredients in foods or fluoride in toothpaste) will not always be automatically acceptable to consumers.

A digital camera can fall into both the dynamically continuous and the discontinuous innovation categories. If it is used to take pictures and the memory card is then taken to a photographic shop for processing, it has little effect on the customer's lifestyle, whereas if it is used by the customer in conjunction with a computer or special printer for processing, it has a more disruptive effect on purchasing and usage, and customers must be educated as to the benefits. For continuous and dynamically continuous innovations, the mass of the market should be easily convinced of the benefits.

The more disruptive the innovation is to the customers' normal purchasing, consumption and disposal patterns, the greater the investment that is needed in marketing communications to educate them in respect of why they need the innovation, how they will benefit from it and how they should use it (and not use it). In the early days, it will be the innovators of the diffusion curve (Figure 4.3) that will be first to see the benefits of a disruptive innovation. It may take the early adopters and early majority a long time to accept the product. Consequently, the take-up of the product may be slower than expected.

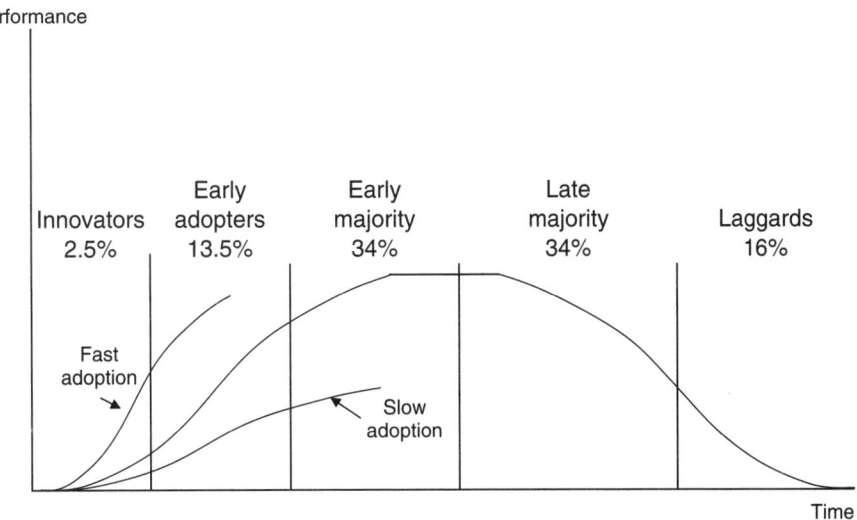

Figure 4.3 The diffusion curve

Major technology change may require a radical change in the firm's management processes such as manufacturing, distribution channel and marketing, and so a re-orientation or even a complete reinvention of the firm's business model might be needed.

Activity 4.1

Assess the innovation capability of your own organization (or one of your choice) and assess the number and quality of successful innovations that the organization produces that reach the market.

Sources of innovation and opportunity identification

Whilst much of our discussion so far has centred on technological breakthroughs, our discussion on industry breakpoints suggests that many breakthroughs are not the result of technology. Other sources of innovation are now highlighted which have the effect of creating industry breakpoints. We then look at the specific techniques that might be used for identifying opportunities. Many of the innovation opportunities come as a result of major environmental change or unexpected events and create the industry breakpoints.

Opportunity identification

Doole and Lowe (2005) have discussed techniques to identify opportunities. These include:

o *Scientific exploration* – that starts with no immediate, obvious application or customer benefit in mind.
o *Analysis of current and anticipated customer needs* – is an obvious starting point. Asking customers what they want usually identifies new product and service developments that will be discussed in Unit 9, but it is often difficult for customers to articulate what they do not know is possible and this is discussed in Unit 7.

○ *Segmenting markets further* – than they have been segmented before is an effective way of developing products and services to meet more precisely the needs of sub-segments of customers.

○ *Identifying a new emerging segment* – that is born out of changes in the mood, attitudes and expectation of customers and dissatisfaction with current offerings.

○ *Applying existing techniques in a new sector* – Managers can make connections between seemingly unrelated ideas or apply a technology, process or technique from one business sector to another.

○ *Vertical integration* – of the supply chain: an organization can eliminate one link in the chain or create a new, better value route to market. A fruit grower in Kent (UK) vertically integrated the business into jam making (Tiptree Jams).

○ *Business rationalization* – or mergers often lead to some products and services being no longer required or a customer segment no longer being satisfied.

○ *Innovation in mature sectors* – The most successful innovations have taken place often in mature sectors by offering customers a quantum leap in value.

Thinking techniques

Creative thinking techniques can be applied by managers in an existing organization to observe trends, understand the underlying causes of common complaints, apply the leading-edge knowledge and expert ideas in the sector, and spot market gaps and unfulfilled requirements.

Ignoring the competition and providing a quantum leap

The fast growth companies do not compete by benchmarking themselves with competitors and trying to match or beat them. They ignore the competition by offering buyers a quantum leap in value, often competing in a quite different way.

Kim and Mabourgne (1997) say that an organization must ask what it would take to win over the mass of buyers without relying on traditional competitive marketing and they propose asking the questions in Figure 4.4.

○ What factors that your industry takes for granted should be eliminated?
○ What factors that your industry competes on should be reduced well below the standard?
○ What factors that your industry competes on should be raised well above the standard?
○ What factors should be created that our industry has never offered?

Figure 4.4 Giving customers a quantum leap in value

In doing this, the most creative organizations set new standards for their industry. Rarely are these organizations the most powerful market leaders but may become leaders. Recent examples of firms offering a quantum leap in value include the low-cost activities of Amazon and Dell.

Case study

Cirque du Soleil's new act

Cirque du Soleil was created in 1984 by a group of street performers who realised the traditional circus format with the pedestrian animal acts and slapstick comedy routines of the clowns was outdated. Cirque created a new industry sector, by eliminating some of the costly and problematic elements, such as the animals and replaced them with spectacular shows that focused on technology, performance arts and musical theatre. They no longer offered low priced entertainment targeted at children but instead aimed at adults with premium priced shows. Cirque now employs 3000 people and has been seen by 50 million people in almost 100 cities.

Source: Adapted from Crainer, S. (2005) 'Plenty more seas to fish', *Observer*, 6 February.

Question 4.2

What assumptions were challenged in this example?

Activity 4.2

Identify the possible techniques for opportunity identification that could be applied to your own organization or an organization of your choice. Use one of the techniques to identify an opportunity.

Insight

Home and mobile media

People wanting to enjoy a variety of home entertainment media, such as radio, TV, music, electronic games and online media, must be prepared to have a roomful of electronic boxes, cables resembling spaghetti and service subscriptions covering a page of a bank statement. If they want on-the-move communications and entertainment, such as telephony, Internet connection, music and radio, they must be prepared to carry pockets or bags full of quickly out-of-date gadgets.

A number of products are emerging to address the confusion, including media PCs, multifunction mobile phones and wireless connectivity but it is difficult still to predict where the next breakpoints in the sector will occur. Use the techniques discussed to suggest where the next innovations and breakpoints might occur.

Innovation throughout the marketing strategy process
Opportunities for innovation can be initiated by challenging current thinking in every aspect of the marketing strategy development process and some examples of areas that can be exploited are included in Table 4.1.

Table 4.1 Marketing strategy process innovations

Innovations	Some examples
Environmental changes	Responding to legal changes (e.g. safety or environmental pollution regulations, market derogation)
	Responding to technological advances
Resources and capabilities audit	Exploiting company competencies in a new way (e.g. using e-business)
Strategy	Segmenting the market further than it is at present
	Repositioning to benefit from changes in customer needs and attitudes
Market entry alternatives	Participating in an alliance to redefine the market
The marketing mix	Focusing on interactive rather than mass communications
Supply chain	Finding new value from supply-chain contributions
Relationships	Redefining the mix to solution provision, rather than selling products and services

The innovation process

The inescapable fact is that the majority of good ideas never become commercial successes. There is a strong possibility that they will fail at every stage of the new product development process. For this reason it is vital to have an established, objective and systematic process to:

- Increase the number of ideas coming forward
- Better manage the process from idea generation to commercialization
- Increase the chances of success for the potential winners
- Screen out potential losing ideas as early as possible in order to avoid wasting effort
- Minimize the early costs of investigating individual ideas
- Tap the organization's creative potential by encouraging everyone in the organization to suggest innovations and improvements
- Increase the speed to market in order to beat the competition
- Maximize the value of the innovation to the organization and its customers.

Developing a systematic process for innovation

The familiar process for new product development suggested by Kotler is detailed in Figure 4.5. Whilst it is intended for new product development, the concepts behind the process can be applied to most areas of marketing innovation. The objectives of the NPD process is to delay the largest investment cost, until it has been shown that the new product or service has a high probability of success so that the risk is reduced as far as possible. Carrying out the process as a linear sequence as shown in Figure 4.5 is time consuming and so many organizations aim to carry out the individual process steps simultaneously, thus reducing the time to market.

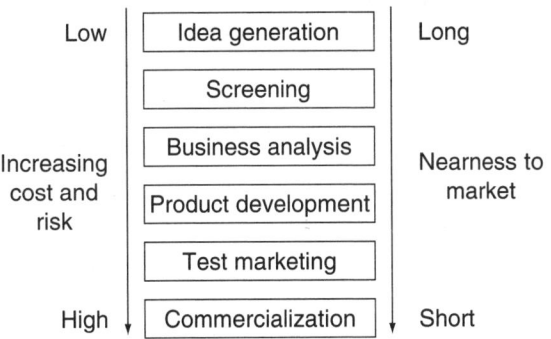

Figure 4.5 The new product development process

Most marketing texts include explanations of how the process should be used and a fuller discussion is included in Doole and Lowe (2005).

Activity 4.3

Design a process for innovation for your own organization or an organization of your choice, from idea to commercialization. What are the major barriers in the process and how might they be overcome?

Diffusion is key

Achieving a commercial success depends on a number of critical factors in the innovation process including:

- Minimizing the early stage costs in the innovation process and only carrying out the high investment at later stages of the process when there is a high probability of success
- Successfully launching the product or service to quickly get a high level of customer first purchases
- Achieving a positive cash flow quickly
- Winning over fast enough a sufficient number of loyal customers who will repeat purchase to generate a sustainable income stream for the product or service
- Using cost-effective market entry methods to build global sales
- Achieving continual improvements after launch through ongoing R&D to keep the product or service fresh.

Research suggests that the reason for failure in innovation is not usually technology failure but is more often marketing related. It is ineffective diffusion of the innovation into the market that is the main reason for failure.

Multinational enterprises may need to launch new products and services simultaneously into many markets. Their considerable resources allow them to tolerate large negative outflows over longer periods. By contrast, smaller organizations need to reach the breakeven point (Figure 4.6) and generate a positive cash flow as quickly as possible merely to survive. Consequently, they need to keep their R&D investment, marketing and fixed costs as low as possible in order to quickly recover them through sales revenue. This may mean that their launch and marketing programmes may need to strike a careful balance between creating awareness and interest through a comprehensive promotional programme and incurring unacceptably high costs.

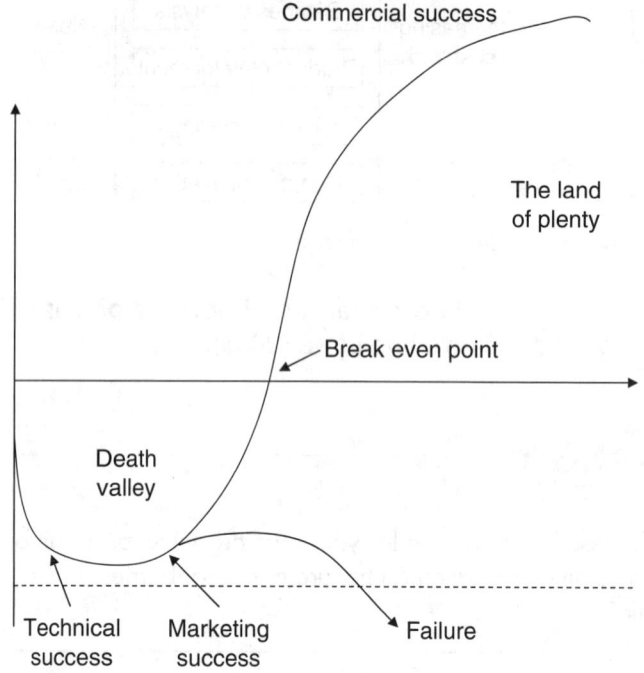

Figure 4.6 Getting to breakeven point

Bolton and Thompson (2000) describe the period up to the break-even point shown in Figure 4.6 as 'death valley', which must be crossed before reaching the 'land of plenty'. In the initial commercialization period for any innovation, there are two critical points in the new business model, shown in Figure 4.6. The first is whether the new business is a technical success – does it work for the customers and deliver the benefits to them that were set out in the original brief? If it is not a technical success then the business will fail. The second point is whether or not the new business is a marketing success – in other words, will sufficient customers from the target segment buy and repeatedly buy to generate the necessary cash flows? If not the business will again fail.

It is worth re-emphasizing that the organization should focus on the opportunity to generate revenue and exploit the market gap rather than stubbornly trying to sell the specific product or service that was originally envisaged. Famously, Honda failed initially to make an impact when it sold large motor cycles in the US, but noticed that people were fascinated by the 50 cc bikes their staff were using. They sold the 50 cc bikes successfully to build up the business and later succeeded with large bikes. They are still the market leader in the US.

The problem for decision-makers arises when the initial product or service offer fails to generate sufficient revenue. The question becomes how long should it be supported before making a significant revision. A further problem is created if a product or service is successful in some less important country or regional operations but fails in the major markets.

Question 4.3

What do you consider to be the critical success factors in achieving a commercial success?

Risk-taking in bureaucratic and entrepreneurial organizations

There are two certainties associated with innovation: as competition increases, growth and even survival in any market sector will become more difficult without innovation; and risk-taking is an inevitable part of innovation. Organizations adopt a stance somewhere on a continuum between being risk-averse, characterized by bureaucratic organizations, and risk-taking typically seen in entrepreneurial companies. Over a period of time, an organization must move out of low to higher value-adding areas through innovation. To develop and grow an organization, one must be a risk taker, but for sustainability, one must also be a risk manager. At any time, an organization should not collapse if one's innovation goes wrong.

Risk-taking in bureaucratic firms

The most bureaucratic organizations recognize the need to take risks but fail to put in place a strategy and process to support it. Large firms often ignore the marketing philosophy of meeting customer needs and instead arrogantly believe that they can influence sales through their market power. They believe that timing market entry is less important than getting their launch right, so bureaucratic firms are rarely first movers if there is a significant change.

In order to become less bureaucratic, firms must recognize that innovators do not follow rules because, at its best, innovation has no rules. Innovation avoids established patterns, standards and controls that tend to be the central pillars of a bureaucratic firm. There is an inevitable conflict between the entrepreneurs who seek to commercialize innovations and the administrators who seek to apply controls. Stevenson (2000) contrasts entrepreneurial and administrative management and emphasizes the differences in strategies, commitment to pursuing opportunity, the commitment and control of resources, management structures and reward systems.

In extreme situations, bureaucratic organizations get into a vicious circle of failing to commercialize ideas, and so develop a discouraging culture. Innovation paralysis results.

Activity 4.4

As a marketing director of a bureaucratic organization that has a poor record of innovation throughout, prepare a list of actions that you would take to encourage your staff to become more innovative.

Risk-taking in entrepreneurial firms

Referring back to the entrepreneurial styles of management the lower the fixed asset and cost base of the organization, the faster the entrepreneurial business is likely to enter new markets, albeit initially less intensively. It is likely to be able to withdraw from unpromising areas more quickly too. Entrepreneurs may be risk takers but they also have greater scope to be risk managers too. They rely on their ability to be more adaptable, flexible and responsive to manage risk.

Large organizations that are risk-averse ultimately may have to take greater risks because of the need to re-orientate a large fixed asset base. For these reasons in a highly competitive fast-changing market, where development and marketing costs are a high proportion of the selling price, outsourcing and partnering may be lower-risk business models than the organization having all the business functions and operations in-house.

Managing innovation and creating the right culture

Creating the right organizational culture is essential and to this there is a need for:

- A sustained commitment to innovation from top management
- A willingness to accept risks
- A degree of flexibility
- An ability and willingness to commit resources
- Individuals to be given more responsibility for new product development
- Innovation to be seen as a corporate-wide task.

Organizing for innovation

The organization structure, management style and culture must reflect the commitment to innovation. However, organizing for innovation can cause problems, given that the innovation process requires contributions from all functions as well as outside organizations, too. There can be some dispute as to which department should take overall managerial responsibility for innovation. Consequently, a range of innovation models exist ranging from R&D, brand, marketing and general managers taking responsibility. Many companies believe that the only way to achieve breakthrough innovation is through 'skunk works', which are set up as entirely separate units physically outside their offices to maximize creativity.

Question 4.4

Choose an organization that you consider to be one of the most innovative. How has it achieved success and how can this be maintained in the future?

Customer-led Internet marketing

Much of the early period of Internet-led marketing was characterized by the idea that somehow technology-driven businesses would replace marketing-led businesses run with traditional business models, simply by setting up a website. However, the majority of the companies set up failed to develop a business model that had predictable costs and quantifiable and sustainable income streams. Few of the dot-com businesses offered customer value and satisfaction. In practice, the (few) winners from the dot-com boom have succeeded by combining good marketing, efficient technology platforms and good business sense. The vast majority of businesses have added Internet marketing onto already successful traditional formats.

Lower costs

E-commerce can be used to reduce costs, for example, by cutting out non-contributing intermediaries in the supply chain, enabling easier access and management of suppliers, and providing better targeting, servicing and management of customers. However, whilst saving on supply and distribution costs, the e-business model usually requires high initial infrastructure investment and some additional costs of running the business. Whilst e-commerce may still lower costs, this may not be enough to provide customer satisfaction.

Strategy redirection

Rather than seeing e-business simply as providing cost savings the more astute firms have used e-commerce as the mechanism for redirecting the business, either to exploit the new opportunities or to gain competitive advantage and so it is essential to decide:

- o How Internet marketing can be used to further add satisfaction and customer value.
- o How Internet marketing can be used to better integrate the organizations' external and internal processes.
- o The future role of Internet marketing in the business sector and the changing nature of business models, which is dealt with in Unit 7.

Innovation in Internet marketing

Opportunities for e-business innovation occur at the interface between customers and the internal operation.

The specific characteristics of the Internet that have facilitated the development of Internet marketing are shown in Table 4.2. These characteristics provide the drivers for innovation in Internet marketing.

Table 4.2 The six-Is of the Internet

Six-Is	Characteristics of the Internet
Interactivity	Customer initiated contact Marketer has 100% customer attention
Intelligence	Can continuously collect and analyse information and make individually focused offers
Individualization	Marketing communications is tailored to meet individual needs so achieving mass customization
Integration	Managing integrated external and internal marketing communications and mixed mode buying
Industry restructuring	Dis-intermediation involves removing the traditional intermediaries from the distribution channel Re-intermediation involves gaining a presence on websites that might fulfil the role of intermediary
Independence of location	Reach can be extended into countries where it is not viable to locate a significant sales support activity

Source: Adapted from Deighton (1996)

Question 4.5

A number of technologies have not lived up to their earlier promise. Third generation mobile phones and consumer purchasing on the Internet have not generated as much revenue as was originally expected. Why do you think this is so?

Case study

The Eden project: showbiz meets science

Among Britain's lottery-funded millennium projects, there were a lot of high-profile flops, including the Dome at Greenwich, Sheffield's rock and pop museum and the Earth Centre in South Yorkshire. But the Eden Project in Cornwall, which opened in March 2001, proved to be a spectacular success. In a year, 645 000 visitors were expected, but it attracted 940 000 in its first six months alone and now has over 1.5 million visitors each year.

The entrepreneur

Tim Smit, an Anglo-Dutch former pop producer, moved to Cornwall in the late 1980s to set up a recording studio. Next door to the studio was a large, neglected garden, which Smit restored as 'The Lost Gardens of Heligan'. Soon after its opening in 1992, it became one of Cornwall's top tourist destinations. Smit's next brainchild was *The Eden Project* and his aim was to create a rainforest and other plant 'landscapes' underneath two giant 'biomes' built in a disused China clay pit. His track record gave the lottery's fund commission the confidence to award the project £37.5 million and helped him to attract the private investment that was necessary to match the lottery funding.

The early success of Eden was attributed to the fact that unlike some of the other lottery-funded projects, it was a good idea looking for money, not money-looking for an idea. Many projects of this type appeared to be the result of the determination of cities to get some of the lottery cash, irrespective of how viable the project was. The Eden Project was the vision of one entrepreneur, rather than the result of planning by committee. The most notorious failure – the Dome – was the product of bureaucratic compromise and inappropriate political intervention. After five years, the Dome still has no real role.

The vision

The Lost Gardens of Heligan had proved to Smit that the study of plants could mean good business in the right situation. Smit realised from his former background, however, that an element of showbiz was needed and his mission was to 'make science sexy'. Science appeals to both children and adults and seems to be good theme-park material. The message of the project was also very serious – that man and plants have co-existed profitably together for centuries and must continue to do so – and this has enabled Eden to make a valuable contribution to education, research, awareness raising of important issues and campaigning. A new £15 million education centre was built in 2005. All the buildings have unique, instantly recognisable designs and are made, where possible, from locally available materials from sustainable sources.

The regional contribution

Eden has a key role and fits in well in the region. There are a number of other garden attractions and so is a 'must' for adults interested in gardening and, given its location in a popular holiday area, it also attracts visitors looking for a day away from the beach. Many lottery funded visitor attractions seemed to be isolated from other attractions and have no emotional attachment to the area, making it more unlikely that people would visit. Moreover, local people resent money that was intended for charitable purposes being spent on what they regard as pointless projects.

Eden employs over 440 people, 90 per cent of them are local. It has contributed significantly to the economy of Cornwall, one of the poorest counties in England. It claims to have appointed 200 local suppliers and have put £150 million into the local economy in its first year. It also had a significant impact on the demand for accommodation, being partly responsible for the 96 per cent increase compared to the previous year.

The potential for conflict

Despite the outstanding success of the Eden project it is does face continual challenges, dilemmas and potential conflicts. Whilst it is not expected to pay off its original grants it does have to continually generate income to pay its way and justify further funding for new projects, some of which will not generate income. The fact that the number of visitors far exceeds the forecast places considerable strain on the facilities and catering – areas where the staff try to avoid compromise and wish to maintain high standards.

Many of its show business activities are high profile and perhaps attract a different type of visitor. The Eden project hosted the 'Africa Calling' concert for 4000 people as part of the 'Make Poverty History' Live 8 campaign in 2005. It was memorable in featuring black artists, answering the criticisms of some of the other concerts. It is planning a repeat event in 2006. It also creates a giant skating rink as part of its winter event to generate additional income. It has been host to conferences and seminars attended by world experts discussing environmental concerns.

Events such as these create considerable disruption and heartache for the horticulturalists at Eden, whose work is devoted to creating the right conditions for the plants to be at their best. Neither the plants nor the staff take kindly to being trampled on or uprooted by the construction workers and electricians working on the next event, so the management team must try to balance the opposing interests and maintain the motivation of the staff that believed, when they joined, that they were working for a science establishment rather than one they feel is increasingly becoming dedicated to show business. Smit emphasises that he is not a horticulturalist and horticulture is not the primary aim of the Eden project.

Source: Robin Lowe from various public sources

Question 4.6

What do you consider to be the marketing aims of the Eden project and how does this fit with the macro and micro environmental factors?

Question 4.7

How can the marketing decisions taken address the different stakeholder expectations?

Question 4.8

How might the spirit of building stakeholder value generated by the Eden project be capitalized upon (1) within Cornwall (2) by the Eden project itself?

Summary

- ○ Technology both drives innovation and provides the means of responding to changing customer requirements and expectations
- ○ There are, however, sources other than technology that drive innovation
- ○ There are categories of innovation from 'new to the world breakthroughs' to minor adaptations to products and these pose different challenges for marketing
- ○ An effective innovation process is essential for managing diffusion of the innovation into the market
- ○ A supportive culture is needed to encourage risk-taking, but innovation also should be carried out within a process that is designed to manage risk too
- ○ In Internet marketing the website and business model are the platforms for innovation
- ○ The reasons for success and failure in innovation have been well-researched and to be successful it is vital to learn the lessons of good practice.

Further study

Birley, S. and Muzyka, D.F. (2000) *Mastering Entrepreneurship*, FT Pitman.

Bolton, B. and Thompson, J. (2000) *Entrepreneurs, Talent, Temperament, Technique*, Butterworth-Heinemann.

Doole, I. and Lowe, R. (2005) *Strategic Marketing Decisions in Global Markets*, Thomson Learning, Chapter 7.

Hints and tips

In studying this subject and answering questions on innovation, it is important to demonstrate that whilst there are some systematic processes and good practice lessons that are at the heart of innovation, fundamentally it is about being creative, thinking out of the box and taking risks that are proportionate to the opportunity identified.

You should build up examples that illustrate innovation in different areas of the marketing process and you should also build good (and bad) examples of management of the innovation process that can be applied to case studies.

Bibliography

Chaffey, D., Mayer, R., Johnston, K. and Ellis-Chadwick, F. (2003) *Internet Marketing, Strategy Implementation and Practice*, FT Prentice Hall, pp. 265–304.

Deighton, J. (1996) 'The future of interactive marketing', *Harvard Business Review*, Nov–Dec, pp. 151–162.

Doole, I. and Lowe, R. (2005) *Strategic Marketing Decisions in Global Markets*, Thomson Learning.

Drucker, P.F. (1985) *Innovation and Entrepreneurship*, Butterworth-Heinemann.

Kim, W.C. and Mabourgne, R. (1997) 'The strategic logic of high growth', *Harvard Business Review*, **75**(1).

Murphy, C. (2003) 'Innovation Masterminds', *Marketing*, 15 May.

Stevenson, H. (2000) 'The six dimensions of entrepreneurship', in S. Birley and D.F. Muzyka (eds), *Mastering Entrepreneurship*, FT Prentice Hall, pp. 8–13.

Strebel, P. (1996) 'Breakpoint: how to stay in the game', *Financial Times Mastering Management*, part 17, pp. 13–14.

Sample exam questions and answers for the Strategic Marketing Decisions module as a whole can be found in Appendix 3 at the back of the book.

unit 5

decisions for a new strategic marketing direction

Learning objectives

The CIM syllabus for Strategic Marketing Decisions requires you to be able to evaluate an organization's current strategy in the light of the context in which it operates and decide whether there is a need for the organization to take a new strategic marketing direction.

In studying this unit you will:

3.2 Evaluate and apply the generic marketing strategies to strategic marketing decision-making in the context of today's competitive environment, including segmentation, targeting and positioning (STP), Porter's three generic strategies.

3.4 Identify and critically evaluate strategic options in relation to shareholder value, using appropriate decision tools. See syllabus section.

3.5 Describe the formulation and evaluation of competitive strategies.

3.3 Critically appraise strategic marketing decisions for pioneers, challengers, followers and niche players.

Having completed this unit you will be able to:

o Appraise a range of corporate and business visions, missions and objectives and the processes by which they are formulated, in the light of the changing bases of competitive advantage across geographically diverse markets.

o Identify, compare and contrast strategic options and critically evaluate the implications of strategic marketing decisions in relation to the concept of 'shareholder value'.

o Demonstrate the ability to re-orientate the formulation and control of cost-effective competitive strategies, appropriate for the objectives and context of an organization operating in a dynamic global environment.

This unit relates to the statements of practice

Bd.1   Promote a strong market orientation and influence/contribute to strategy formulation and investment decisions.

Bd.2   Specify and direct the strategic marketing planning process.

Key definitions

Five definitions of strategy

Strategies can be intended
1. **Strategy as a plan** – a consciously intended course of action
2. **Strategy as a ploy** – just a specific manoeuvre to outwit rivals.

Strategies can be realized through behaviour
3. **Strategy as a pattern** – a stream of consistent behaviours, whether intended or not. It is worth comparing strategic intent with strategic reality. Strategic intent is often only partially realized in the form of a delivered strategy (the reality). There is often an unrealized part of this strategy, which leaves gaps that are often filled by emergent strategies that are not part of the initial intentions.

Strategy can be about external focus
4. **Strategy as a position** – a unique location for the organization within its environment achieved by matching up the organization (internal context) with the environment (external context).

Strategy can also be an internal focus
5. **Strategy as a perspective** – an ingrained way of perceiving the world.
    Source: Mintzberg et al., 2003.

Study Guide

This unit is concerned with the ways in which an organization can assess the appropriateness of its current strategy in its current context, and design new strategies to exploit opportunities in the global market. We focus upon an evaluation of why strategies fail or wear out. We then go on to identify the key decisions in the formulation of a new strategy, beginning with a redefinition of the business and its markets. An understanding of the success criteria for a strategy is followed by a discussion of the decisions involving the generic strategies, which should be central to the strategy. We have highlighted the Porter generic strategies and STP marketing. We have ended by referring briefly to decisions regarding competitive stance and competitive strategy.

Before starting on the unit, students should familiarize themselves with the planning process before addressing this unit by reading one of the recognized texts, such as the Strategic Marketing Management coursebook, that are identified in the 'Further study' section.

Strategy evaluation: the reasons for marketing strategy failure and wear-out

Few, if any, marketing strategies can remain the same forever. The evidence for this comes from the fact that from time to time some of the best-known and previously successful organizations go through a period of crisis in which they underperform against the expectations of their customers and other stakeholders make huge losses or, at worst, fail completely. At these times the marketing strategy that the company has pursued for a long time no longer delivers the required results and needs to be changed. In this section we consider the various reasons for failure, including the organization's inability to respond quickly enough to changes in the market environment. Some other organizations may well have the right marketing strategy for the context in which they are operating but they fail to implement it effectively because of weaknesses in their management and availability of resources.

The reasons for strategy failure and underperformance

There are many reasons why marketing strategies fail and organizations underperform, and we have grouped these into:

- Poor general management and inability to implement an appropriate strategy
- An inability to cope with market changes or the strategy taking longer than expected to succeed in the market
- Ineffective marketing management
- Removal of a protected environment.

Poor management

The most obvious evidence of underperformance comes in the form of poor financial performance or profit warnings made by the management to the city and investment fund managers. Whilst there may be many reasons for underperformance it is the senior management who are held responsible.

Operational inefficiency and poor cost control leading to uncompetitiveness

The causes of underperformance can include high production costs, poor use of fixed assets such as buildings and facilities, poor customer service, inefficiency in outsourcing and ineffective financial management.

Poor leadership and management

It can be argued that the problems highlighted above are merely symptomatic of indecisive leadership and weak management leading to lack of direction and control.

Lack of investment

Because of a lack of direction and a failure to generate profits, organizations fail to invest in projects to secure the future growth. They fail to invest in facilities, equipment, product and service development, brand development and market development.

Inability to cope with market changes

Firms in crisis often compound the error by making unwise and inappropriate investments as a panic reaction to the situation.

The nature and intensity of change in the sector environment

Different sectors experience change at different rates. For example, change in the industries that are driven by high technology, such as computer hardware and software marketing, is likely to be more dramatic than industries dependent on well-established technology such as specialist engineering. Over time, industries that are regarded as luxuries experience greater variability in demand than necessities, such as the utilities. The level and patterns of demand in the travel sector are affected by the economic situation and unexpected events, such as war and terrorism.

The problems that can contribute to strategy failure are, therefore, the inability to:

- o Manage an economic downturn or an industry sector cycle
- o Anticipate and plan for legislative and technological changes
- o Cope with slower than expected growth in a key segment, country or product
- o Cope with slower than expected diffusion of key products and services
- o Cope with changes in the route to market and distribution channels.

Ineffective marketing management

There are a number of areas where underperformance in marketing management can lead to strategy failure including:

- o Ineffective use of marketing tools and resources.
- o A competitor innovation or the emergence of a new, unexpected competitor.
- o Overdependence on one key customer. Small firms can become overdependent on one customer, and with the increasing concentration of retailers, distributors and manufacturers even larger suppliers often become increasingly dependent on fewer large customers and a narrow product range, at worst putting them at risk of going out of business, or at best making them targets for takeover.
- o Overdependence on one major product. Smaller firms and especially those that are new start with one innovative new product or service tend to be over-reliant in the early days on one or two major products. In a highly competitive market, competitors quickly copy new ideas and quickly remove the organization's market lead. Despite their limited resources, they must quickly develop additional or improved products and services in order to build a sustainable business. Even large businesses that provide one component or service in the supply chain of a global company can become vulnerable to the introduction of alternative products.

Removal of a 'protected' environment

A number of organizations operate in a protected environment and the strategy for this situation will be inadequate for a new competitive environment.

Imminent end of a monopoly

Governments around the world have privatized state-owned utilities often without fully thinking through the implications for the services, existing organization and its staff. An example of this in the UK is the privatization of the railways.

Change of customer needs and fashion

The main reason for strategy wear-out, however, is the failure of organizations to respond quickly enough and adapt to changes in the market and, particularly, respond to changes in customer needs and fashion, the emergence of a new competitor or changes in the structure of the market. In looking for one over-riding reason for the failure of a marketing strategy, most observers would place the blame firmly on the organization being too internally and not sufficiently externally focused.

Lack of customer and competitor focus

Senior managers often become preoccupied with managing staff, internal systems, structures and processes rather than using the resources that are available or could be accessed to add customer value. Efforts should be made to concentrate on the activities that yield the best results for all stakeholders and avoid the activities that simply maintain the current position or at worst drain resources from more value-adding activities in order to try to save dying products and services.

Question 5.1

If you look in the business press for a few days you will find reports of underperformance of a major global organization. Examples in 2003 included McDonald's, Marks & Spencer (again) and Sony. Choose one organization to study. Using newspaper reports and the checklist of reasons highlighted in this section analyse the cause of the underperformance in the organization.

 ## Activity 5.1

Strategic wear-out usually follows a quite long period of good performance. Often the signs of strategic wear-out are there but the management fail to respond. Assess the vulnerability to strategic wear-out of the marketing strategy of your own organization or an organization of your choice. Where is the greatest risk?

Redefining the business

Having considered the possible reasons for marketing strategy failure we now consider what preventive action should be taken. First the organization should have in place an effective marketing information system for collecting and monitoring information. Organizations that might be affected by this type of market environment change must decide whether they need to make major changes to the nature of the business and its place within its chosen market sector. In doing this, it is necessary to ask a number of questions. In order to ensure the sustainability of its business model, does the organization need to:

1. Stay in its current business and make only incremental changes to the marketing strategy, by broadly maintaining its current position in the market, focusing on its current contribution to the value chain, relying on its current source of competitive advantage and targeting its current and closely related market segments?
2. Make some major modifications to its role and contribution in the current market; perhaps through new product or market development initiatives, further differentiation of its products and services, increasing value added in the supply chain and enhance the source of competitive advantage?
3. Carry out some significant restructuring, perhaps by vertical integration or by outsourcing, redefining the basis of competitive advantage or moving into another market?
4. Completely reinvent its role and contribution through diversifying into a completely new sector?

Some examples of the above might include the following:

o Public sector organizations and organizations that have very specific responsibilities enshrined in law do make incremental changes but have little room to change their fundamental business model. Professional organizations, such as law firms, accountants and health care organizations, do experience substantial changes and initiate innovations but essentially they stay in the 'same business'.
o Supermarkets also essentially stay in the 'same business' of retailing but the successful ones continually innovate in order to stay ahead of the competition, introduce new products and services and enter new product categories. They have always outsourced products but are constantly finding new ways of adding customer value, often through supply-chain developments.
o A number of businesses, including banks, airlines, telecommunications and manufacturing businesses, have found it necessary to embark on major restructuring by outsourcing activities to lower-cost suppliers. They are concentrating more on their knowledge assets including market, customer, process technology, R&D capability rather than on operations.
o A number of businesses have reinvented themselves, with varying degrees of success. GEC was a large and highly profitable manufacturer of electrical engineering and communications products, and during the dot-com era it reinvented itself as Marconi in order to exploit the emerging IT market. The gamble (which it was) failed, the company only just avoided bankruptcy and years after is still struggling to regain a sustainable position.

Insight

Defining the business model

It may be necessary to redefine the business and in order to do this it is useful to address the following questions. The key factors in the business model are:

- What the organization will do and what tasks it will carry out.
- How the organization will connect with the market.
- What the offer is, how it is positioned and communicated to the customers.
- What the income streams will be.
- How the organization arranges its resources and what the cost streams will be.
- The organization's role within the value chain.
- How surpluses will be generated for further investment.

Selecting target markets

Before considering in detail the segmentation, targeting and positioning strategy, it is necessary to decide where the market focus should be. Hooley *et al.* (2004) discuss market attractiveness and the competitive position of the company in each market to distinguish between core, peripheral, illusion and dead-end business.

Case study

A new direction for IBM

Periodically an organization must review its strategy and decide if it is still pursuing a direction that will continue to generate value for its stakeholders. In 1981 IBM introduced the first personal computer to the market and was essentially responsible for turning computing into a mass market. However, very quickly competitors started to sell 'IBM compatible' copies and over time IBM has been unable to stop the PC hardware becoming a commodity. It is now a highly competitive market in which only very focused, specialist companies are able to compete.

Perhaps the biggest mistake that IBM made, however, was failing to realize that the profits from the industry would be made from the software. Unfortunately it allowed Microsoft, at that stage a fledgling business, to provide the software that would control its PC.

Eventually IBM had little competitive advantage and realized that it could no longer operate on the slender profit margins in the PC industry, against competitors such as Dell. In 2004 IBM sold its PC hardware division to the Chinese firm Lenovo (formerly known as Legend) for $1.75 billion. 10 000 IBM staff transferred to the new company, which moved its HQ from Beijing to upstate New York.

Lenovo believes that this deal will help it create a global brand. IBM's new direction means it will concentrate on large systems and providing consultancy and business solutions for organizations that wish to outsource their IT management.

Source: Adapted from 'Chinese firm buys IBM PC business', BBC News Online, 8 December 2004.

Question 5.2

Identify the benefits, threats and future challenges for IBM and Lenovo for this radical step.

Turnaround strategies

The most urgent need for a redefinition of the business occurs when the underperformance in the organization is so acute that its very survival is at risk. A turnaround strategy is needed to reverse the underperformance and put the firm back on a more secure path. Usually the poor performance is accompanied by a lethargic or 'blame' culture, lack of leadership and team-working, demoralized staff and management not focused on results. Often there is conflict between top managers on what needs to be done to improve the situation and this often leads to changes of personnel. The action usually taken focuses largely on cost cutting as a short-term measure to improve efficiency and competitiveness and ensure survival. However, for the turnaround strategy to deliver long-term improvement it is necessary to take action to address the more fundamental causes of poor performance such as redefining the segmentation, targeting and positioning strategy, rationalizing the portfolio, making customer service and satisfaction a priority, improving channel effectives and obtaining better value from marketing communications.

Generic decisions for a successful strategy

Whilst it is not our intention to discuss in detail the marketing strategy and planning process you should refer to the particular coursebook to remind yourself of the key decision points, such as objective setting and strategy evaluation criteria and the key models that help in setting the criteria by which the key strategic decisions should be made. We have highlighted here some important criteria for a successful strategy and the Porter generic strategies before considering STP.

Criteria for a successful strategy

The starting point in this section is to emphasize that in making strategic marketing decisions it is vital, first, that organizations are quite clear about the purpose of the strategy. Mintzberg *et al.* (2003) suggest that a strategy is needed when the potential aims or responses of intelligent opponents can seriously affect the endeavour's desired outcome. A strategy comprises patterns from the past and plans for the future and comprises a set of objectives, policies and plans that taken together define the scope of the enterprise and its approach to survival and success. The criteria for a successful strategy should include as a minimum:

- ○ *Clear decisive objectives* – although subordinate goals may change in the heat of the campaign or competition, the overriding goals must remain clear and understood.
- ○ *Maintaining the initiative* – it must allow freedom of action, enhance commitment and maintain the pace and determine the course of events, rather than reacting to them.
- ○ *Concentration* – it must be capable of concentrating superior power at a particular place and time to be decisive.
- ○ *Flexibility* – it must keep in reserve resources and capabilities in order to allow flexibility and manoeuvrability.

- ○ *Co-ordinated and committed leadership* – leaders must be appointed for each of the goals, and their interests and ambitions must match the needs of their roles.
- ○ *Surprise* – it must make use of speed, secrecy and intelligence to attack unprepared competitors.
- ○ *Security* – it must secure resources to support the actions.

 Activity 5.2

How would you define the strategy of your own organization or an organization of your choice in Mintzberg's terms and how does it score on Mintzberg's criteria for success? What steps are needed to ensure better levels of future success?

Porter's three competitive strategies

To compete effectively, Porter proposed that organizations need to select one from the following three generic competitive strategies and pursue it consistently:

1. *Cost leadership* – involves proactively seeking to lower costs in each element of the supply chain with the intention of outperforming rivals.
2. *Focus strategy* – involves creating a strong, specialist reputation in a very small number of customer segments.
3. *Differentiation strategy* – involves the delivery of superior customer value in one or more activities supported by a strong brand.

Wilson and Gilligan (2004) discuss the ways in which the strategy can be achieved, the benefits and the possible problems of each, and the danger of not pursuing any of the three and so being 'stuck in the middle'. It should be pointed out that a low-cost strategy does not necessarily mean a low-price strategy too, and many organizations following a focus or differentiation strategy work hard to achieve low costs too.

 Activity 5.3

Which of Porter's three generic strategies is being pursued by the strategic business units of your own organization or an organization of your choice? Is there any evidence of the strategic business units being stuck in the middle?

STP decisions

The fundamental process in marketing strategy development is segmentation, targeting and positioning and this should be at the core of all marketing strategies. Consequently, these are the areas where the key decision-making occurs. Before we do that, it is worth emphasizing the key areas of decision-making identified in Table 5.1.

Table 5.1 Key decisions in the STP process

Stages	Key decisions
1. Segmentation	
Choose the variables upon which the segmentation will be based	Build a deep understanding of the customer requirements and purchasing behaviour and reflect this in the variables used
	Avoid simple, single segmentation variables that do not achieve precision in targeting and positioning
Create segments for the whole market	Ensure the segments are measurable, substantial, accessible, stable and useful (Kotler, 1984) Dibb (2003)
Profile the segments and understand their needs and expectations	Ensure the profile is an accurate reflection of the key elements of customer attitudes, values and behaviour
2. Targeting	
Devise a targeting strategy	Determine the criteria for selecting the target segments, based on a deep understanding of the customers and company capability
Prioritize the segments and decide how many to serve	Apply criteria that will enable selection decisions to be made on the basis of the segments the organization is best able to serve or will be the most profitable
	Only target the number of segments that can be effectively resourced
3. Positioning	
Understand the target segment perceptions	Understand the customers' perceptions of the organization, brand or products and where they diverge from the organization's intended image and value proposition
Create a positioning approach that meets the target segment perceptions and expectations	Decide on a value proposition that emphasizes the customers the tangible and intangible benefits offered and how they are differentiated from competitor offerings
	Determine whether repositioning is needed and, if so, whether the necessary investment could be recouped
Design or redesign the marketing mix to meet the segment perceptions and expectations	Assess the contribution of each element of the marketing mix in delivering the value proposition to the customer groups

Source: Doole and Lowe (2005)

Insight

Breakthroughs in business models

By using creativity in STP approaches and combining this with innovation in the business proposition it is possible to create 'breakthrough' business models. Examples include:

Business models	Examples
Bait and hook	Low margin basic product with high margin refill, for example razor and blades, mobile phone and air time, computer printer and cartridges
'No frills'	Yield management processes to maximise revenue by using flexible pricing, at South West Air, EasyJet and Ryanair
Online retailing	Easy purchasing on line with customised recommendations at Amazon
On line auctions	Organiser takes percentage from advertiser and completed deal, for example e-Bay and Betfair

Source: Http://digitalenterprise.org/models/models.html

Segmentation hierarchies

Fundamental to the STP process is the need for the organization to obtain a deep understanding of the customers. Customers all have different expectations of the products and services that they receive, and segmentation identifies groups that have similar needs and make similar decisions in the purchasing process. The typical consumer base variables that are used for segmentation are listed in Figure 5.1. The choice of variables is key as it represents not only what is common amongst the individual customers that make up the segment but what is also distinctive from other segments. Segmentation variables based on characteristics that are relatively easy to collect, such as age, gender or income, may provide an approximation to predicted purchasing behaviour but it will be far from precise. Behavioural segmentation will be more predictive of purchasing behaviour and customer satisfaction criteria, but in most circumstances, the information needed about customers for behavioural segmentation will be much more difficult and expensive to collect.

> ***Demographic***: sex, age, income level, social class and educational achievement
>
> ***Psychographic***: lifestyle factors – activities, interests and opinions
>
> ***Behavioural***: patterns of consumption, loyalty to product category and brand

Figure 5.1 Consumer segmentation base variables

Faced with this obstacle Dibb (2003) emphasizes the need to choose the base variables that will truly discriminate between customer needs and buyer behaviour, and avoid a segmentation approach that is simple to apply but does not really provide the benefits of directing the marketing strategy. The implication of this is that a single variable approach is unlikely to add real value.

Using multiple variables, a hierarchy of segmentation can be created to form the basis for a marketing strategy, in which further segmentation or subsegmentation will achieve an even better match between customer needs and the specific elements of the marketing mix, such as promotion and distribution channels.

In international marketing, a hierarchy of segmentation variables provides the basis for an international strategy that balances the need for standardization of the marketing activity, where possible, but facilitates adaptation to meet customer needs more precisely, where necessary. For example, a global segment of wealthy customers need and want similar luxury products worldwide and the producers of such products will be able to obtain some economies of scale by developing and producing standardized products that have appeal worldwide. However, advertising may need to make different appeals according to the culture of customers of the region, and different languages may be needed for the packaging of products that are going to be sold in specific countries. Too often, it is assumed that the appeal will be the same in all markets, but managers need to consider self-reference criteria and overcome their preconceived ideas of the perceived benefits, which at one level may be similar, but at another different for different cultures. For example, a perfume may have a worldwide appeal but a sexy provocative advertisement may be unacceptable in some cultures.

For a full discussion of the segmentation of B2B and B2C markets read Hooley *et al.*, 2004.

Question 5.3

How can better methods of segmentation assist in decision-making in global markets?

Targeting the most profitable customers

A number of texts identify the criteria for assessing segment attractiveness and offer processes for a systematic approach to segment selection in some detail. However, following the theme of this unit it is essential to regularly review the targeting criteria and process, because of changes that impact on segment attractiveness.

- o Companies change as markets develop and so their views change about the attractiveness of segments.
- o Markets change, for example the next generation of consumers have different views about preferred products.
- o Competitors change. Dyson quickly took 58 per cent of the market in the high end of the vacuum cleaner market against established competition.
- o Market reinvention takes place, for example Amazon reinvented book selling.
- o Market boundaries change. Supermarkets have rapidly increased their share of petrol sales and entered the financial services market.

Positioning and repositioning

The concept of positioning can be applied to companies, brands, products and services. The key points of positioning are:

- The positioning must be as distinctive as possible and must clearly differentiate the organization's position from that of the competition. It is the customers' perception of positioning that is important and perceptual mapping is useful for positioning research.
- The organization's image is projected through all its activities, not just marketing but also such things as staff recruitment and working conditions. All of these influences must converge with the customer's perception of the company, brand or product.

Increasingly it is through the imagery rather than the product specification, quality or pricing that the organization confirms the positioning. In doing this it must make choices. Organizations put a value proposition to one customer segment that makes promises about the quality of the products and level of service that might be expected. The positioning might suggest that customers like the one in the segment (with the same demographic, lifestyle or behavioural characteristics or aspirations) are likely to buy the organization's products and services. By inference, the organization might also be saying that customers who do not have these characteristics or aspirations probably do not buy this product or service.

In cross-cultural marketing either in the domestic or international market, organizations must take care with this type of positioning. Particular problems exist where the imagery is created for one target market segment but is unacceptable to another segment with a different culture.

Repositioning

Organizational underperformance can be associated with a failure to appeal in sufficient volume to the target segment resulting in insufficient sales as the organization comes under increasing attack from competitors. Alternatively the target segments are simply not large enough to sustain a growing business. As a result it may be necessary for the organization to reposition. This decision should not be taken lightly as the investment and commitment necessary to carry it through effectively can be huge. Effective positioning is achieving a convergence between customer perceptions and the organizations' positioning delivered through the marketing mix, and this is difficult enough. Effective repositioning requires the organization to reformulate every aspect of its marketing mix, neutralize the old customer perceptions and recreate and influence new perceptions by actions and communications. Changing well-entrenched customer perceptions is a very lengthy process, and subtle repositioning communicated through promotional messages is unlikely to be understood by many customers who do not have high involvement in the organization, brand or product. Whilst some repositionings, such as Lucozade and Guinness, have been very successful, many others have left customers confused.

The use of STP and segments of one

The determination and capability of organizations to gain greater customer insights and to manage customer data allows ever-smaller sub-segments to be profiled, targeted and served as niche markets. In the limit the sub-segment size can be one, giving rise to one-to-one marketing and this is discussed in Unit 10.

Question 5.4

Select a B2B organization whose products and services you are familiar with. Write down the criteria that might be a meaningful basis for segmentation of the customers in its overall market sector. Identify the criteria that appear to have been used by the company as its target segment. Finally evaluate the market mix that it uses and decide whether it communicates clear and distinctive positioning to its customers.

Growth strategies and decisions

Other generic strategies that are important in decision-making relate to the alternative growth options identified by Ansoff. The strategic options tend to increase in terms of the investment cost and risk of achieving success in the following order: penetration, market development, product development and diversification. The market leaders must simultaneously pursue all of the first three options. However, many organizations do not have sufficient financial and management resources to proactively and aggressively pursue more than two of these options at the same time.

The decisions on which growth option to pursue will be influenced by the macro-environment, market changes (customer and competitor factors) and the organization's capability, ambitions, choice of marketing approach and competitive stance, which now follow.

Alternative marketing approaches

As part of the fundamental review of the business the firm should consider its approach to marketing.

Approaches to marketing

○ *Product-push marketing* – is an approach that concentrates on persuading customers to buy the products and services that the firm can produce, deliver and further develop easily, largely using their existing realm of knowledge and resources.
○ *Customer-led marketing* – is typified by those organizations that do everything they can to satisfy customer needs. Some organizations have taken this to extremes and set out to deliver customer needs almost irrespective of cost.
○ *Resource-based marketing* – is considered to be a balanced strategy between meeting the market requirements and exploiting the organization's capabilities to serve the market. Resource-based marketing takes into account the competitive situation, the full range of assets, skills and competencies of the organization and aims to exploit the organization's role within the supply chain.

o *Entrepreneurial marketing* – Entrepreneurs tend to focus on the opportunity or market gap, irrespective of whether or not this will make use of existing assets and resources. Entrepreneurial marketing usually takes the form of a new business start or a new spin-out from within an existing firm. Increasingly large firms realize that it is difficult to develop a breakthrough innovation within the firm and resort to managing diversification by setting up separate entities.

o *Network marketing* – is becoming increasingly significant as organizations, desperate for growth, use connections through alliances, partnerships and equity participation in other organizations to exploit opportunities that are not deliverable through their directly owned assets. The rationale for network marketing is that in conjunction with partners an organization can increase the overall size of the potential market that can be served by the two or more companies.

In practice, the appropriateness of the choice of approach depends upon the context of the organization and its market.

Question 5.5

Using appropriate examples, explain the different marketing approaches of firms and how they might build competitive advantage in these areas.

Case study

Apple goes for the low-price market

Apple, led by its charismatic, entrepreneurial founder, Steve Jobs, has traditionally produced products that have focused on design and ease of use rather than price. The result has been a niche marketer selling to purchasers that are probably better described as fans and devotees rather than customers. Apple's main products, the iMac and iPod, have achieved almost iconic status.

For many potential customers the price of Apple products has prevented them buying and so, in an effort to attract a mass market, in 2005, Jobs announced that the company was going to offer low price versions of its key products in order to convert users to Apple products. The cheapest Mac mini went on sale for $499 (without monitor, keyboard and mouse) and the cheapest iPod Shuffle, which holds about 120 songs, went on sale for $99.

Although many saw this change of direction inference on as one of the most courageous moves the company had made, but it very quickly proved successful, adding significantly to Apple's profitability. In the fourth quarter, 24 September 2005, Apple quadrupled its profits as revenues rose 56 per cent to $3.68 billion compared to the previous year. Global sales of iPods were 6.5 million units. New products had quickly followed with an iPod phone hybrid and iPod video player. Not everything proved to be instantly successful as the credit card-sized iPod Nano was heavily criticised by customers because of the product's susceptibility to scratches.

Source: Adapted from public sources.

Question 5.6

What might be the possible consequences of this move?

Adopting the right competitive stance

Against the background of the assessment made earlier in this unit there are a number of alternative competitive stances that organizations might adopt and these are discussed in the marketing strategy texts by Wilson and Gilligan (2004). The main competitive strategies are:

- ○ *Leaders* – keep ahead of the field by developing an ever-stronger selling proposition and competitive advantage to build customer loyalty, discouraging other possible market entrants.
- ○ *Challengers* – develop a strong alternative proposition and challenge the leaders' weaknesses continually, often by aggressive pricing.
- ○ *Followers* – imitate the other competitors at lower cost. They look for unexploited opportunities.

See CIM SMD Examination June 2005, Question 2

This question examines the value disciplines of Treacy & Wiersma (See Unit 1 and Doole & Lowe Chapter 3). In this question, you have to critically evaluate the three value disciplines. The question is specific in nature and requires the candidate to apply conceptual knowledge to best practice examples in these disciplines that are developed in this and previous units.

Whilst these are the main competitive stances, there are specialist strategies too that do not necessarily fall into the above categories.

- ○ *Pioneers* – are innovators and tend to be the first into new opportunities. Some may also be market leaders but others may not maintain a consistent strategy and may fail to consolidate their pioneering efforts and build their business.
- ○ *Market nichers* – survive and grow through specializing in a part of the market that is too small to be attractive to larger firms or in a market niche that they define and create themselves. With globalization some market nichers have built substantial businesses through creating a global niche.

Companies must decide whether their current competitive stance is appropriate for the present and the future. Clearly, if the organization redefines its business it must also decide whether or not it should attempt to change its competitive stance and adopt new competitive strategies. The competitive strategies that are adopted to attack and defend are usually described in terms of planning military campaigns and Wilson and Gilligan (2004) and Hooley *et al.* (2004) discuss the alternatives in some detail.

It is useful to have an understanding of these strategies as they help to articulate a proposed strategy and there are a number of examples in the texts of their use by leading companies. Their appropriateness for a particular situation requires considerable analysis and is therefore beyond the scope of this coursebook.

Activity 5.4

> How would you characterize your organization or an organization of your choice? Is it a market leader, challenger, follower or nicher? Is it also a market pioneer? What competitive strategy is it pursuing?

Case study

Bidding for the Olympic games

When the International Olympic Committee awarded the 2012 Olympic games to London many enterprising people could rightfully claim some of the credit. Although Lord Coe, the chairman of the London Organising Committee, a famous Olympian, himself was praised as the main architect of the success, many others made significant contributions and were heralded as winners from the Prime Minister, Tony Blair, who worked particularly hard in the final stages to convince the Olympic committee members, to Princess Anne and David Beckham, who lent their unswerving support, to children from Langdon School in East Ham, East London, who were in Singapore for the announcement, to the many tireless workers that were part of the team.

The entrepreneur

Perhaps the person who was not quite so much in the limelight at the ceremony to award the games was Keith Mills, the vice-chairman. But the insiders said that it was his steady leadership and pragmatism that was at the heart of the bid, his confident practical approach, getting on with the job and quiet determination to tackle the seemingly impossible tasks. He had done the numbers and was so confident of success in Singapore that 200 planning meetings had already been arranged for after they had won.

He was hired by Barbara Cassini, the then chairman of the bid team, at a time when no one was really interested in bidding for the games. She chose Mills because he was 'self-made' and passionate about sport. Coe adds that he is not traditional or strongly corporate, but instead is creative, seeing the world in a different way. Mills recognised that his 25 years of experience in marketing products throughout the world was appropriate for the bid. A technically excellent product had to be created and marketed domestically and internationally. Mills had invented customer-loyalty schemes, selling Air Miles to British Airways in 1987 and later, coming up with the Nectar reward scheme. He had already amassed a fortune of £200 million by the time he was appointed.

Despite his success, Mills will not continue as chief executive of the newly formed London Organising Committee of the Games. He recognises that his skill is in marketing and an executive is now needed that has experience in a consumer-facing, fast-moving business based on managing logistics, perhaps retailing to plan and implement the next stages of the preparation. The 'leg-work' for the Olympics is now beginning but he prefers starting companies to running them and he has already got new ambitions – to challenge for the America's Cup sailing competition.

The preparation for the games

A huge area of East London needs to be cleared in order to build the village and this requires the relocation of many people and over 200 businesses. Major construction work is required to create the venues, accommodation, training, media and support facilities and infrastructure. Entrepreneurs will exploit opportunities to provide additional services and goods that will be Olympics related such as improved local shopping, leisure and accommodation facilities. A month after the games were awarded the planning team had a list of 8500 jobs that would need to be done before the games began.

The games themselves

Fairly obviously at what will be the biggest supported event there will be huge challenges to co-ordinate all the elements necessary to make it a successful games including competitors, visitors, service providers and media. Already 50 000 people have signed up as volunteers to help. The London bombings that immediately followed the announcement reminded everyone that ensuring security would probably become the biggest headache.

The potential legacy

The potential legacy of the games could be increased interest in sport and better facilities, and improvements in health of the population. The construction work will create many tens of thousands of jobs and providing pre-event training facilities and services to the foreign teams will benefit all parts of the UK. The hope is that a neglected area of East London will benefit from the regeneration that will result and so improve the lives and prospects for the local community.

Enterprise and planning

It is very rare that any organisation has the luxury (or worry) of having 7 years to plan an event, knowing that everything must be ready for peak performance during a very short period of time, and the potential for financial failure is great, given the experiences of recent Olympics.

This project requires co-operation between many different interests, public and private, large and small, those that will benefit and those that will be inconvenienced. This will result in the need for entrepreneurship and innovation as well as tight control and monitoring to avoid overspend, fraud and negative publicity, often a danger with projects such as this.

Source: Adapted from Armistead, L. (2005) 'Britain's real Olympic hero', *The Daily Telegraph*, 7 August.

Question 5.7

What are the key issues that needed to be considered in bidding for the Olympic games?

Question 5.8

What marketing competencies are needed to (1) bid for and (2) plan for the Olympic games?

Summary

○ There are a number of reasons for organization underperformance and strategy wear-out. Whilst external factors, such as changes in the market, customer requirements and competition, might be the cause it is the management of the organization that must anticipate and respond to likely changes.

○ From time to time, therefore, it is necessary to redefine the organization's role in its chosen market sector and decide on an appropriate approach to the market.

○ Generic strategic approaches are essential in determining the organization's competitive approach (Porter), its customer targets, positioning and marketing activity (STP).

○ Increasingly, organizations need to develop a hierarchy approach to segmentation especially in international marketing.

○ Having assessed their competitive capability, organizations must then adopt an appropriate competitive stance that will secure their position in the market.

Further study

Doole, I. and Lowe, R. (2005) *Strategic Marketing Decisions in Global Markets*, Thomson Learning, Chapters 5 and 6.

You should ensure that you have a full understanding of marketing strategy and planning process by studying the following texts:

Hooley, G., Saunders, J. and Piercy, N. (2004) *Marketing Strategy and Competitive Positioning*, 3rd edition, FT Prentice Hall.

Wilson, R.M.S. and Gilligan, C. (2004) *Strategic Marketing Management, Planning, Implementation and Control*, 3rd edition, Oxford: Elsevier Butterworth-Heinemann.

Hints and tips

Build a collection of examples that illustrate to you the diversity of strategic decisions that companies make together with a brief explanation of the reasons. Try to find examples from different industries from those that you are most familiar with, as this will help to broaden your experience and possible management solutions for your own situation. It will also help you to recall examples in the exam.

As STP marketing is central to the marketing process ensure that you have a full understanding of the key decision areas in the STP process.

Bibliography

Dibb, S. (2003) 'Marketing segmentation: changes and challenges', in S. Hart (ed.), *Marketing Changes*, London: Thomson Learning, pp. 205–237 (ISBN 1861526733).

Doole, I. and Lowe, R. (2005) *Strategic Marketing Decisions in Global Markets*, Thomson Learning.

Hooley, G., Saunders, J. and Piercy, N. (2004) *Marketing Strategy and Competitive Positioning*, 3rd edition, FT Prentice Hall (ISBN 0273655167).

Mintzberg, H., Lampel, J., Quinn, J.B. and Ghoshall, S. (2003) 'Strategies', *The Strategy Process, Concepts, Contexts, Cases*, Pearson Education, pp. 2–29 (ISBN 027365120X).

Wilson, R.M.S. and Gilligan, C. (2004) *Strategic Marketing Management, Planning, Implementation and Control*, 3rd edition, Oxford: Elsevier Butterworth-Heinemann.

Sample exam questions and answers for the Strategic Marketing Decisions module as a whole can be found in Appendix 3 at the back of the book. Examination question B2 from the December 2004 examination includes some of the issues discussed in this unit.

unit 6
strategic decisions for global development

Learning objectives

The CIM syllabus for Strategic Marketing Decisions expects you to have an appreciation of the different contexts for marketing decisions. Whilst it is important to recognize that international marketing should be considered throughout the syllabus, this unit focuses on the strategic decisions that international players must take.

In studying this unit you will:

3.1   Examine the issues of decisions to build competitive capability and approaches to leveraging capability to create advantage across geographically diverse markets.

3.10   Leverage individual and corporate learning across geographically diverse markets for competitive advantage.

3.6   Determine the lessons of best practice from strategic decisions made by successful global companies.

Having completed this unit, you will be able to:

o   Appraise a range of corporate and business visions, missions and objectives and the processes by which they are formulated, in the light of the changing bases of competitive advantage across geographically diverse markets.

o   Demonstrate the ability to develop innovative and creative marketing solutions to enhance an organization's global competitive position in the context of changing product, market, brand and customer life cycles.

o   Define and contribute to investment decisions concerning the marketing assets of an organization.

o   Demonstrate the ability to re-orientate the formulation and control of cost-effective competitive strategies, appropriate for the objectives and context of an organization operating in a dynamic global environment.

This unit relates to the statements of practice

Bd.1 Promote a strong market orientation and influence/contribute to strategy formulation and investment decisions.

Bd.2 Specify and direct the strategic marketing planning process.

Cd.1 Promote organization-wide innovation and co-operation in the development of brands.

Key definitions

Export marketing – The marketing of goods and/or services across national/political boundaries.

Multinational marketing – The marketing activities of an organization which has activities, interests or operations in more than one country and where there is some kind of influence of control of marketing activities from outside the country in which the goods or services will actually be sold, but where the global markets are primarily perceived to be independent markets and profit centres in their own right.

Global marketing – Where the whole organization focuses on the selection and exploitation of global marketing opportunities and marshalls resources around the globe with the objective of achieving a global competitive advantage.

Study Guide

This unit is concerned with making strategic marketing decisions in the global context to exploit new opportunities in the global market through leveraging capability and sharing learning. Organizations adopt different approaches depending on their resources, ambition and market context. Understanding the factors that have contributed to globalization is essential in understanding how the very largest firms grow. It is important too to recognize the times when activities can be standardized or should be adapted for local markets. Smaller firms also succeed in global markets provided that they take appropriate decisions on strategic approaches for their situation, for example niche marketing. In both large and small firms, we also emphasize the importance of corporate learning to ensure that the lessons learned in the market can be shared as widely as possible.

Many students are unfamiliar with international marketing and therefore before starting on the unit students should familiarize themselves with this aspect of marketing by reading one of the recognized texts that are identified in the 'Further study' section.

Building competitive advantage through globalization

International marketing

Companies develop international marketing strategies in order to improve corporate performance through growth and strengthening their competitive advantage. The strategies are driven by the increasing trend to globalization. However, companies differ in their approach to international marketing strategy development and the speed and progress they make in achieving an international presence.

International marketing is often defined largely in terms of the level of involvement of the company in the global marketplace, and three levels are considered: export, multinational and global marketing.

Exporting is the simplest form of international marketing activity and is the preferred approach for many firms. However, the latter definitions are more complex and more formal. They indicate a revised attitude to international marketing and suggest fundamental changes in the basic philosophy.

Global marketing

Over the last few years, the importance of international marketing has increased as globalization has increased the range of possible opportunities for proactive organizations with aggressive growth strategies. The downside of globalization, of course, is that reactive companies are now much more likely to be attacked in their home market. Whilst some domestic businesses might be able to stay unaffected, the majority of businesses are experiencing direct or indirect international competition. In this section, therefore, we focus on how the globalization of markets is affecting the strategic decisions of both large and small firms. Doole and Lowe (2004) explain the themes that are leading to globalization and thus are important considerations in the development of international strategies.

Exploiting the globalization drivers

The most successful global businesses are aggressively building their global strategies around the following themes:

- Increased market access because of the opening up of markets in China, Central and Eastern Europe.
- Increased market opportunities because of the deregulation of many markets, such as the financial market and privatization of state-owned utilities.
- Greater uniformity of industry standards, encouraged, for example, by the EU.
- Sourcing of products and components initially, but more recently services, too, from a wider range of countries, particularly those emerging markets with a high ratio of skills to cost.
- More globally standardized products and services, particularly in areas of new technology, but increasingly in more culturally sensitive product areas, such as food.
- Common technology used in many more markets, particularly in areas of information technology, bioscience and pharmaceuticals, where there is a high cost of R&D that must be recovered through sales in many countries.
- Similar customer requirements leading to transnational customer segments, resulting from increased communication and travel.

- Competition from the same organizations in each major market and thus interdependence of markets.
- Co-operation between organizations from different parts of the world, leading to companies competing with each other and co-operating with each other in different niches of the same market.
- Worldwide or regional organization of distribution, ignoring country boundaries.
- Communication generated and received almost anywhere in the world.
- Global organization strategies that increasingly treat the world as one market.

Insight

Marketing to the poor

Many marketers assume that the world's poor are of no interest. For many sophisticated products designed for western consumers, this may be so, but Prahalad and Hart (2002) explain that for the right products there is substantial global demand:

	Global population (m)	Purchasing power ($)
The wealthy	800	15 000
The emerging middle class	1500	1500–15 000
Low income markets	4000	<1500

Source: Adapted from Prahalad, C. K. and Hart, S. L. (2002) 'The fortune at the bottom of the pyramid', *Strategy and Business*, 26(54), 67.

Activity 6.1

For an organization or an organization of your choice, assess the current and future impact of the globalization drivers on the business.

The benefits and challenges of developing strategies for globally diverse markets

The benefits to organizations of increased globalization are increased profit through market growth and a reduced cost base due to economies of scale and the experience effect (the more times you do the same operation the more efficient you become). There are intangible benefits too from a much more visible brand and its associated imagery, achieved through the sheer volume and consistency of communications and extensive distribution.

Associated with globalization is the increasing presence of global companies as they enter more country markets and achieve greater worldwide reach through communications, alliances and distribution partnerships. External factors too, such as the increase in regional trading blocks creating greater interdependence of marketing, enable global firms to increase their power, influence and competitiveness.

There are significant challenges too in developing a worldwide strategy and these can be addressed in terms of the firm's response to three fundamental questions.

1. In what circumstances is it best to adopt a standardized approach (the same marketing actions in as many markets as possible) or a highly adapted approach (different marketing actions for each country market)?
2. How can a firm achieve regional or worldwide exposure of products and marketing messages with large but finite resources?
3. What is likely to be the basis of future global competitiveness in the sector?

In answering these three questions, the first involves the choice for a company between a global, regional or multi-domestic strategy; and these different approaches are defined below. The answer to the second question involves considering a number of options for responding to market opportunities through the marketing mix and other marketing activities. An important issue, however, is concerned with market and product coverage, and the decision the firm makes must also take into account the strategies of their competitors and particularly their power within the market sector. The third question is about the nature of future global competitive advantage and, for example, how important it will be for the major players to have a large fast-growing home market or a low operational cost base in order to be competitive in global markets.

See CIM SMD Examination June 2005, Question 1

This case study question enables you to prepare for examination questions on the global competitiveness of larger companies. It looks at the changing dimensions of the global market in which Dyson operate and how their market position has been threatened by the changing competitive landscape and new entrants into the market from China.

Strategy alternatives for global firms

Whilst we have emphasized the potential benefits for MNEs of standardizing the marketing strategy and actions, a worldwide strategy does not necessarily lead to globally standardized marketing. Instead, it could mean developing a separate strategy for each international market. The conditions in the international trading environment are an important factor in this decision and influence the choice of strategies for both large and smaller firms.

The concepts of global, multi-domestic and regional strategies (Figure 6.1) reflect the different approaches. Global strategies assume that there is one global segment to be served. In contrast, the multi-domestic strategy assumes that market conditions are so different in each market that a different strategy is required for each. Regional strategies recognize the emergence of regional trading blocks as essentially 'home markets'. You should familiarize yourself with these concepts as they underpin international strategies.

In practice, the very largest and the most complex organizations have business units, brands, joint ventures, products and services that are at different stages of market development, so it is unlikely that in practice a global or multi-domestic strategy will be appropriate for every part of the organization. The corporate brand identity and products may be globally standardized, but the services may need to be adapted for each country and so the services brand manager may be pursuing a multi-domestic strategy. Such composite strategies are referred to as 'transnational strategies'.

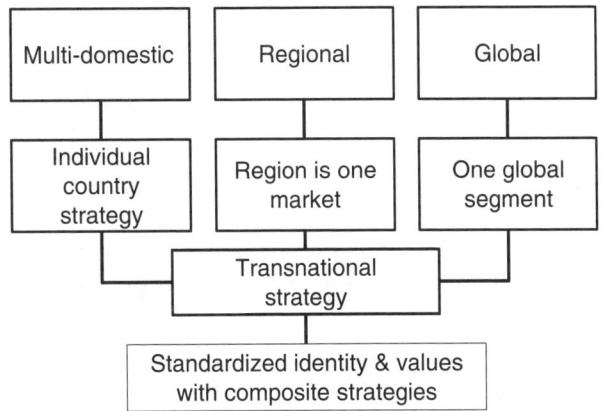

Figure 6.1 Alternative worldwide strategies
Source: Doole and Lowe (2004)

Leveraging capability in global markets

Clearly, the benefits for a firm are increasing its scale of operations through increased global activity. They include:

○ Better knowledge of the requirements and expectations of customers worldwide
○ The economies associated with increased scale of operations and R&D
○ Improving efficiency and effectiveness through repeating programmes and processes and, as a result
○ Building the capability and knowledge of the organization that can be applied to new business and marketing initiatives.

Insight

Toyota overtaking the gas-guzzlers

Over the last few years, the fortunes of the leading carmakers have changed significantly. In 2005, Toyota took over the No. 2 position in the league table from Ford. At the same time it was becoming clear that General Motors would not beat its 2005 forecast of 9.12 million cars, Toyota was forecasting an 11 per cent increase in production in 2006 to 9.2 million The Japanese car makers have focused on being profitable and responding quickly to market changes. By contrast, the US carmakers have lost out as high fuel costs hit demand hard for 4-wheel drive Sports Utility Vehicles and other large cars. They have also been crippled by very high healthcare costs.

The Japanese carmakers have developed a policy of manufacturing where they sell. By contrast, the US carmakers are basing their strategies on manufacturing in partnership with other firms in lower cost markets. They seem to be transforming themselves into marketing businesses that import, export and market products rather than manufacture.

The lessons of best (and worst) practices in global firms

In Activity 6.1, we suggested that you might consider the concept of globalization and its implications for strategy development. One key issue in globalization is to what extent it is possible and desirable to standardize products and services in response to the globalization push and pull factors.

Standardization gives the potential benefits of economies of scale and the effects of the experience curve, but the disadvantage of supplying products that may not have local appeal. The question then facing firms is whether it is better to standardize and attempt to 'educate' consumers to accepting the new product or whether it is better to supply an equivalent to the traditional local product.

The issue of standardization has absorbed many writers over the last decade, but the truly globally standardized brand or product – a highly desirable objective for some firms – is still rare. An indication is given of the elements of global marketing that are relatively easy to standardize (see Doole and Lowe, 2004).

There are many reasons why it might be necessary to adapt elements of the marketing mix including legal, cultural differences and usage conditions. Consequently, a product might need to be modified for different markets because of different safety standards, its packaging and advertising because of legal requirements, language differences and culture may dictate that certain colours, symbols and brand names would have the wrong meaning. Distribution tends to be difficult to standardize because companies must make use of the traditional distribution channels that are often very slow to change. Prices are almost impossible to standardize because of the fluctuating currency exchange rates and the differing stages of economic development of countries, leaving customers with differing abilities to pay the same price.

Achieving uniform positioning of a product or service, too, is extremely difficult. Countries are at different stages of economic development and few firms practise truly effective global segmentation, so a product may be an everyday purchase in one country and a luxury in another.

Programme and process standardization

In practice, it is useful to distinguish between programme and process standardization. By 'marketing programme' we are referring to using exactly the same new product launch programme or advertising campaign, for example, across all the countries in Europe and by 'marketing process' we are referring to taking the same steps, but the nature of the steps may be adapted to the local situation. For example, a market research study might be made in a number of countries to achieve the same objectives but it would be necessary to change some aspects of the study, because of differences in culture. It may be appropriate to adopt the same overall process for an advertising campaign but adapt the creative elements to local requirements and media to what is available and preferred in each country. So whilst it might be possible to save money by standardizing the programme, it may not be advisable, as the standard product or campaign may not be successful in all the countries. However, using the same process may facilitate corporate learning of good practice and make savings on such things as setting up evaluation procedures.

Question 6.1

What do you consider to be the benefits of standardization? Explain why it is difficult to find a truly standardized product.

International marketing challenges

Throughout the international marketing process, there are pitfalls and challenges, some of which are detailed below. These give rise to creating the lessons of good and bad practice. Good and bad practices are discussed in greater detail in Doole and Lowe (2004).

Opportunity analysis and marketing research – are essential to decide which countries are most commercially attractive, offer the most potential and can most effectively be served by the company. However, emerging markets carry risks, first because of the risks associated with unstable environments and second because of the unreliability and difficulty in obtaining information.

Sensitivity to different cultures – is essential throughout the process, including customer research, product and service development, and communications. There are many examples of organizations offending customers and underperforming because of their cultural insensitivity.

Transnational segmentation – Over-focus on country characteristics segmentation rather than transnational benefit segmentation can seriously curtail global development because of the failure to benefit from scale economies. Good practice requires a hierarchy approach starting with transnational segmentation followed then by country-based segmentation but, typically, few managers have the vision to carry out transnational segmentation effectively.

Market entry strategies – Arguably the most critical decision for organizations is deciding which market entry strategy to adopt. Choosing between the options, such as using agents or distributors, licensing or acquiring a local company, requires an appropriate balance to be struck between the organization's desire for host market involvement and control, and the level of investment and risk it is prepared to take.

Marketing mix – As we have already indicated there are a series of decisions about the marketing mix, the level of standardization that is possible and adaptation to local market needs that is necessary. Decisions are required on the product portfolio; new product development, distribution, communications and pricing strategy and each of these are critical. Each decision could well be influenced by different factors, including the stage of economic development, cultural demands, legal controls, usage conditions and ethical considerations.

Insight

The size of the informal economy

For marketers selling to less developed countries, what is known as the informal economy, which frequently involves covert and often illegal activities, seriously distorts the apparent market size. In Africa, it makes up 42 per cent of GDP, and is as high as 58–59 per cent in Zimbabwe, Tanzania and Nigeria. In Latin America, the informal economy in Bolivia is 67 per cent compared to Chile 20 per cent. In Asia Thailand's informal economy is 53 per cent compared to Japan's 11 per cent. In the UK, it is estimated to be 13 per cent.

Whilst much of informal economy comprises criminal activity, such as stolen goods, drug dealing, prostitution and smuggling, it also includes tax evasion and tax avoidance associated with legal business activity. This often occurs because the local government is corrupt or overly bureaucratic for small business owners that might be too poorly educated to follow complex procedures. All these activities present problems for legitimate marketers seeking to do business in these markets.

Source: Adapted from Schneider, F. 'Size and measurement of the informal economy in 110 countries around the world', July 2002, accessed at www.worldbank.org on 8 September 2005.

Question 6.2

Outline the market entry methods and the levels of involvement associated with the development of a company's globalization process from initial exporting through to becoming a global corporation. Specify what you consider to be the important criteria in deciding the appropriate entry method.

Activity 6.2

Carry out an audit of the organization's international marketing mix elements (the 7Ps plus market entry). To what degree are the elements standardized? How much scope is there for further standardization and what would you expect the benefits to be?

Choices and investment decisions

For relatively simple niche marketing organizations that target one segment, offer a relatively limited range of products and services, it is possible to develop a relatively straightforward STP strategy based on largely standardized marketing processes throughout the operation. It may be possible to develop some standardized programmes too, for example, in marketing research, R&D of new products, and even communications across a region. Even for these organizations, investment decisions are complex, because the profit impact of product or market development and supply-chain choices may be significantly different in the short and long term. Moreover, the barriers to implementation and level of success will be significantly affected by the turbulent international environment.

The largest and most complex businesses operate in most countries and are subject to a myriad of often-conflicting influences. They target multiple segments with large product and service portfolios and must motivate and galvanize their workforces into taking appropriate action. The decisions they make must reinforce the global corporate strategy, standards and values, and must be logical, justifiable and understandable to their staff. At the same time, they need to be sensitive to local and national situations and deliver stakeholder value in both short and long term.

International planning and organization

Having just given a flavour to the sheer diversity of problems in managing the marketing strategy implementation, it is also important to recognize the problems organizations have in planning and managing the organization. The problems arise from misunderstandings about the different environments, miscommunications, lack of cultural sensitivity, lack of a planning culture and the difficulty of maintaining meaningful controls.

Organization structure for global firms

The establishment of a suitable organization structure should reflect the firm's wishes to integrate individual activities to ensure effective communication, planning and implementation. Small firms can simply decide whether to set up a special department to handle exports or include exports within the general management of the firm. As the business develops, so different market requirements and internal pressures force changes in the organizational structure.

The organization structure must respond as the roles of managers are constantly adjusted to meet new marketing challenges, and seek to maximize the contributions from individual managers, no matter where they are located. The organization structure must also seek to avoid duplication and bureaucracy and, instead, constantly seek to encourage innovation. The complexity of these organization issues is greater in transnational companies, where the organization structure has taken on an entirely new meaning with advanced forms of networking and matrix organization structures.

The organization structure can either help or hinder the firm in delivering its objectives and can contribute to the international marketing problems identified earlier.

Question 6.3

Marketing environments are changing faster and more dramatically. This makes the planning and control activity difficult to manage across global markets. What is causing the faster change, what are the implications of this and how can planners attempt to improve the process?

Skill and capability development

In thinking about learning, it is useful to revisit the sequence of decisions in international marketing strategy and the three broad issues that managers need to address:

1. The identification, analysis and evaluation of opportunities
2. The establishment of a strategic perspective and development of a global marketing strategy
3. The approach that is to be used in the implementation and operation of the global strategy.

It is these issues that form the base of the management process that underpins the development of a global marketing strategy and so these are the key areas for knowledge, skill and capability development. To be successful in international markets, firms must have managers that have the ability to *think, analyse* and *plan* on an international scale. To operate effectively a global marketing manager needs:

o   Proactive marketing skills
o   A global outlook and positive attitude to the international arena
o   A broad knowledge of the global marketplace.

It is necessary to develop the management skills to manipulate the interface between the marketing mix and the complex environmental factors. However, it is difficult for individual managers to take the local country approach at the same time as a regional/global view.

Leveraging corporate learning across geographically diverse markets

Markets around the world are subject to many influences. Whilst it is possible to identify those influences that are common to many country markets, the real difficulty lies in understanding the specific nature and importance of influences within markets. Understanding the apparently conflicting nature of these influences is essential in order to develop appropriate strategies.

This is particularly problematic in the largest and most complex companies, which are referred to as 'transnational companies'. They aim to standardize some elements of the marketing activity and adapt others, and so end up with composite strategies. These transnational companies aim to achieve superior performance by pursuing three strategic aims:

1. Global-scale efficiency and competitiveness
2. National level responsibilities and flexibility
3. Cross-market capacity to leverage learning on a worldwide basis.

The strategies that transnational firms develop in order to achieve global competitive advantage need to accommodate some or all of the following:

o   Simple and complex individual product and market policies, which may be independent or interdependent in different parts of the organization.
o   Customer segments that may be specific or unique to a specific or transnational market and valid across borders.
o   Co-operative relationships with firms that might also be customers, suppliers and competitors at the same time, whilst simultaneously ensuring that the distinctive values and positioning of the company are maintained by building meaningful value-added relationships in the supply chain.

Question 6.4

Explain the concept of transnational strategies and what competencies transnational organizations must have in order to succeed.

Building competitive capability in SMEs for global markets

Smaller firm patterns of involvement in Smaller firm patterns of involvement in global markets

Smaller firms are involved in international marketing in a variety of ways (Doole and Lowe, 2004).

- Domestic marketing is for those firms that have confidence in providing niche products and services that satisfy their loyal, local customer base. Ideally, they can claim competitive advantage over their local competitors and there are significant barriers to entry for foreign competitors. These companies might adopt international marketing skills, attitudes and sensitivities to cross-cultural domestic markets.
- Exporting is primarily concerned with selling domestically developed and produced goods and services abroad.
- International niche marketing is concerned with marketing a differentiated product or service overseas using the full range of market entry and marketing mix options available.
- Domestically delivered or developed niche services can be marketed or delivered internationally to potential visitors.
- Direct marketing, including e-commerce, allows firms to market products and services globally from a domestic location.
- Participation in the international supply chain of an MNE can lead to SMEs piggybacking on the MNE's international development. This may involve either domestic production or establishing a facility close to where the MNE's new locations are established in other countries.

Insight

UK supermarkets pushing South African workers into poverty

UK supermarkets have long been criticised for their unethical business practices in their dealings with farmers. In August 2005, 65 per cent of South African grape farmers were estimated to be operating at a loss. Although the strong rand and bad weather was contributing to the difficult situation, British supermarket price wars were a major reason for the high level of financial hardship and bankruptcies. Supermarkets demand high standards of production but are not prepared to pay the price it costs to produce them. For some farmers prices have more than halved. 'Buy one, get one free' promotions or sudden discounts result in farmers being paid even less. Often, the promotions and what price the supermarket will pay are only decided by the supermarket after the grapes have left. They appear to retain their profit margin at the growers' expense.

It is South Africa's poorest people who suffer, living in near poverty earning less than the South African minimum wage of £4 per day. The campaigning charity, Action Aid and the South Africa's Women in Farms trade union want supermarkets to abide by the ethical codes that most of them have signed up to.

Marks & Spencer and Waitrose behave ethically and pay realistic prices to their suppliers. Asian supermarkets also pay realistic prices. Of course, their shoppers have to pay a realistic price too, but they do this knowing that, as a result, the workers on the farms have an acceptable standard of living.

Source: Adapted from Emmett, S. (2005) 'South African grape farmers face squeeze', BBC News Online 12 August.

Whilst some of these models are determined by the market context, in which the organization is operating and the nature of the products and services, others are dependent upon the aspirations and attitudes of the owners and senior management of the business.

For smaller firms, internationalization is typically concerned with entering new markets and modifying their products to meet the needs of these markets but the greater determinants of success are likely to be the firms' capability, willingness and ambition to exploit the international opportunities that are available to them. Frequently, firms with promising products and services fail to exploit them internationally because they lack one of these key elements. For smaller firms, the owner, manager or the senior management team is likely to have a profound influence on the development of the business and consequently it will be their ambitions that will be of paramount importance. It is possible to categorize firms by their stage of internationalization, particularly their commitment to international markets, and the most important elements for success are the degree to which the firms:

o Have effective relationships with stakeholders such as suppliers, customers and others in the supply chain.
o Have a clear competitive focus, which means not just being clearly positioned and aware of competitor activity but also seeking to offer customers a significant added value – the source of competitive advantage.
o Have a well-managed organization, which values its staff and encourages them to be committed to learning good practice.

Case study (Universities and international students)

Decline in Chinese applications for UK university places

In the UK as in other countries, government funding is failing to keep pace with the increasing demands for income from universities and colleges, as higher education is expanded.

Over the last few years, universities and colleges have turned to the international market to attract foreign students to boost income. Indeed, in 1999, the UK government set a target of doubling non-EU students in British universities and colleges by 2005. To do this many have been quick to capitalize on the booming Chinese economy and large numbers of Chinese students have been recruited. Some courses have a significant majority of Chinese students.

However, things are changing and applications are suddenly declining. First, the Chinese economy is showing some signs of overheating and, coupled with the improvement in the quality of Chinese education, there is less justification for financing students abroad. Secondly, the Chinese currency is linked to the depreciating US dollar. This has meant that the cost of tuition fees and accommodation has increased by more than 40 per cent in 2 years. Thirdly, the UK authorities have made entry more difficult as they have tightened up on the granting of student visas, as evidence has emerged of organized crime taking advantage of a more relaxed approach to granting student visas. The international competitive situation is also changing with other countries including the US, Canada, Australia and other EU countries competing strongly in providing English taught degrees.

Some observers comment, however, that another reason for the current decline in applications from Chinese students is the UK universities and colleges are failing to provide the experience that Chinese students are looking for. Often the students are placed on courses that have few students from other nationalities and so are unable to mix with students from other cultures. They are given inadequate pastoral care, insufficient support in learning English and do not get sufficient chance to gain social and work experience.

Question 6.5

As a university international development officer suggest how you would address this situation.

The geographic development of SMEs

Given the different patterns of internationalization identified earlier, it is inevitable that the geographic development can be significantly different (Doole and Lowe, 2004). It is worth reflecting on the alternatives (Figure 6.2) between, first, market spreading by the traditional expansion and concentration methods and, secondly, internationalization through networking, which is driven by the nature of the firm's family and business contacts and, thirdly, through the new market development of the firm's supply chain.

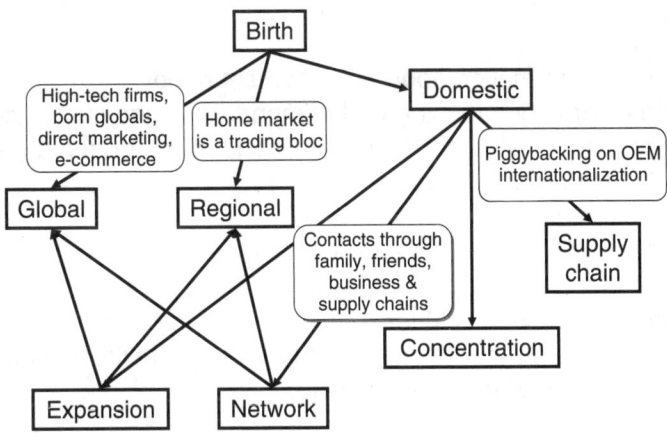

Figure 6.2 The different models of SME involvement in international marketing

The most significant development in the internationalization of SMEs is the phenomenon of the Born Global in which the new firms consider their market to be the world, rather than one or two countries. There are two factors driving the Born Global firms. The first is 'market-pull' because in new technology markets, the firms' customers and competitors will tend to be global and the firm must find a global niche in which to operate. The second factor is that information and telecommunications technology are enabling firms to communicate instantly and do business around the world using e-commerce.

The importance of niche marketing

Activity 6.3

Using Table 6.1 assess an organization of your choice in terms of it being an exporter or a niche international marketer.

Table 6.1 Difference between exporting and niche marketing

	Exporting	International niche marketing
Marketing strategy	Selling production capacity	Meeting customer needs
Financial objective	To amortize overheads	To add value
Segmentation	Usually by country and customer characteristics	By identifying common international customer benefit
Pricing	Cost based	Market or customer based
Management focus	Efficiency in operations	Meeting market requirements
Distribution	Using existing agents or distributors	Managing the supply chain
Market information	Relying on agent or distributor feedback	Analysing the market situation and customer needs
Customer relationship	Working through intermediaries	Building multiple level relationships

Source: Doole and Lowe (2004)

Building and sustaining the niche

To sustain and develop the niche the firm must:

- o Have good information about the segment needs
- o Have a clear understanding of the important segmentation criteria
- o Understand the value of the product niche to the targeted segment(s)
- o Provide high levels of service
- o Carry out small-scale innovations
- o Seek cost-efficiency in the supply chain
- o Maintain a separate focus, perhaps, by being content to remain relatively small
- o Concentrate on profit rather than market share; and evaluate and apply appropriate market entry and marketing mix strategies to build market share in each country in which they wish to become involved.

Leveraging learning in SMEs

The SMEs can be characterized by their proactivity in international marketing typically and categorized as passive, reactive, experimental, proactive or world-class international marketers as shown in Figure 6.3.

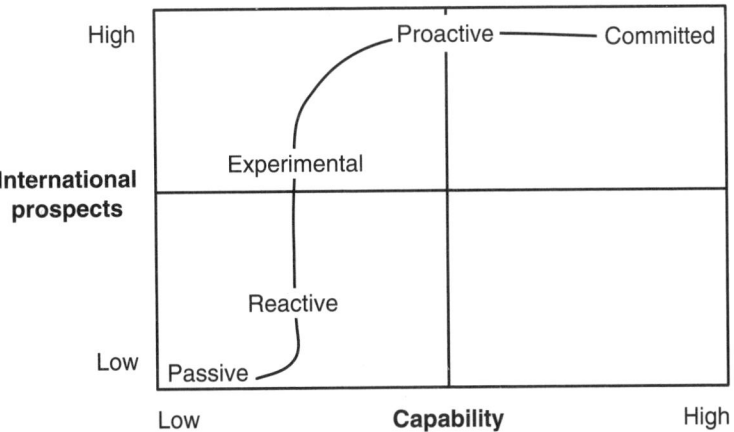

Figure 6.3 Levels of internationalization

Successful SME international marketers share with their larger counterparts the characteristics of being very customer-oriented and having a strong international competitive focus. However, their small size and lack of resources means that they build success in international markets in other ways too. They learn by developing very effective relationships, often personal, with customers, suppliers, contacts and experts that can bypass more lengthy ways of collecting information.

They also develop a culture of learning throughout the firm, invest in skills development, share experiences and knowledge and this allows them to be very flexible in their international market development. Staff invest high levels of emotional energy in the firm and are usually very innovative.

Activity 6.4

Thinking about your own organization or one of your choice (large or small) how would you categorize the firm in terms of international marketing (Passive, reactive, experimental, proactive and committed)? What evidence do you have to justify this categorization? How does the organization learn from its international marketing activity?

Summary

- Companies adopt different approaches to international marketing depending on the way they view international markets, how they organize themselves to exploit the opportunities and how they expand internationally.
- The very largest firms are exploiting the globalization drivers to develop the customer appeal of the business on a worldwide basis, but they decide on different strategic approaches, depending on their situation.

- A key challenge is improving global efficiency and competitiveness, local responsiveness and leveraging corporate learning across their global operation.
- The most successful international small firms focus on developing a global niche that they can defend and exploit.
- To be successful, it is necessary to get the worldwide operations to take and 'buy into' a planned approach, but not one that is inappropriately standardized and centralized, so that local staff have little scope for innovation and decision-making.

Further study

For further reading on this unit, you should refer to.

Doole, I. and Lowe, R. (2005) *Strategic Marketing Decisions in Global Markets,* Thomson Learning, Chapter 6.

Before starting this unit you should familiarize yourself with international marketing by reading the following recognized texts:

Doole, I. and Lowe, R. (2004) *International Marketing Strategy*, Thomson Learning.

Hints and tips

The unit assumes that you have built up a good understanding of the global environment, trends and issues and you should also make sure that you understand cultural issues and know how they impact on strategic marketing decisions.

Bibliography

Doole, I. and Lowe, R. (2004) *International Marketing Strategy*, Thomson Learning.

Sample exam questions and answers for the Strategic Marketing Decisions module as a whole can be found in Appendix 3 at the back of the book. Question B3 from the December 2004 examination focuses on some of the issues raised in this unit.

unit 7

developing innovative strategies to achieve global fast growth

Learning objectives

The CIM syllabus for Strategic Marketing Decisions requires you to be able to suggest specific strategies that will achieve fast growth, by developing innovative marketing approaches, for example, to the delivery of service and by using e-business.

In studying this unit you will:

3.8 Critically, appraise innovative marketing strategies in small and large companies operating on global markets.

3.7 Evaluate the use of e-technology to build and exploit competitive advantage.

Having completed this unit, you will be able to:

o Appraise a range of corporate and business visions, missions and objectives and the processes by which they are formulated, in the light of the changing bases of competitive advantage across geographically diverse markets.

o Identify, compare and contrast strategic options and critically evaluate the implications of strategic marketing decisions in relation to the concept of 'shareholder value'.

o Demonstrate the ability to develop innovative and creative marketing solutions to enhance an organization's global competitive position in the context of changing product, market, brand and customer life cycles.

This unit relates to the statements of practice

Bd.1   Promote a strong market orientation and influence/contribute to strategy formulation and investment decisions.

Cd.1   Promote organization-wide innovation and co-operation in the development of brands.

Ed.1   Promote corporate-wide innovation and co-operation in the development of products and services.

Gd.1   Select and monitor channel criteria to meet the organization's needs in a changing environment.

Key definitions

Assets – are the 'things' that the organization possesses, including the physical facilities, the customer database and brand.

Competencies – are skills that exist within the organization's staff, including brand management, IT and supply chain.

Core competencies – are the skills that pervade the organization and are those areas and activities in which the firm has a very high-developed ability.

Study Guide

In this unit, we focus particularly upon the development of innovative marketing strategies in small and large firms, and the strategies that lead to fast growth in global markets. Over the last few years, much of the fastest growth appears to have been driven by technology and particularly e-commerce developments. However, in developed markets, many products have reached commodity status. Competition comes increasingly from countries with a lower cost base for production and services. In order to survive and grow, organizations are increasingly building their competitive advantage around superior knowledge of their customers and markets, customer service enhancement and efficient and effective management.

This unit is concerned with making decisions that are innovative and, therefore, might challenge the often highly planned, conventional marketing strategies of many organizations. In order to better understand entrepreneurial marketing and motivate themselves to be more innovative, students should read how entrepreneurs have successfully identified and exploited new opportunities. Suggestions for further reading are included at the end of this unit.

Entrepreneurial and fast growth strategies

There are a number of firms that manage to achieve above-average performance and grow even during periods of economic recession, and in this unit, we explore how this can be done. At the end of this section, you may conclude that there are no secrets to achieve fast growth and that entrepreneurial or fast-growth strategies are largely founded on common sense and good management. The problem is that common sense is not always common; and as managers spend so much time in dealing with daily crises, the mundane activities and routine marketing, they lose focus and do not have time to apply common sense and innovation. This section is therefore intended to reinforce some fundamental principles in the context of fast growth.

Proactivity and hypergrowth

Typically within a market, firms usually adopt one of four stances in their approach to market innovation.

'Pioneers' are the entrepreneurial marketing firms that endeavour to be first in. 'Second-in' firms tend to follow the pioneers in innovation, but improve on their initial offering. The 'imitators' are those firms that copy the product and service innovations but try to offer lower-priced alternatives. 'Defensive firms' tend to ignore the innovations in the market except when there is no choice.

In evaluating their behaviour, it is possible to place firms on a continuum between those that adopt a proactive approach to innovation and those that adopt a reactive approach. Of course, the nature of the industry often influences the stance on innovation that firms adopt.

Activity 7.1

Classify your own organization and its competitors in terms of their innovation proactivity. How do you expect your classification to change over the next 5 years?

Entrepreneurial firms

By studying the characteristics and strategies of entrepreneurial businesses, lessons can be learned and applied much more broadly. Indeed many large organizations recognize the need to behave more like a smaller firm. As we saw in Unit 4, large firms are able to apply their power and influence in the market to build their business, but they are often slow in identifying and exploiting new opportunities. Because of their limited size and power in the market, smaller firms must be risk takers and learn how to rapidly exploit new market opportunities.

In Unit 4 we compared entrepreneurial and administrative approaches to management and it is useful to think about how entrepreneurial firms achieve fast growth. Roure (2000) explains that dynamic, entrepreneurial firms produce high growth in both old and new companies and come from all business sectors. The dynamic entrepreneurs that run them are of all ages and educational levels. These firms are built by teams or a partnership with a professional approach to management and entrepreneurs rely on people whom they carefully recruit, train and develop. They compete with high quality products and superior service. They typically target markets where they can be leaders or strong challengers and target a significant proportion of their sales to export markets, where they can learn and grow.

In Units 2 and 3, we discussed the challenges of achieving above-average performance and discussed the research in this area. We have also emphasized the short life of marketing strategies in many firms. Achieving sustained above-average performance over years results from building fast-growth characteristics into the competitive strategy.

Hypergrowth businesses

Hypergrowth businesses are those fastest growing firms that have turnover and number of employees growing at more than 100 per cent over the last 3 years.

The characteristics of the fastest growing businesses (hypergrowth businesses) are that they:

o Focus on being unique and offer exceptional customer value
o Define and exploit a niche, which they can defend
o Have products or services that are 'leading edge'
o Lead in competitor and performance benchmarking
o Compete in areas that require speed, flexibility and exceptional customer service
o Diversify into related products and adjacent markets
o Leave the industry before the window of opportunity closes.

These may be the exceptional firms but many more firms exhibit above-average performance and we now turn to how this can be achieved.

Competitive advantage

In looking at firms with above-average performance and the most significant sources of competitive advantage (Figure 7.1), Wilson and Gilligan (2004) focus on beating the competition by giving customers exceptional value.

Product differentiation advantages	Cost advantages
o Superior quality	o Consistent investment in R&D
o Superior levels of service	o High levels of process technology and production efficiency
o Strong brand names	o Patents
o High levels of brand loyalty	o Access to scarce or low cost resources
o Distribution strengths	o Vertical integration
o High cost to the customer of switching	o Distribution efficiency

Figure 7.1 Building competitive strategies

Focusing on beating the competition

As the pace of change in the environment and the nature, source and bases of competition change, markets become more complex and it becomes increasingly difficult to achieve exceptional sustained performance. Despite this difficulty, it is essential for organizations to try to manage the competitive situation, for example, by using the following ways:

o Firms should never ignore new competition. Low-cost airlines have won at least in the short term against bigger rivals and names unknown in the telecommunications business 20 years ago now dominate it.
o Firms should always exploit and seek to continually build their competitive advantage.
o Firms should know how to manage competitor responses to their new product launches or strategies to increase market share.

Customer value philosophy

The simple fact is that, in general, successful businesses persuade more customers to buy their products more than unsuccessful ones. Research findings suggest that successful organizations achieve higher market shares than others in their defined niche. It is important to remember at this point that frequently the best product in terms of specification and performance may not gain the highest market share. For example, Pepsi has often claimed victory over Coca-Cola in blind taste testing. Beta was generally thought to be a better technology than VHS for video recording but was not successful commercially.

It is essential, therefore, to build a total customer value proposition and not rely simply on the performance of the core product or service. Central to this is managing the complete customer interaction and, as far as possible, customer experiences in dealing with the firm.

Implementation – the drivers of entrepreneurial companies

Much is written about the growth sectors; particularly those relating to major technological leaps forward and we discuss this in other units. However, many firms are involved in markets that are in the mature phase. These provide the greatest challenge for entrepreneurial companies that wish to grow fast without the need for product invention. However, even in these markets, some important decisions need to be made about allocating resources to what is important and this is shown in Figure 7.2.

Figure 7.2 Resource allocation in mature markets

Customer management

These fast-growth businesses focus on high levels of customer management:

- Segmentation and sub-segmentation to better satisfy more specialized customer needs leading ultimately to one-to-one marketing.
- Understanding the lifetime value of customers and the need to build customer loyalty.
- Exploiting the opportunities for cross-selling, when the level of trust of customers in the company is high.
- Managing customers through the entire process of information search, purchasing and consuming the product or service and post-purchase customer service, in order to ensure a satisfactory experience.

- ○ Building appropriate relationships with all the stakeholders that might influence purchasing decisions.
- ○ Focusing on providing the very highest levels of service at the customer interface throughout the purchasing process.

Improving the process

As companies increasingly offer similar products and services, it becomes harder to differentiate products and services on the core attributes. Consequently, achieving fast growth becomes a more difficult challenge and there are few options for increasing market share. One remaining differentiator is providing superior customer satisfaction and service at each point of customer–supplier interface.

Activity 7.2

Carry out an audit of the customer management process of your organization or one that you have dealt with. Is there a clearly stated and implemented customer service strategy? Is the strategy designed to provide competitive advantage? You may wish to refer to Table 7.1.

Table 7.1 Areas for customer management process improvements

Quality	Being right
Speed	Being fast
Dependability	Being on time
Flexibility	Being able to change
Cost	Being productive

Question 7.1

What do you consider to be the characteristics of a fast-growth organization? What prevents many large organizations achieving above-average growth performance?

Strategy decisions for a new direction

Going beyond customer-led: taking customers in a new direction

The conventional marketing approach is that it is essential to be customer-led, and we use the term periodically in this coursebook. However, in Unit 4 we discussed discontinuities in technology and industry breakpoints and observed that it is innovative businesses, often new to the sector, rather than the existing firms that exploit the opportunities. They take the market in a new direction by anticipating what might be important to customers in the future instead of carrying out research to find out what they want and need. Customers rarely have a detailed vision of what they would like in the future and do not know what is possible. Products such as the Sony Walkman would not have been developed, if Sony had relied on customer research.

An innovative organization should therefore exploit the areas of opportunity that go beyond defined customer needs as shown in Figure 7.3.

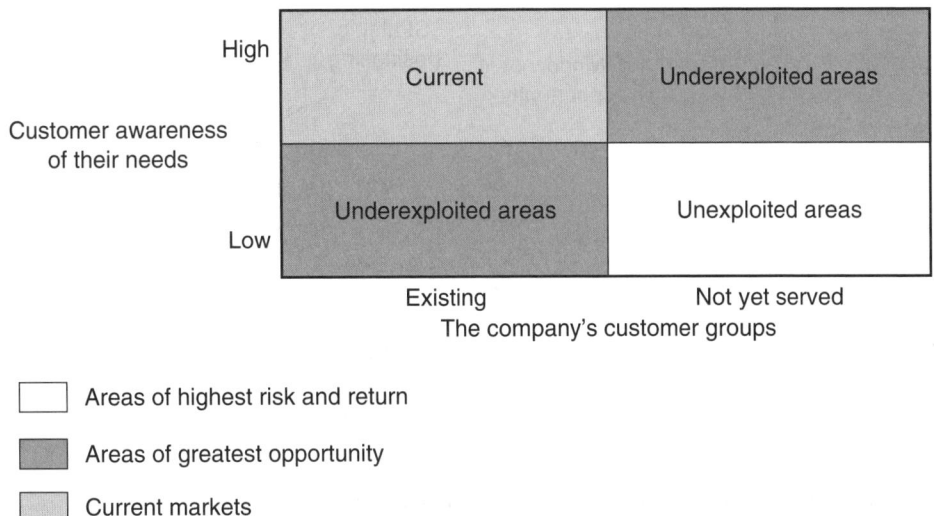

Figure 7.3 Identifying new market opportunity

Building and sustaining the strategy

Bolton and Thompson (2000) have clarified the steps, from having the initial idea through to developing a sustainable business (Figure 7.4). Having the idea and spotting the market gap is not enough. Skills, knowledge and competence must be applied in order to achieve distinctive positioning in the market. The positioning must be unique in order to offer customers a 'quantum leap' in benefits. The firm must build competitive advantage and increase the barriers to the entry of competitors. For example, a new product can be quickly copied but if its positioning is distinctive because of its design and image, and if it has been launched and marketed well, then there will be a lead time before it comes under serious attack from the competitors. By then, it could have established a secure position in the supply chain.

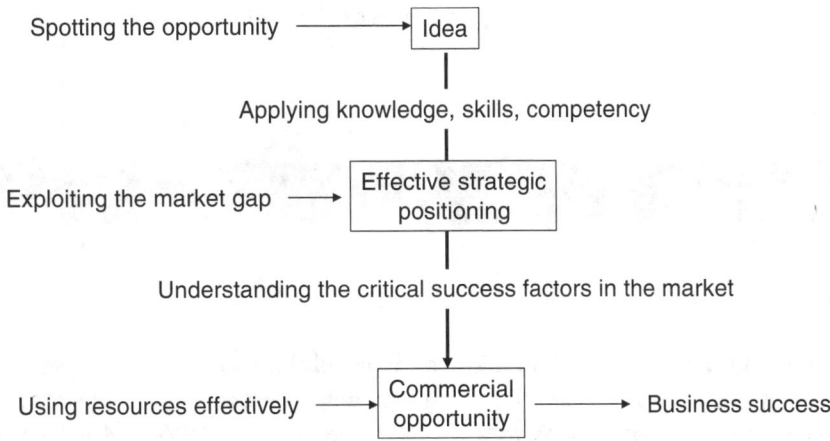

Figure 7.4 The development stages for a new business

However, the entire firm's resources and capabilities must be mobilized to achieve the result. As Figure 7.5 shows, the firm must be capable of recognizing the opportunity and be willing to change and apply competencies and resources in new ways to achieve this strategic positioning.

Figure 7.5 Entrepreneurial management and strategic positioning

After establishing an initial market position through a visionary leap forward, too many firms sit back instead of building a sustainable business and reinforcing the competitive advantage and strategic positioning through continuous small-scale innovations. Furthermore, to reduce its risk exposure, the firm must improve management effectiveness and learn good practices by reflecting on successes and failures.

There are many challenges in the early stages of a new business or innovation within an existing business. Doole and Lowe (2005) discuss this in greater detail.

Question 7.2

A significant number of organizations achieve fast growth for short periods, especially after start-up but many of them fail to maintain the growth rates. Why do you think this is?

Case study

Playstation

Being 'second' into a new market can allow established firms to learn about the market and use their resources to grow fast when they finally do decide to enter. Before Sony's Playstation entered the market in 1994, Nintendo, Sega and Atari were the main players. By 1996, 3.4 million units of Playstation were sold. In 2004, Sony made its 100 millionth Playstation sale.

Sony is credited with achieving the spectacular growth because it targeted a new segment, adults, by changing gaming from being a child's toy played in the bedroom to an all-family entertainment gadget that sits alongside the Hi-Fi and DVD recorder in the main family room. The Playstation created a media star, Lara Croft, became part of mass popular culture but also managed to maintain the technological interest.

Sony got its timing right for market entry and, by appealing to grown-ups too, ensured that its young devotees would continue to play into adulthood. Gaming is now a mainstream alternative entertainment and this will continue as new segments, which would never consider themselves as gaming enthusiasts, are targeted, for example, by dance mat and karaoke games, such as SingStar. The more diverse audience, of course, does pose new challenges for games design.

Source: Adapted from Twist, J., 'Decade of dominance for Playstation', BBC News Online, 3 December 2004.

Question 7.3

What do you attribute Sony's fast growth with Playstation to?

Search for greater competitiveness

What is clear from the re-evaluation of the organization's activities is that organizations will have to find new ways of competing in the future. The basis of competitiveness in many market sectors is changing rapidly and this was the subject of the book on competing for the future (Hamel and Prahalad, 1994). Subsequently, much has been written on the subject by other authors but some of the main conclusions about how to achieve future competitiveness are:

Dropping losers and backing the winners – Perhaps one of the great fallacies in marketing management is that more products or business units should be retained because they make a contribution to the overall costs of the operation, even though they are not particularly profitable. In practice, unprofitable areas can be a huge (often hidden) drain on resources and management time, so their realistic costs can be much higher than reported. There are additional costs too – the opportunity cost of not putting resources into areas of greater future profitability, and the damage to the brand of not using resources to build future value for the brand.

Business restructuring for flexibility – Backing winners not losers can be applied to all aspects of the business. So it is not just the product portfolio that should be restructured, but the decision might be made to move out of lower productivity business areas. Also outsourcing might be used for certain activities, the workforce might be reduced to make the company more flexible, adaptable and more sharply focused.

Continuous improvement in quality and service – Redesigning business and customer management processes is essential to make the organization better and faster and gives the customer ever-better value and experience.

Organization and sector reinvention – Many market sectors could be (and are being) reinvented and the organizations with the best industry insights will take the lead in determining the future.

Increasing globalization – Greater globalization means that the future opportunities for organizations lie in global market development, leveraging the current value-adding, highly productive competencies and assets into new markets and reducing resources applied to lower productivity activities, by outsourcing manufacturing.

The consequences of this are that the most valuable future organization capabilities are to be able to instigate, manage and capitalize on change. At the heart of this is having a clear idea about what assets and competencies will be required in the future. The most valuable organizational competencies and assets are those that can be leveraged into the future business processes, and the worthless competencies and assets are those that are locked into the business models of the past.

Activity 7.3

Classify your organization's products and services into:

- ○ Yesterday's successes and money generators
- ○ Today's successes and money generators
- ○ Tomorrow's successes and money generators
- ○ The also-rans
- ○ The failures.

What implications does this have for redefining the organization's source of competitive advantage in terms of superior, more effectively applied knowledge, capabilities and assets?

Insight

Equant – awards for customer service but poor results

Equant is an international telecoms group with 9500 staff operating in 165 countries, providing networks for companies such as Rio Tinto, Electrolux and Allianz. It has won many awards for its high levels of customer service. Indeed, it won five awards a few days before the new boss, Charles Dehelly, took over.

However, the first words from the new boss were not congratulatory. Instead, he shocked employees with the news that the firm was in a mess. 2004 had been a very bad year, the company failed to deliver the budget, the revenue was down, losses had increased and a large amount of cash had been burnt, resulting in a fall of the share price by 48 per cent.

The company needed to be turned around and this needed reducing costs and aligning costs more closely to the development of the market and company.

Whilst to receive the awards is satisfying, sustaining the business and fast growth require results to be delivered too.

Source: Adapted from Durman, P., 'Happy New Year from the boss – you're about to be fired', *The Sunday Times*, 9 January 2005.

Knowledge management

The process of identifying and effectively managing competencies and assets (knowledge management) will therefore become increasingly important.

The areas of knowledge that might provide the organization with competitive advantage are very context-specific but might include:

- Detailed understanding of customer needs and future expectations
- Customer databases and the ability to analyse them
- Key contacts and knowledge of the market
- Supply-chain management and partner relationship
- Process technology
- Research capability
- Intellectual property creation and protection
- Brand value creation
- Cost and price dynamics.

Question 7.4

How will the innovative organizations compete and win in their chosen sector in the future? Choosing one industry sector, explain what the future critical success factors will be?

See CIM SMD Examination December 2004, Question 3

Strategy development can take different forms depending on whether it is being developed in a large or small organization. This question allows you to explore some of those differences and helps you prepare for the varying organizational contexts which are presented in the examination.

e-Business innovations

During the late 1990s, e-business innovations were expected to create a new generation of fast-growth businesses, eliminate many firms with traditional business models and change forever the way in which business is done. In practice, this is all happening, but not at the same pace and on the same scale in all market sectors as was predicted. Some of the most significant e-business innovations have been in improving the customer management process in mature sectors, such as the purchase of travel, books, music and financial products. By defining new routes to the market, some innovative companies in the sector have managed to provide a quantum leap in value for customers.

We have discussed the drivers of Internet marketing in Unit 4, and concluded that innovations must be customer-led, with technology playing a supporting, enabling role. It is essential to maximize the value contribution of the technology advances (systems, processes etc.) to customers and the organization through innovative website design and new business models.

Innovation in website development

Table 7.2 shows four main categories of websites. In thinking about their purpose it is possible to see how their value contribution can be enhanced by linking the external website with internal business processes and databases, in order to provide better customer service (e.g. faster, more relevant and complete information, simpler processes and interactions) and organization cost savings (e.g. in customer management, staff time devoted to service delivery, and eliminating duplicated and unnecessary processes).

For a fuller discussion of this topic, you should refer to Chapter 8 of Doole and Lowe (2005).

Table 7.2 Four categories of websites

Website type	Purpose of the website
Site to provide organization information (e.g. www.Philips.com)	o Explains the origins, business mission and areas of activity, standards and values, brands, financial performance, job opportunities and contact points o Information about products and their applications
Site to provide service online (e.g. www.bloomberg.com and www.fedex.com)	o Puts customers in control of their accounts, and enables them to track inventories, orders, transactions and deliveries from anywhere in the world o Provides real-time information, for example, on travel and share prices
Site to provide information online (e.g. www.bbc.co.uk)	o Provides access to current and archived past files of news, data and images o Media organizations can maintain and build relationships with their consumers beyond the scheduled content and provide content to areas where it is not accessible by traditional communication methods
Site to carry out business transactions (e.g. www.expedia.com)	o Facilitates fast, convenient, interactive online transactions through a variety of business models (see below)

Further enhancing the website

Once the purpose of the website within the overall company strategy has been decided there are considerable opportunities for innovation in order to ensure that the website is further developed to increase the value added. Chaffey *et al.* (2003) define the characteristics of successful marketing-led websites that will appeal to customers. While basic website requirements, ease of navigation, attractiveness, interactivity and usefulness (such as reliability and security) are fundamental, others (such as multi-language options, sensitivity to local cultures and knowledge of local laws) are essential for global development.

 Activity 7.4

A number of texts discuss good website design (e.g. Chaffey *et al.* 2003, Chapter 7). List the characteristics of good websites and use them to assess three websites that you regularly use. Apply these and critically evaluate your own organization's website. How could innovation in website design be used to significantly improve the customer management process (refer to Table 7.1)?

Internet business models

In moving beyond information provision to business transactions online, the main e-business models are B2C and B2B. However, Chaffey *et al.* (2003) note that 11 different models have been developed and these are shown in Table 7.3. Of these, the two most significant developments are C2C and C2B and we discuss these later.

Table 7.3 Eleven types of e-business models

1. E-shop
2. E-procurement
3. E-mails
4. E-auctions
5. Virtual communities
6. Collaborative platforms
7. Third party marketplace (hubs)
8. Value chain integrators
9. Value chain service providers
10. Information brokerage
11. Trust and other services

Source: Chaffey *et al.* (2003)

Business to consumer (B2C)

Many customers are prepared to use the Internet to carry out their information search on companies, products and services but are still unwilling to pay for products and services online because of fears about the security of online payment and the potential for fraud. It is useful to be able to refer potential customers to telephone sales or a physical store to make their purchase and collection. A key challenge for firms is to ensure that their website address is prominent when search engines are used for key-word searches. This has led to innovative communication strategies by many firms and this is discussed in Unit 10.

A key decision for firms is the degree to which their products and services lend themselves to online retailing perhaps because they:

o Require low customer involvement in the purchasing process
o Can be delivered online (e.g. software and financial services)
o Are sold on the basis of proven design or quality of manufacture
o Do not involve considerable negotiation between supplier and purchaser
o Are neither large nor perishable which may give fulfilment (physical delivery) problems.

The boundaries between what can and cannot be sold online are becoming less clear as innovation in websites and business models develop. Stores with physical and online retailing are integrating their activities. However, some organizations still try to keep their physical and online stores separate, frustrating customers who wish to deal with the company using both routes in the process. There are still many challenges for online and integrated stores. For example, setting prices that are appropriate to both physical and global virtual markets but different inevitably leads to comparisons being made. Often the disparities in pricing simply cannot be explained to customers.

Business to business (B2B)

The transactions in the B2B virtual marketplace differ from the B2C marketplace because:

o   B2B transactions are typically more complex and the developments in B2B business models reflect the changing process needs of the participants.

o   Some B2B transactions are relatively routine repurchases or frequent reordering of commodity items that are simply to manage.

o   For many of the participants the driver of the B2B market is the need to match supply and demand in real time, usually because of the inflexibility of product capacity.

o   Interactions involve the exchange of significant amounts of information between the seller and customer before, during and after any transaction and it must be shared between many departments. The information includes such things as specifications, designs and drawings, purchase contracts, manufacturing and delivery schedules, inventory control, negotiation of price and delivery.

o   Some of these purchases will be core to the business, such as raw materials and essential maintenance services, and others will be occasional or peripheral, such as facilities management or purchase of office equipment.

The Internet enables a far wider range of data to be exchanged without restriction on the number of participant organizations. Web portals are the means by which the exchanges take place and business can be transacted through them. There are the 'hubs' where all the interested participants congregate. Typically, there are two types of hubs:

o   Industry specific hubs, such as automobile or aerospace manufacturing

o   Function specific hubs, such as advertising or human resource management.

Using e-hubs, firms improve the efficiency of the processes of transactions and thereby ensure lower costs. The hubs can reduce the transaction cost by bringing together all the purchasing requirements of many hundreds of customers worldwide. E-hubs also attract buyers who are able to negotiate bulk discounts on behalf of a range of smaller individual buyers.

Transacting business through hubs has a significant effect not just on the way that business is done but also on the way that the company must be organized to respond more quickly to business opportunities and the culture that must be developed throughout the organization.

Question 7.5

What do you consider to be the advantages and disadvantages of business transactions in the B2B market through e-hubs? Explain the characteristics of organizations that you would expect to be successful?

Other models

Online auctions (C2C) have become extremely popular and e-Bay is the most successful site for trading between individuals who buy and sell antiques, collectible items and memorabilia, by virtual bidding. e-Bay provides the website at www.ebay.com and takes a fee to insert advertisements and a further fee based on the final value. C2B works in reverse to the normal type of auction as consumers join together to reduce the prices they pay through bulk buying. A final date is set and the price falls as more customers join the buying group. One example is Letsbuyit.com. Priceline.com is similar but provides a mechanism for consumers to say what they are prepared to pay for an airline flight. Suppliers decide whether they are prepared to accept the offer.

It is increasingly recognized that, whilst online retailing has many benefits as a route to market for international development, a combination of virtual and physical routes to market might deliver the best results for many businesses.

Further value-adding activities using communications and information technology innovation

The interactivity of the Internet allows service delivery and product promotion offers to be made closer to the point at which customers might be prepared to buy, for example, through product placement in films, on television and on websites.

The technologies are being further integrated albeit at a rather slower speed than might have been expected, when the 3G licences were bought by the phone network companies to enable services to be supplied to hand-held devices. Innovations in mobile phone technology are enabling still and moving images, data and audio clips to be transferred to mobile phones resulting in e-business service delivery, sales promotions and communications being used in a much wider range of situations. Further opportunities come from tracking customer movements using Global Positioning Systems and offering products and services in their new location.

Permission marketing

Many e-business innovations will increase the targeted marketing messages directed to individual customers and it is unlikely that traditional marketing will be phased out. Godin (2002) has suggested that customers in future will see up to 3000 messages per day, the majority of which will come using the new communications technologies. Because very few of these messages are requested, Godin calls this 'interruption marketing'. Godin has introduced the term 'permission marketing' to suggest that the communications will be more effective if customers agree to receive communications from a particular firm, because it will develop the ongoing relationship.

It is suggested that this opt-in approach, in which firms would need to seek permission from recipients before sending electronic mail, is preferable to an opt-out approach in which the customer would have to take the initiative in asking a firm **not** to send messages that were of no interest, as this would be more difficult to implement, would not help 'policing' and would be unlikely to reduce the unwanted mail to a sufficient degree. Implementing the opt-in approach could be the first step in controlling spam – the unwanted, messages that are blocking up the Internet. Of course, it would prevent customers from receiving a wide range of information too.

Viral marketing takes this one stage further by encouraging people to pass along an electronic marketing message to a friend. A high pass rate from person to person will result in a 'snowball' effect, but a message will soon fizzle out if there is a low pass rate. Hotmail achieved great success with viral marketing but there have been few campaigns since that have achieved outstanding success.

Case study

The future of alcopops

After a lot of experience in running pubs and bars, Steve Perez set up his own distribution business in the 1980s, selling premium imported bottled beer from the back of a van. By the early 1990s, the business had sales of £10 million per year. But the environment turned against him and the business nearly went bankrupt. There was a recession, the opening up of the EU made it possible for cross-channel shoppers to buy cheap beer from France, the breweries started importing beer themselves and young people started turning away from beer.

In response, he set up a new business in 1997, GBL International, and 2 years later launched Vodka Kick (VK). Vodka Kick is known as a Fab (flavoured alcoholic beverage), which became part of the growth of so-called alcopops, popular with young people. The company has grown from four people at the start to 100 now, with a turnover of £70 million and sales in 30 countries. GBL was placed third in the 2003 *Sunday Times* Fast track among 100 fastest growing UK businesses.

Perez now owns a Ferrari and several Porches but his future ride may not be too smooth:

o GBL spends £7 million on marketing, a fraction of that spent by market leaders Smirnoff Ice (Diageo) and Bacardi Breezer (Bacardi-Martini), both of which outsell Vodka Kick eight to one.
o In response to a spate of under-age drinking of alcopops, the government applied punitive excise duties on the drinks. The drinks are still popular with the young.
o The population is ageing and adults are going off Fabs.
o People are drinking less alcohol and more than half prefer to drink at home.
o There is a chance that duties will be further increased and the EU may ban advertising.
o The company has done well with very limited advertising to get into supermarkets but they are less profitable than selling to bars and clubs.
o The company is based in the north of England; and although UK sales are countrywide, the brand has failed to penetrate London.

Source: Balland, M.A., 'Capital wheeze for alcopops', *The Sunday Times*, 15 February 2004.

Question 7.6

What should Perez do to maintain his impressive growth?

Summary

○ Organizations adopt different levels of innovation proactivity in the market and the strategies that they choose to pursue must reflect this.

○ When compared with average performers the characteristics of the fastest growth organizations show differences in ambition, attitudes to business, management style, awareness of customer value and approaches to dealing with competition.

○ Critical to early stage fast growth is the need to orientate the organization to achieving initial growth but then rapidly building distinctive positioning and a management approach that will build a sustainable future.

○ It is harder to achieve fast growth and rapidly increase market share in larger businesses in mature markets. Critical for success is better customer management processes to give exceptional service and satisfaction.

○ Future competitiveness will depend on picking winners and dropping losers, and focusing on opportunities for adding greater value. Knowledge, competencies and assets will provide the basis of competitive advantage and routine operations will be outsourced.

○ e-Business provides the mechanism to exploit many of these knowledge assets ultimately to provide personalized marketing. There are, however, a number of obstacles to overcome.

Further study

For a more detailed discussion of the topics in this unit you should refer to

Doole, I. and Lowe, R. (2005) *Strategic Marketing Decisions in Global Markets*, Thomson Learning, Chapter 8.

For further treatment of strategic marketing you should refer to

Wilson, R.M.S. and Gilligan, C. (2004) *Strategic Marketing Management*, Elsevier Butterworth-Heinemann.

For Internet marketing you should refer to

Chaffey, D., Mayer, R., Johnston, K. and Ellis-Chadwick, F. (2003) *Internet Marketing: Strategy, Implementation and Practice*, FT Prentice Hall.

Bibliography

Bolton, B. and Thompson, J. (2000) *Entrepreneurs, Talent, Temperament, Technique*, Butterworth-Heinemann.

Chaffey, D., Mayer, R., Johnston, K. and Ellis-Chadwick, F. (2003) *Internet Marketing: Strategy, Implementation and Practice*, FT Prentice Hall.

Doole, I. and Lowe, R. (2005) *Strategic Marketing Decisions in Global Markets*, Thomson Learning, Chapter 8.

Godin, S. (2002) *Permission Marketing: Turning Strangers into Friends and Friends into Customers,* Free Press.

Hamel, G. and Prahalad, C.K. (1994) *Competing for the Future: Breakthrough Strategies for Seizing Control of your Industry and Creating the Markets of Tomorrow,* Harvard Business School Press.

Roure, J. (2000) 'Ten myths about entrepreneurs', in S. Birley and D.F. Muzyka (eds), *Mastering Entrepreneurship,* FT Prentice Hall, pp. 20–22 (ISBN 0273649280).

Wilson, R.M.S. and Gilligan, C. (2004) *Strategic Marketing Management,* 3rd edition, Elsevier Butterworth-Heinemann.

Sample exam questions and answers for the Strategic Marketing Decisions module as a whole can be found in Appendix 3 at the back of the book.

unit 8
building portfolio value: branding, products and services

The CIM syllabus for Strategic Marketing Decisions includes the requirement to understand the decisions that are required to build the revenue streams that come from a strong portfolio of products and services. However, stakeholder value is also generated through its intangible assets and principally the brand.

In studying this unit you will:

- o 4.2 Assess the nature and dimensions of branding /brand decisions, their role in the development of advantage and their significance in global markets.

- o 4.3 Examine product strategies and the role of new product development in competitive strategy.

Having completed this unit, you will be able to:

- o Evaluate the role of brands, innovation, integrated marketing communications, alliances, customer relationships and service in decisions for developing a differentiated positioning to create exceptional value for the customer.

- o Demonstrate the ability to develop innovative and creative marketing solutions to enhance an organization's global competitive position in the context of changing product, market, brand and customer life cycles.

- o Define and contribute to investment decisions concerning the marketing assets of an organization.

This unit relates to the statements of practice

   o **Cd.1**   Promote organization-wide innovation and co-operation in the development of brands.

   o **Ed.1**   Promote corporate-wide innovation and co-operation in the development of products and services.

Study Guide

This unit is concerned with making strategic marketing decisions that add value for the organization and its stakeholders, principally customers, through portfolio development. We start by explaining the importance of integrating all the marketing mix activities, supply-chain developments and relationships with customers and other companies in the process of adding value. You should, therefore, keep in mind the links between the subjects considered in this unit with those in Units 9 (communications and relationship building) and 10 (pricing, supply-chain and partnership development) in order to fully understand the value benefits of integrating the marketing mix.

In this unit, we focus on portfolio management, maintenance and development, and specifically on the decisions that are made on branding, both at a strategic level to increase brand awareness, impact and equity and at an operational level, in the application of branding to products and services. We then turn to the management of the portfolio of products and services, and focus on the management decisions of maintaining and building the portfolio, where necessary, carrying out rationalization, new product development and service enhancement.

Before starting this unit, students should familiarize themselves with the issues of branding, product and service, and new product development concepts, using the reading mentioned in the 'Further study' section.

Key definitions

A successful brand – is an identifiable product, service or place augmented in such a way that the buyer or user perceives relevant, unique, sustainable added values that match their needs most closely (de Chernatony, 2001).

Product portfolio – is the collection of products and services that are managed together rather than as individual products.

Brand equity – is the net present value of the future cash flow attributable to the brand name.

Intangible assets – non-material assets such as technical expertise, brands or patents.

Adding value through branding

Previously, in this coursebook, we have emphasized that for many global companies today, it is their intangible assets that provide their most significant source of future competitive advantage. Of these intangible assets, the brand is the most significant. For example, the brand equity of the Coca-Cola brand was estimated by Interbrand to be worth $70 billion in 2002. The brand has been created through sustained marketing investment in advertising and promoting a consistent message for over 100 years.

At the outset, therefore, it is possible to categorize firms according to their approach to branding:

- o Those firms for which the brand is pivotal to their strategies and investing in protecting and building the brand is (almost) the most critical activity.
- o Those firms that use their existing and already established brands as an asset to be used to promote additional products and services but do not have a strategy to invest and develop them.
- o Those firms that merely 'name' products, fail to manage and support the name through focused marketing activity and so do not create a brand that has future value.

Most of the world's most valuable brands have received heavy and sustained investment over decades in every aspect of their marketing strategy – from customer research, segmentation and positioning through to every aspect of marketing mix activity. Usually the investment includes a large commitment to advertising but other factors, such as totally consistent quality, reliability and continuous innovation are just as important to achieve widespread customer loyalty and referrals.

Careful consideration should be given to whether a new or improved product, line extension or modification will enhance the overall brand as well as helping with the initial sales of the product. In many less sophisticated organizations, managers use the name or brand on new products, line extensions or modifications without any real thought to whether the name will enhance or erode the value of either the product or the firm's overall reputation. Their purpose is often very short term. They simply want customers to buy a product or service presented under the brand name. These kinds of decisions at best do little to enhance the brand and at worst devalue the brand by confusing customers as to what it stands for. Even with well-known brands, there are many examples of inappropriate brand extensions, product modifications and failed repositionings.

The purpose of brands

The purpose of brands is to create value for customers by helping them to make purchasing choices from the increasing range of competitive offerings available and help to reduce the risk of choosing the wrong product or service.

Customers expect brands to be a 'guarantee' of satisfaction right through the purchase decision-making process, from obtaining information through to delivery and post-purchase support. In some sectors, customers do not differentiate between the brand owner and the brand distributor, so it is essential to manage the brand throughout the supply chain.

Whilst organizations try to create a distinctive positive image in consumers' minds through their marketing activities, ultimately customers make up their own minds and build their own individual perception of the brand. Different customer segments may build up different perceptions of the brand because of their different demands and expectations. The organization needs a sufficient volume of customers to be prepared to pay a price premium to offset the investment that is made in the brand.

The real question and the subject for the remainder of this section is how can the brand be leveraged to add value for customers and the organization in the future and how can erosion of value be avoided.

Customer brand perception

The customers' positive perception of the brand is built from various sources:

o *Experience* – of previous use of the product and satisfaction with its performance.
o *Personal referral* – from friends and acquaintances; peer pressure, such as wearing the 'cool' brand, can be critical.
o *Editorial and other public sources* – such as the media, consumer reports and endorsement by experts or fashion gurus.
o *Communications* – by the organization, both through interactions between its staff and customers through the promotion mix.

The organization must make strategic marketing decisions that influence customer perceptions and reinforce a positive image.

Categories of brands

Brands (Doyle, 2000) can be categorized as:

o *Attribute brands* – that build confidence amongst customers where the functional attributes such as quality and performance are important, but are difficult for consumers to assess.
o *Aspirational brands* – that convey to customers images about the type of people who purchase the brand. Such brands do not simply deliver the customers' functional requirements of the products and services but also deliver status, recognition and esteem.
o *Experience brands* – focus on a shared philosophy between the customer and brand.

The choice of approach is dependent upon the context and particularly whether customers are able to distinguish between the product attributes and how 'involved' they are with the product purchase and use.

For example, in global markets, some cultures place more importance on the attributes, functionality and specification, whereas in other cultures, aspirational branding might be more appealing. Where appropriate, organizations must be prepared to modify their approach.

Car branding issues

Branding is central to much of the promotion communication work carried out and it is possible to see some of the dilemmas faced by brand managers simply by watching and reflecting on the nature of their advertising and the messages being put out – and then thinking about the implications for brand management. Renault, for example, has been very successful in building the Clio brand through successive TV commercials. For many existing and potential customers, the Clio brand is more recognizable than the Renault brand. Whilst this might be good for Clio sales, it may not help in the promotion of other models.

Money spent on promoting a small car, especially when it has such a strong sub brand, may not allow brand equity to be leveraged for the benefit of niche products, such as the Renault Espace, the sales of which will not justify mass promotion methods.

Renault has been very successful in designing and engineering their cars to high safety standards confirmed in official safety tests. The question is how can Renault achieve the maximum impact in its promotion and differentiation from its competitors from safety, something that consumers would either take for granted or prefer not to think about.

Country of origin (COO) effect

Brands give confidence to the buyers in situations where the buyers' knowledge about the product and its design and manufacture is limited, for example, because they are not able to assess the quality of the technology. In such situations, the country-of-origin perceptions can influence their buying decisions by creating trust in the particular expertise of firms and workers from that country. Increasingly, of course, the MNE's headquarters, the brand's perceived 'home', the location of product design and places of manufacture and service centres may all be in different countries as the supply chain is developed. However, consumers are becoming much more aware of these differences and are making increasingly sophisticated decisions based on COO perceptions.

Global branding

Strategically global branding offers the opportunity for the organization to benefit from economies of scale and the experience effect and is the response to targeting a global customer segment. To build and maintain a strong global brand requires every decision throughout the marketing process to be consistent with the brand standards and values. The decisions range from the need to gain deep insights into customer brand perception through to careful selection of celebrity endorsers that might be used to personify the brand.

The difficulty in global branding is to maintain consistency through standardization, where possible, but also be able to make adaptations to the mix, where necessary, because of cultural, legal or usage reasons without distorting the brand identity.

Specific benefits to the organization

If well-managed brands have the potential to add value to the organization by providing the following benefits (Doyle, 2000):

○ *Price premium* – Branded products should allow higher prices to be charged than for products that have an equivalent specification but no brand.
○ *Higher volumes* – Alternatively branded products can generate higher volumes than non-branded products if they are priced at market rates, rather than at a premium.
○ *Lower costs* – High volumes should lead to cost reduction because of the economies of scale and the experience effect.
○ *Better utilization of assets* – The predictably high level of sales should lead brand managers to make more effective use of assets, such as equipment, the supply chain and distribution channels.

Question 8.1

What are the benefits to customers and the organization of having a high profile, distinctive brand?

Factors contributing to brand value erosion

Over the last two decades, brands have come under increasing pressure. Some have been devalued and others have been discontinued. We have categorized the factors that have contributed to brand value erosion as external factors outside the organization's control including unexpected events and internal factors as poor brand management.

External factors
Private branding
As the major retailers have become more powerful and improved the quality of their own label products, so the private brand share of the market has increased significantly, as consumers perceive private brands to provide better value for money. The key decision for branded product producers is whether or not they should also manufacture for private label brands too.

Brand forgery
Brand forgery not only reduces the revenues for brands through lost sales but customers also sometimes associate poor quality of the forged brand product with the legitimate brand. Reducing or eliminating forgery is costly and time-consuming for governments and companies. It is widespread and in some product areas, such as CDs and software copying, is very mobile and difficult to close down.

Negative brand associations
As part of the strategy to explain the brand attributes to customers, firms make associations with the personalities, who encapsulate the standards, values and beliefs of the brand. For some brand, associations are made with the owners, such as Richard Branson and Bill Gates, and for others it is sports and media celebrities. Whilst these are generally positive, the brand can be damaged if the personalities are associated with inappropriate behaviour.

Product or corporate brands can also become too closely associated with sponsored events that disappoint visitors or are badly organized. Public relations activity that is designed to achieve a better relationship with governments and politicians can backfire if they are shown later to be corrupt and high-profile alliances with organizations that fail can also have a negative impact.

Insight

Kate Moss, the undesirable face of fashion

Using celebrities to endorse products can be risky if the celebrity's behaviour is inappropriate. In 2005, Kate Moss, one of the most successful fashion models, was photographed snorting cocaine, resulting in considerable media publicity. She had a number of valuable contracts to promote brands, such as Chanel, Burberry and Dior. H&M, the fashion store, many of whose customers are teenage girls, dropped her, as the publicity did not fit in with their clear dissociation of drugs.

Unacceptable business practices
A number of brands have been associated with unethical business practices such as environmental pollution, exploiting child labour and misleading customers. Often this is due to malpractice by contractors who must be very carefully policed. The problem in this area is that what is acceptable and unacceptable is often a very personal view and is affected by different stakeholder values, culture, affluence levels and understanding of business practices.

Unexpected crises
High profile brands are vulnerable to unexpected crises that occur from time to time. These events are often outside the organization's control, for example tampering with products, attacks on IT systems and anti-company propaganda through protests and websites, and accidents such as airline crashes.

Customers expect (sometimes unreasonably) to have systems in place that will prevent many of these events. Even with unavoidable events and where no blame is attributed to the firm, the brand can still suffer from being associated with negative publicity. It is vital that the organization has in place an effective strategy for responding fast and managing effectively any crises.

Grey marketing
Branded products that reach the market through unauthorized channels are often sold to customers at much lower prices than the authorized channels and can lead to customers believing that they have been 'ripped off'. There are three types of grey marketing: parallel importing, re-importing and lateral importing and for a fuller discussion read Doole and Lowe (2004).

 ## Activity 8.1

> For your own organization or an organization of your choice carry out a critical evaluation of the company's brands and the value they contribute to customers and the organization.

Insight

Exclusive brands with mass market appeal

Luxury brands are facing difficult decisions: whether to maintain exclusivity or increase their appeal to the mass market. For years Chanel, Gucci and Louis Vuitton have produced 'one-off, hand made' creations for the extremely rich and the brand value has been built upon exclusivity. However, as the brands have pursued fast growth strategies they have had to target new customer segments, by offering cheaper lines that would compete with those products at the top end of the high street chains.

There is considerable demand from consumers wanting a little of the 'bling' lifestyle of their celebrity idols, perhaps £20 Versace underpants to go with a supermarket outfit or a £54 Louis Vuitton keyring for the ageing motor that is probably worth about the same amount.

The theory is that recruiting customers young by offering a low entry price to the brand could be important in building long-term loyalty, given their potential, lifetime purchasing power. Equally cheap lines may help to discourage customers from buying counterfeit products.

There are dangers, however, as the brand image can be devalued if exclusivity is lost. An extreme version of this occurred when the Burberry baseball cap became the favoured dress of football hooligans and the company decided to withdraw the line.

Source: Adapted from 'Bling or bust', BBC News Online, 29 September 2004.

Brand building and management

At the start of the section, we distinguished between brands as assets to be built or brands as names to be used with products and services. It is essential to develop a strategy to create future brand value for the organization and customers.

Brand strategy – There are a number of brand strategies that you should be familiar with, including corporate umbrella branding, range branding and individual brand names. The use of these differs according to the context and company approach.

Brand portfolio management

A number of actions can be taken to improve the portfolio:

Brand building – Building knowledge of customer perceptions through research is used to strengthen the brand essence and identity and thus reinforce brand value in customers' minds through effective brand communications.

Brand positioning or repositioning – Customer insights are needed to more clearly define brand positioning or repositioning in order to avoid customers being unclear what the brand stands for.

Brand extension – Brand names with positive appeal can be applied to new products and services, but it is important to ensure that they fit with customer perceptions otherwise they will be devalued.

Brand rationalization – To be successful brands require substantial and sustained marketing support. Companies that have acquired many new brands or have carried out regular brand extension find that the portfolio can become unfocused and action is required to delete products. However, the decision to delete old products can be risky if they offend too many loyal customers.

Brand innovation – and new product development is essential to keep the brand fresh in customers' minds through continual innovation and occasional new developments.

Global branding – offers the chance to provide support on a much higher level and creates the expectation that considerable additional sales will result. Of course, as we have mentioned earlier, the global success of the brand depends on consistency of image and customer appeal, but customers from different cultures may have different expectations and beliefs about the brand that might make consistent positioning difficult.

Brand management

Over the last decade, there has been increasing evidence that many brands have come under pressure, as it has become more difficult to charge premium prices. Khashani (1995) identified the customer and competitor factors that have increased the pressure on brands and listed the actions that must be taken to address the problems. One of the main problems identified was a failure of management to invest and build the brand.

See CIM SMD Examination December 2004, Question 1

Branding is an important issue in the SMD syllabus and arises in varying guises in different types of questions. You need to ensure you understand the important characteristics of building a global brand and be able to assess the strategic implications of a company's branding strategy and how it could be improved. It is this issue which is examined in the Lego case study in this examination.

Business-to-business branding

So far, the discussion has focused largely on global consumer branding, but branding is increasingly important in B2B marketing too. The rationale for the existence of brands in business-to-business marketing is the same as in consumer goods marketing, to clearly communicate the attributes, values and standards of the company, product or service and to resist the decline into commoditization of products, which leads to decisions being based only on price.

Branding is a focus for building relationships. Purchasers and users value the commitment of suppliers to the product and service, and benefit from the added value from dealing with a firm with strong brands. In some situations, there may be benefits for low-profile brands from an association with globally recognized branded components (e.g. Intel microprocessors in computers or Lycra in garments). This trend is becoming increasingly important as consumers become more influential in the supply chain and demand products which contain branded components.

Branding in the not-for-profit sector

As with many aspects of marketing branding is becoming increasingly important in the not-for-profit sector, as the brand provides a 'short cut' in explaining the promised customer experience. We give two examples of the need for branding decisions in the UK charity sector in Unit 9 (Barnardos and the Soil Association) in order to assist in improving stakeholder communications. In destination marketing the branding is affected by media images. Despite its recent problems New York promises a positive experience for tourists. By contrast, the positive image of Prague of a few years ago has been eroded recently by stories of badly behaved young visitors, attracted by low alcohol prices and low-cost airline tickets.

 Activity 8.2

> Choose a brand from your own organization or an organization of your choice. Explain the appeal of the brand to customers and how effectively it adds intangible benefits. In what areas of brand management is there scope for increasing added value through the intangible benefits?

Product and service portfolio decisions

Much of what has gone earlier in the study guide has focused on the company's situation, capabilities, resources, markets, customers and competition, and how this can drive the strategic direction, growth and thus lead to successful performance.

However, it is the products and services of the company that generate the income streams on which the company's performance is judged. Efficient distribution and memorable communications are important in adding value, but cannot make a success of an unwanted product or service. For this reason, both proactive product and service management are critical.

Product and service analysis

There are many concepts and techniques, such as product life cycle and portfolio analysis that are referred to in the pre-reading that are used to analyse the product and service portfolio. Answers are required for a number of questions, including:

- Which products and services are performing well or badly, in terms of volume, value contribution to overheads and profitability?
- Which phase of the life cycle and cell of the portfolio matrices each product and service is in and what implications this has for future investment and revenue generation?
- Which market segments, including geographic segments, are best for generating demand for existing and new products and services?
- Which products and services generate the greatest volume, value and profitability through the various customer segments and distribution channels?
- How successful are the introduction of new products and services measured by the diffusion rates?
- For which product and service areas are there the best opportunities for new development?

Answering these questions will enable managers to reach conclusions about the strategies that should be adopted for each individual product and category of product and service both globally and in specific market segments. The implications of this might be that decisions will be required about which products need to be eliminated, reinvigorated or replaced with a new development. Some alternative strategies follow.

Rationalization of product range

There are a number of reasons for the rationalization of products within the portfolio and these include:

o When products and services have reached the end of the life cycle and support instead should be given to growth products
o When the marketing budget is limited and cannot effectively support all the products in the portfolio
o When there is a need to standardize products, for example in international markets, to reduce costs through scale economies
o When there is a need to reduce inventory and product line changeover time in manufacturing.

Retention of poorly performing products

There may be reasons why poorly performing or unprofitable products should be retained. A low volume sales product might be an essential part of a range. It might be a loss leader and leverage sales of complementary, higher volume or value products. The product might be what everyone remembers the brand for and therefore to discontinue it could lead to brand damage. Not choosing to discontinue the product might be important in retaining some residual customer loyalty until a replacement is developed and introduced. In other cases, keeping the product might ensure the production line; skills and knowledge are retained until the next big order materializes. This is often necessary in sectors such as shipbuilding, aircraft manufacture or defence equipment manufacture.

Decisions need to be taken about whether contributing to overheads is sufficient reason to retain a product. It is worthwhile remembering that discontinuing a product that contributes to overheads will result in other products having to share an additional overhead burden that could lead to them becoming loss making as a result.

Question 8.2

What might be the reasons for rationalizing the product/service range in the portfolio? What factors should be taken into account when deciding which products and services to delete from the range?

The downward spiral into commoditization

Having been around for a long time many products in widespread use have reached the mature phase of the life cycle. The product and services are well known and are often taken for granted by the customers, and the organization may see very little opportunity for innovation or product development. It becomes increasingly difficult for some organizations to continue to differentiate their product and add customer value; and in desperation, they resort to price-cutting. Competition often remains intense as firms attempt to hang on to market share. This problem is compounded by e-commerce which has increased price transparency, allowing customers to more easily compare prices and buy from the lowest priced supplier, forcing the higher priced alternatives to lower their prices or risk going out of business.

As supermarkets become more powerful, they are able to apply pressure to suppliers to force them into offering volume discounts. This is made worse as they put further pressure on branded goods suppliers by offering own label across an ever-broader range of products.

Becoming the lowest cost supplier of commodities

Firms that supply commodities have no alternative but to aggressively and continuously reduce costs throughout their supply chain and be prepared to source components and services from the lowest cost supplier no matter what the location is. For many years the textile and garment-making industry has been driven by cost advantage to source from emerging countries. Banks and insurance companies are lowering their costs by making staff redundant in high-cost locations and relocating their service operations to low cost countries. As we have seen earlier, e-hubs will further increase the pressure towards commoditization in the B2B sector.

Differentiation by adding value

It is easy for a firm to be drawn into believing that they are in the business of selling a specific product or service made to a specific design with the inevitable consequence of trying to achieve ever-lower prices. But some of the most successful firms have been able to manage customer perceptions of lower prices, whilst differentiating products and adding value. For example, TESCO has grown from being the 'pile it high, sell it cheap' food retailer of the late 1960s to become the leading UK food retailer. It has achieved this through continually differentiating the relatively mundane activity of food shopping by adding customer value through a whole range of successful, often small initiatives. However, it is also building a value brand designed to give customers every day low prices (EDLP).

Activity 8.3

For your own organization or an organization of your choice carry out a critical assessment of the value added throughout the portfolio. Which are the areas where the portfolio is underperforming?

The global portfolio

We have discussed earlier some product portfolio issues in making international marketing decisions and it is worth returning to them at this point:

- Global standardization/local adaptation product and service decisions because of, for example, cultural, legal and usage reasons in different countries.
- The fact that the products may be at different stages of the life cycle in different countries. This adds an additional complication for new product development and portfolio rationalization decisions because the global perspective must be considered. In some countries, it may be desirable to cut the old product and replace it with a new development, whilst in other markets, it may be preferable to promote the existing product.
- Emerging markets may require a more basic version of the product compared to more technologically advanced countries.
- In emerging markets, it may be possible to 'leapfrog' one technology completely as is happening with mobile phone technology.

New product and service developments (NPD)

In Unit 4, we introduced the NPD process as a framework for the innovation process and the various elements contained within it. The idea is that the process is linear and a series of single gateways at which decisions are made. As a linear process the next stage is not begun until the previous one is completed, assessed and the decision taken to proceed, usually by senior management. Whilst in concept this provides the necessary discipline, cost containment and control, it can be a lengthy process, particularly if decision-making in the company is slow and bureaucratic. Often the time to market launch is critical because of:

- The importance of being first mover in a market, to set the new basis for competing
- The speed at which information and intelligence about new developments spreads through markets
- The speed with which competitors copy and introduce new product and services
- The demands of customers and their dissatisfaction with old products.

Some companies do not have these pressures and so the linear process is appropriate. However, an increasing number of firms must undertake the various stages in the NPD process simultaneously in order to reduce the time to market, so marketing launch and commercialization plans might be needed in concept in early stages. It may be that the company is committed to a new product launch but the final product features may depend on differentiating the product from competitor products that are introduced to the market during the period up to the firm's launch. The packaging design concepts may be produced at the same time that the product features are being finally developed.

New product development categories

There are a number of categories of new products and these are shown in Table 8.1. These reflect the fact that the majority of new developments made by companies are needed to update and refresh the portfolio through incremental improvements. In fact, new-to-the-world products are not too common, so the firms that wait for the next big R&D breakthrough to improve their fortunes are likely to be disappointed.

Table 8.1 New product categories

Category	Contribution
New to the world	10%
New product lines	20%
Additions to product lines	26%
Revisions/improvements	26%
Cost reductions	11%
Repositionings	7%

Aligning NPD to the marketing strategy

A key task in developing new products is ensuring that the time and resources spent on new developments are aligned with the marketing strategy. It is therefore necessary to answer a number of questions and these are highlighted in Table 8.2.

Table 8.2 Aligning NPD to the marketing strategy

Fit with mission	Will all stakeholders understand the new idea?
Fit with product/market scope	Can the ideas be contained within an identified and easily communicated area?
Match between growth strategies and resources	Are the resources being used effectively within the growth options?
Delivery of competitive advantage	Is the advantage tangible or in the mind of the innovator?
Synergy between firm and target market	Will this add value to the current customer segment?
Fit with positioning	Does this reinforce or enhance the current positioning? Does it fit with the brand image?
Market entry alternatives	Could the idea be better exploited by alternative collaboration in order to reduce risks?
Is the timing right?	Should the product be launched now or should the firm wait for others to create the demand?

Question 8.3

In marketing international services, the elements of the extended marketing mix 'physical evidence', process and people provide the basis for adding value for customers. As a consultant to a global bank, explain how these should be used within the marketing mix to build competitive advantage.

Service enhancement

There is considerable difficulty and uncertainty in the development of new products and we have already emphasized in Unit 7 that many fast growth businesses are successful through adding very high levels of customer service into their product and service offer, but this is an area where organizations often fail to maximize the use of their assets and competencies. Services can either be regarded as 'add-ons' to a product offering or a service offering alone. Services also involve the process management of information (e.g. financial services), people (airlines) and physical objects (e.g. laundry). As we have indicated with the examples, the balance between each of these varies according to the context.

However, what is quite clear is that the quality of service is becoming ever more important as the differentiator between product offerings and between competing service offerings. Many organizations are focusing on the customer 'experience' and this is where portfolio enhancement can be increased. Whilst it would seem relatively straightforward to enhance service delivery, in practice the cost of improving processes, systems and staff training to achieve the required levels can be extremely high.

Success and failure in NPD

The problem with NPD is the high risk of failure. Griffin (1997) found that although failure rates had been reduced during mid-1980s and mid-1990s, only one in five ideas made it through to success.

Griffin suggests that products and services are often abandoned during the NPD process because of:

o A lack of available technology
o A change in the firm's strategy
o A competitor pre-emptive new product launch
o Market information suggesting that the new product or service will not meet customer needs or expectations.

However, 55 per cent of products and services that are launched also fail. The reasons for this include:

o The size of the market is frequently overestimated and the adoption curve misunderstood
o The product fails to perform
o Competitors prove to be too firmly entrenched
o The product is poorly positioned, inadequately promoted, or priced at too high a level
o Distributors lack commitment
o The new product is pushed through despite market research findings.

Case study

New product problems at Coca-Cola

For Coca-Cola, the year 2004 was bad. On two occasions, the company was forced to warn the stock markets that it would not meet its sales targets. The share price had continued to decline sharply during the year and the newly appointed Chairman and Chief Executive, Nevell Idsell, was forced to reduce the company's volume, operating income and earnings per share growth targets. At the same time, its main rival, Pepsi, was reconfirming double-digit-earnings growth – the result of Pepsi beating Coke in innovation over the last few years.

Coca-Cola has had a number of innovation failures recently. Backed by a $50 million advertising campaign, its C2 low carb, low caffeine beverage was seen as the most exciting development since the launch of Diet Coke in 1982. But C2 was premium priced at a time when regular Coke was being discounted and sales have failed to take off.

In the UK Coca-Cola launched its Dasani, purified bottled water brand. However, the product had to be withdrawn when the press publicized the fact that the source of the water was the main supply and the Dasani water was found to have high levels of the carcinogen, bromate. In Europe, the main selling point of bottled water is the source and is expected to be natural.

Source: Adapted from Rusche, D., 'Coke's latest idea falls flat', *Sunday Times*, 2004.

Question 8.4

Suggest some possible reasons for the failure of major brand new product introduction.

Achieving success in NPD

The key to success is an effective NPD strategy, which will create a flow of new products that might vary in market impact, but will include some high revenue or high-margin generators. This approach is preferable to trying to spot one blockbuster new product.

In order to do this Griffin suggests three fundamental requirements of the process:

1. Uncover unmet needs and problems.
2. Develop a competitively advantaged product.
3. Shepherd the products through the firm.

 Activity 8.4

For your own organization or an organization of your choice, assess the effectiveness of new product development in the company. Where in the process do you believe there is scope for improvement and why?

NPD, platforms and 1:1 marketing

We have discussed the need for 1:1 marketing and customization and advances in technology makes this increasingly possible. The challenge for organizations in the future is to be able to create common product platforms and a computer-aided, modular approach to building the final product for the individual customer. The modular approach not only ensures cost-efficiency but also allows a high degree of customization, especially when applied along with other marketing mix elements.

Question 8.5

You have a consultancy contract to provide advice to a medium-sized specialist engineering company that supplies equipment to the energy generation business. The business is efficiently run but is losing money and needs to reassess its ageing portfolio. Prepare, with justification, a list of actions and areas of investigation that you would undertake.

Case study

Unilever's global brands

In 2004, Niall Fitzgerald, the then Chairman of Unilever, was the main architect of a 5-year growth strategy which focused on achieving growth through 400 leading brands. The strategy has involved disposal of many minor local country brands and non-core activity. Although the strategy had hit 11 out of 12 targets for margins, cost savings and debt reduction the firm has failed to meet its target of 5–6 per cent growth from its leading brands, which include Magnum, Ben and Jerry's and Hellmann's mayonnaise.

As a result of this, the company announced that it would switch its focus to increasing shareholder returns through share buy-backs and dividend increases. Although some brands such as Knorr soups, Lipton tea and Dove soap had achieved their growth forecast, other brands had performed less well, so that in fact the top 400 brands only achieved 2.5 per cent growth overall in 2003. The main underperforming brands were Slim Fast, Calvin Klein fragrances, Cif and Domestos household range and frozen foods. Slim Fast was purchased in 2000 for £1.44 billion but sales have suffered recently because of the success of the Atkins Diet.

Question 8.6

The Unilever strategy was based on concentrating on the development of global brands. What do you consider to be the arguments for and against this strategy?

Question 8.7

What should Unilever do now?

Summary

- Brands are a major means of differentiation of one product or service from those from the competition.
- It is the customers' perception of the brand that ultimately determines the true brand value. This is the reason why the brand becomes a valuable intangible asset of the organization.
- Every aspect of the marketing mix must be managed effectively to build the brand and this requires continual investment, consistent communications, innovation and service enhancement in order to create exceptional value for the customer.
- It is essential to have a product and service portfolio strategy and use appropriate criteria for making portfolio decisions that involve rationalization and new development.

- ○ In international markets, the challenge is to maximize company performance by developing a portfolio that is balanced between globally standardized products and services and locally adapted ones.
- ○ New product development and service enhancement should be a continual process to which the organization is committed. A high proportion of products fail and so it is essential for organizations to have an effective new product development process.

Further study

de Chernatony, L. (2001) *From Brand Vision to Brand Evaluation*, Elsevier Butterworth-Heinemann, branding and brand management.

Doole, I and Lowe, R. (2004) *Strategic Marketing Decisions in Global Markets*, Thomson Learning, Chapter 9.

Wilson, R and Gilligan, C. (2004) *Strategic Marketing Management, Planning, Implementation and Control*, 3rd edition, Oxford: Elsevier Butterworth-Heinemann, provides a fuller discussion of product and service management.

Bibliography

de Chernatony, L. (2001) *From Brand Vision to Brand Evaluation*, Elsevier Butterworth-Heinemann, pp. 19, 261.

Doole, I. and Lowe, R. (2004) *International Marketing Strategy, 2*, Thomson Learning, Chapter 11.

Doole, I. and Lowe, R. (2005) *Strategic Marketing Decisions in Global Markets*, Thomson Learning, Chapter 9.

Doyle, P. (2000) *Value-based Marketing*, Wiley.

Griffin, A. (1997) 'Research in new product development practices: updating trends and benchmarking best practices', *Journal of Innovation Management*, **14**(6), 428–458.

Khashani, K. (1995) 'A new future for brands', *Financial Times*, 10 November.

Sample exam question and answers for the Strategic Marketing Decisions module as a whole can be found in Appendix 3 at the back of the book. The Lego case study from the December 2004 examination is concerned with a number of the issues covered in this unit.

unit 9
integrated communications and relationship development

Learning objectives

The CIM syllabus for Strategic Marketing Decisions recognizes that, in an environment of competing messages, organizations must connect more effectively with their key stakeholders, by integrating their communications and building stronger relationships.

In studying this unit you will:

4.4 Evaluate the role of integrated marketing communications in competitive global strategy.

4.5 Understand the concept of relationship marketing and the role of long-term customer relationships in creating and delivering value.

4.6 Determine the importance of managing marketing relationships in generating customer commitment.

Having completed this unit, you will be able to:

o Evaluate the role of brands, innovation, integrated marketing communications, alliances, customer relationships and service in decisions for developing a differentiated positioning to create exceptional value for the customer.

o Demonstrate the ability to develop innovative and creative marketing solutions to enhance an organization's global competitive position in the context of changing product, market, brand and customer life cycles.

o Define and contribute to investment decisions concerning the marketing assets of an organization.

This unit relates to the statements of practice

Dd.1 Develop and direct an integrated marketing communications strategy.

Key definitions

Integrated Marketing Communications – Shimp (2003) provides a definition of IMC, which focuses on five features:

1. Start with the customer or prospect.
2. Use any form of relevant contact.
3. Achieve synergy through consistency across the communication elements.
4. Build relationships.
5. Affect behaviour.

Relationship marketing – is creating and building mutually beneficial relationships by bringing together the necessary stakeholders and resources to deliver the best possible perceived value proposition for the customer.

Study Guide

This unit is concerned with the ways in which an organization builds competitive advantage by developing an integrated strategy for communications and relationship building with all its stakeholders. In doing this we consider the challenge of increasing the effectiveness of communications by recognizing the need to be aware of the positive and negative messages that are received by customers and appreciating how planning, using the right communication methods, can achieve success. We then focus on taking decisions in relationship marketing that can be used, where appropriate, to build customer loyalty.

The purpose of communications

The purpose of communications is for the organization to present and exchange information with its various stakeholders (individuals and organizations), according to its defined objectives and in order to deliver specific results. This means not only that recipients must accurately receive and understand the information conveyed but also that they may be subject to some persuasion too. This aspect of communications is the traditional promotion P (promoting to external stakeholders) of the marketing mix and includes advertising, personal selling, PR and sales promotion.

The communications role goes further, however, as it implies the need for a two-way dialogue with customers. This has led to the concept of relationship marketing with the objective of building interactive relationships with the most profitable and valuable customers and other influential stakeholders. Because all staff of the organization will have a direct or indirect role in communicating and building relationships with stakeholders, it is vital that they work towards the organization's overall objectives and always meet the standards and values of the organization in all their interactions.

Co-ordinating the Tsunami appeal through integrated communications

The success of the appeal for donations for the communities affected by the Tsunami in December 2004 exceeded the expectations of most observers. The level of donations per head of population involved was considerably higher than for other major disasters in recent years. There are many reasons for this and you may wish to consider the motivations of those donating funds.

However, one significant difference was the fact that the main charities working in this area, such as Save the Children, Oxfam, Christian Aid and the Red Cross, campaigned for funds under one organization, dec.org (Disasters Emergency Committee), with one set of appeal advertisements, website and telephone number. The agreement was that the funds would be shared out between the charities that were providing help for those affected.

Internal, interactive and external marketing

Figure 9.1 shows the importance of considering three dimensions in communications: external, internal and interactive or relationship marketing.

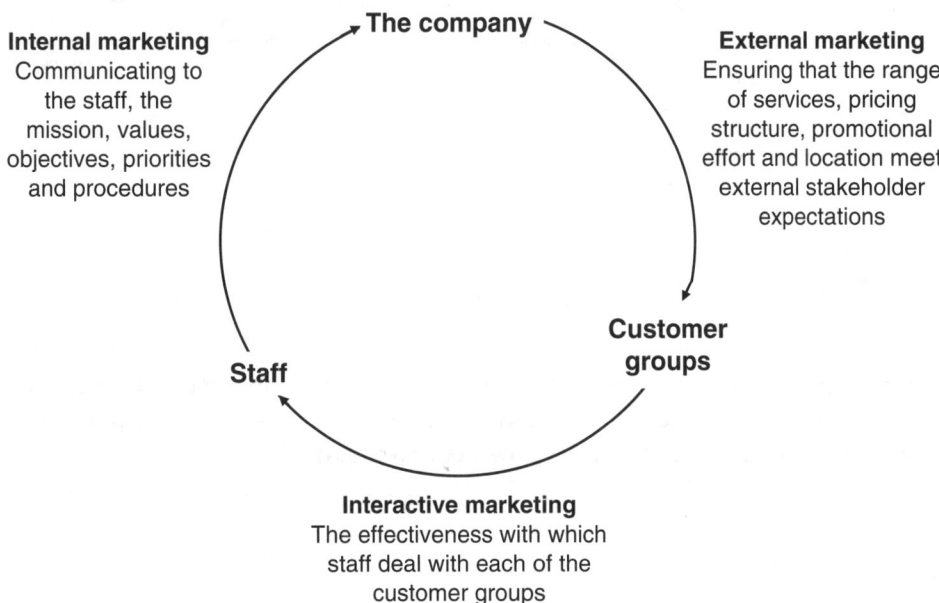

Figure 9.1 External, internal and interactive marketing

Internal marketing ensures that all staff employed in its business units, and supply-chain partnerships, are aware of the strategies, tactics, priorities and procedures to achieve the firm's mission and objectives. This is particularly important for staff who are in different world-wide locations and often subject to cultural and language boundaries in the same way that external audiences may misunderstand the firm's external communications.

Interactive marketing ensures that every contact between staff and customers is consistent with the organization's service standards and values, and that the decisions taken by individual members of staff are consistent with the organization's strategy.

External marketing is the traditional role of communications with external stakeholders, and can be summarized by the DRIP factors (Fill, 1999).

- o **D**ifferentiate products and services.
- o **R**emind and reassure customers and potential customers.
- o **I**nform.
- o **P**ersuade targets to think or act in a certain way.

Four levels of communications and relationship building

Communications and relationship building activities in the organization embrace four distinct strategic elements and these are shown in Figure 9.2. Distribution will be discussed in Unit 10.

Figure 9.2 The dimensions of external marketing communications

 Activity 9.1

Carry out an audit of communications in your organization under the headings of external, internal and interactive marketing. How consistent are the communications and where could improvements be made to improve their effectiveness?

The integration of communications

Stakeholders receive messages, both intended and unintended, from every part of the organization's activities, from the clothes that customer facing staff wear, the packaging design, the delays in answering the telephone at the call centre to stories in the newspaper about the chief executive's extravagant partying habit.

The ways of communicating

Davidson (2002) explains that an organization communicates in eight ways:

1. Actions – what it does?
2. Behaviour – how things are done?
3. Face-to-face by management – through talks, visits and meetings it shows what the management thinks is important.
4. Signals – from the organization's actions, facilities and objects, including executive bonuses, dress, buildings.
5. Product and services – and particularly their quality.
6. Intended communications – such as advertising, which is not always received as the organization expects.
7. Word of mouth and word of Web (including e-mail).
8. Comments by other organizations – such as pressure groups, competitors and the media.

As the number of communications have increased dramatically and customers have become more critical and sceptical, the importance of IMC has been emphasized in order to avoid conflicting messages and instead communicate consistent and mutually supporting messages. Kotler (2003) says that 'companies need to orchestrate a consistent set of impressions from its personnel, facilities and actions that deliver the company's brand meaning and promise to its various audiences'.

Activity 9.2

Thinking about a company with which you have communicated recently, list the areas that you received negative and mixed messages. What could have been done to improve the experience?

The areas of integration

Corporate strategy – It is essential to communicate the standards and values, objectives, strategies and performance of the organization to external and internal stakeholders, including shareholders and staff.

The management style, the organization culture, human resources and recruitment policies convey important messages, such as openness, integrity or creativity to a variety of stakeholders.

Brand strategies – It is vital to clearly convey to customers what the brand stands for and reinforce this by ensuring that all brand activities communicate a consistent message. Communications often go further and define the direction of the brand strategy. For example, the success of many of the world's greatest brands can be attributed to consistent promotion sustained by investment over decades.

Global integration – As organizations operate more internationally, travel and communications become more global because of the Internet and satellite television, so the consistency of communications across borders becomes essential. This means that organizations must standardize some elements of their communications programmes and processes. However, Doole and Lowe (2004) explain that there are many disadvantages and pitfalls associated with overstandardization across borders of communications.

Marketing mix integration – Customers continually receive communications from every element of the marketing mix, such as product specification, leaflets and advertising, service centre efficiency and friendliness, the appearance of a distributor's delivery driver. Some are intended and some are unintentional.

It is important to remember that non-verbal communication in many markets has greater impact than verbal communications and inconsistencies may be culture based. For example, the colours and styles used in creative work communicate non-verbally with the customers, reinforcing the positive or negative images and customer perceptions. Customers pick up small errors in colour, matching the corporate colours and design and, in different cultures, the significance of colours, symbols and numbers is so great that they alone could deter customers from buying a product.

Question 9.1

Explain the concept of integrated marketing communications, and using examples of good and bad practice show how value can be added or removed.

Success and failure in marketing communications

All forms of marketing communication have a fundamental purpose, which is to ensure that the intended messages (those which are part of the firm's strategy) are conveyed accurately between the sender and the receiver, and that the impact of unintentional messages (those which are likely to have an adverse effect on the firm's market performance and reputation) are kept to a minimum. Noise might devalue or discredit the intended message or simply cause it to be lost in the volume of communications.

International marketing communications are particularly difficult. Mistakes in the use of language, particularly using messages, which do not translate or are mistranslated, are a particular problem, but more serious is a lack of sensitivity to different cultures amongst international communicators. Failures of the high profile firms are highly visible and can show the firm to be incompetent, insensitive or arrogant.

The problems that prevent effective communications can be within or outside the organization's control.

Within the organization's control:

- Inconsistency in the messages conveyed to customers by staff at different levels, in different locations
- Different styles of presentation of corporate identity, brand and product image can leave customers confused
- A lack of co-ordination of messages, such as press releases, advertising campaigns and changes in product specification or pricing

o Failure to appreciate the differences in the fields of perception (the way the message is understood) of the sender and receiver
o Ignoring the needs of different audiences
o Achieving little impact from a single message
o Lack of synergy and reinforcement from multiple communications
o More than one message communicated together, so confusing the recipient
o Setting unclear objectives
o Trying to achieve too much with one communication to justify the high cost
o Inconsistency within the distribution channel
o Advertising agencies focusing on their creative work rather than selling the product.

Some problems outside the organization's control include:

o Counterfeiting or other infringements of patents or copyright causes the firm to lose revenue and suffer damage to its image if consumers believe the low-quality goods supplied by the counterfeiter are genuine.
o Grey marketing, which is distribution through channels that are not authorized by the organization, communicates contradictory messages that damage the brand and confuse consumers, often because prices undercut the official channel.
o Competitors, governments or pressure groups attack the standards and values of organizations by alleging, fairly or unfairly, bad business practice.

Marketing communications planning

The framework for communications planning is shown in Table 9.1. Situation analysis should establish a clear, current and desired future position for the organization within its market environment context. The analysis should also confirm the organization's current communications capability within its market. It should be possible to establish from this the organization's ability to influence and persuade its stakeholders through its integrated communications strategy.

Table 9.1 The marketing communications plan

Situation analysis	Environment market: stakeholders, competition, customers, structure
Objectives	The short- and long-term objectives
Messages	Target audiences and messages
Communications	The media, the promotions mix and integration of the channels
Budgets	Basis of allocation
Control	Measurement, evaluation and correct deviations

It will also enable decisions to be made about the communications objectives and budgets to be set (as these must be different from the overall marketing strategy objectives), the target audience, the tools and media and the measurements made to evaluate progress.

Audiences

Profiles of all stakeholder audiences need to be prepared. A clear understanding of the target buyers, their background, experience, preferred information sources, purchasing behaviour and processes will help in the creation of the message and selection of appropriate marketing tools and media. In B2B markets, organizational purchasing is a more formal process and involves a buying centre shown in Table 9.2. Each member of staff has a separate responsibility and motivation for buying and therefore requires a different message.

147

Table 9.2 The B2B Buying centre

Users	Often initiate the purchase and define the specification
Influencers	Help define the product and evaluate the alternatives
Deciders	Decide product requirements and suppliers
Approvers	Authorize the proposals of deciders and buyers
Buyers	Have the formal authority for selecting suppliers and negotiating terms
Gatekeepers	Can stop the sellers reaching the buying centre

Question 9.2

Identify the key decisions that would be needed when developing an outline communications plan for the launch of a new low-cost airline and what factors would be the key when making the decisions.

Case study

The Soil Association

The Soil Association is a charity that campaigns to promote sustainable organic agriculture in the UK. It has an income of £7.4 million and employs 146 full-time and 25 part-time staff. Its main activity is encouraging consumers and, for farms that meet the criteria, providing certification and allowing them to use the Soil Association logo.

In the UK, the organic sector is the fastest growing part of the food and drink market, showing 10 per cent annual rise with sales now over £1 billion. The association currently has 25 000 subscribers but the charity would like to increase it to 100 000 within the next 5 years. If the idea really caught the imagination of consumers, it could become a very influential charity indeed.

To increase subscriptions on which its survival largely depends, however, the soil association must change the public's perceptions. Last year, just a few hundred new members joined. Most people think that the Soil Association is a government body, not a membership organization. It has no large marketing or advertising budget and instead relies on the PR that results from campaigns. Its 'Food for Life' campaign hit the headlines recently because it showed that more was spent on lunches in jails than in schools but this did not lead to an increase in membership.

At the moment, the assumption is that the subscribers are contributing to a good cause. They only receive a magazine in return for their subscription. More might join if they could perceive more benefits.

Source: Adapted from Terry, F. 'Green food campaign sows seed of success', Sunday Times, 14 November 2004.

Question 9.3

How might the Soil Association increase its membership and public profile?

Communication tools and media

The key decisions in media planning are the choice of media

- o *Reach* – is the percentage of the target audience exposed to the message at least once during the relevant period.
- o *Coverage* – is the size of the potential audience that might be exposed to a particular medium vehicle.
- o *Frequency* – is the repetition level of the communication.
- o *Gross Rating Point (GRP)* – is the reach multiplied by the frequency and is a measure of the total number of exposures of the communication.
- o *Efficiency* – is a further key dimension of decision-making, given the need to reach as many potential customers as possible, given a constant budget.

Decisions on media planning involve a trade-off between reach, frequency and the impact and different buying situations require different patterns of advertising.

- o *Recency* – The concept of recency suggests that it is important to plan the communication to reach potential customers that are ready to buy. Some suggest that the main stimuli to purchase is running out of the product and so there may be little point in advertising at other times.

The communication tools

It is essential to be familiar with the main communication tools and have an understanding on their use and for a fuller discussion read Doole and Lowe (2005). In practice, the choice of tools will be determined by the specific communications context and the following four selection criteria: cost, communication effectiveness, credibility and control.

Advertising – The role of advertising is to inform, persuade, remind and reinforce. It has been the mass communication method for consumer products and services and has been used to build brands over decades but it is a one-way communication. It is more difficult to target effectively than more interactive communications tools, such as Internet marketing. TV is the main advertisement medium but audiences are becoming more fragmented due to the increase in number of TV channels; advertisements are typically becoming shorter, placed together and there are more of them, and it has become easier for viewers to switch between channels, so reducing their impact. Kotler (2003) suggests that few advertisements are likely to cover their costs in increased sales and should not be expected to deliver the sales targets of inferior products.

Sales promotion – Kotler maintains that sales promotion is concerned with transaction marketing, not building relationships, as it is a short-term trigger to act and build current sales rather than build the brand. Indeed, sales might be increased short term, but in the long run, profitability will be hit. Sales promotions are typically used with weaker brands and attract brand switchers. Firms must decide whether frequent sales promotions are either necessary or useful in growing sales, because they will not help to build the brand.

PR – is perceived by customers as 'news', more authoritative and believable than advertising. PR is underused and undervalued by many firms and has a variety of uses. Whilst it is apparently 'free' to place, it requires long-term relationships to be built, for example, with editors. The disadvantage of PR for firms is that it is difficult to control. For example, a story can be published rather differently from how it was intended.

One of the key roles of PR is managing crises that might adversely affect the company or brand value from time to time, for example product contamination, lapses in quality control and design faults.

Sponsorship – Many firms sponsor events or individuals and the key decision is whether it will be regarded as a cost or investment. Sponsorship (Shimp, 2003) consists of the event exchange, which is the fee paid to be associated with the event and the marketing of the association by the sponsor. To obtain the maximum benefit a sum two or three times the cost of the sponsorship is needed for pre-event and follow up activity. Overall, success is likely to be greater if there is a match between the event audience and the firm's target customers. Sponsorship of sports and media celebrities can backfire if they engage in inappropriate behaviour.

Insight

For Sunseeker 'The World is Not Enough'

Product placement in films and television programmes is becoming an increasingly important promotion tool.

In 1968, Robert Braithwaite founded his boat building company, Sunseeker, with a team of seven. Despite many set backs, they kept trying but without real success. Then Braithwaite made an important strategic marketing decision. He decided to focus on powerboats, rather than sailing boats and invested in innovation, technology and design.

Braithwaite recognized the importance of building the brand and his ambition was to make Sunseeker the 'Hoover' of the luxury powerboat industry. This seemed to have been fully achieved when, in the opening sequence of the film *The World is Not Enough*, James Bond churned up the Thames in front of the familiar London sites in his Sunseeker boat as he pursed an attractive female assassin.

The harbour area in Poole, its home, seems to be dominated by Sunseeker boats worth up to £5 million each awaiting delivery to millionaires, world rulers sports stars and successful marketing directors (?). Of the boats, 99 per cent are exported. It now employs 1500 employees, a turnover of £172 million.

Personal selling – Personal selling is necessary where complex negotiation and persuasion are needed, and where there is sufficient margin to cover the four or five visits that might be needed to make the sale. It is, however, becoming ever more expensive and organizations have other ways of communicating with customers to collect orders, such as telephone selling, sales agents, and direct and e-marketing. Consequently, personal selling is being used more selectively and is usually managed better with emphasis given to salesperson motivation, direction and control.

Direct marketing – Direct marketing traditionally took the form of direct mailing and telephone selling, supported by database management of the information but the major change has come from e-business development. For many firms their direct marketing strategy means using a combination of direct marketing techniques (traditional and e-business), different routes to market and Web-based promotion, integrating the initiatives and responses through customer relationship management.

B2B – For most B2B communications decisions, there is a small target audience and so the mass-market tools, such as advertising (apart from trade press advertising) and sales promotions, would not normally be used. Direct marketing, PR and personal selling are likely to be more effective methods.

Constraints – It is important to re-emphasize that there are a number of constraints in the use of communications, particularly in international marketing, including cultural, political, infrastructure and legal issues which affect the availability, acceptability and usage of media.

The tools are widening all the time with promotion through websites, e-mail and text messaging. Global positioning systems (GPS) coupled with mobile telephony offer further possibilities.

Question 9.4

Choose two communications tools. Explain for what purposes they are most useful and, using examples, show when they are most effective.

Messages

Most messages in the B2C market must be simple and Kotler (2003) suggests, where possible, they should be based on a single benefit or story or a character that the customers know and can associate strongly with the proposition. Customers need to be taken through a number of stages during the purchasing process.

To achieve the best effect different messages, marketing communication tools and contributions from the whole marketing mix might be required at different stages in this purchasing process. In a B2B situation, even a different member of the buying centre might need to be targeted at each of these stages. There are a range of communications models (see Fill, 1999; Shimp, 2003), including 'AIDA' (Awareness, Interest, Desire, Action).

It is suggested that such rational and detailed customer decision-making models are often difficult to apply and may be only appropriate for high involvement decisions, such as the purchase of a car, but not for low involvement decisions, where impulse buying replaces the measured process.

Budgets

Wilson and Gilligan (2004) identify the various approaches to budgeting:

  o What the organization can afford
  o Matching competitors' spend or the norms for the industry
  o A fixed percentage of past sales

- A fixed percentage of past profit
- A fixed amount to carry out a specific objective or task.

The decision about which approach to take is determined by the organizational context and often reflects the company's view about the marketing communications budget, and whether it is regarded as a cost or an investment.

Measuring the effectiveness of marketing communications is difficult because many of the tools do not precisely target specific customers nor can the effect of the single tool be isolated. In consequence, the budgets of many firms are decided in a rather ad hoc way often leading to internal battles about priorities.

See CIM SMD Examination June 2005, Question 4

This question allows you to show you how to practice in an applied manner the implications of a company moving from a traditional promotional strategy to one that is a more innovative Web-based strategy, discussed in Unit 7.

Measurement and control

The difficulty of measuring effectiveness

Organizations that are driven by measurement often over-compensate for this difficulty by selecting the marketing communications tools that can most easily be measured. In consumer markets, sales promotions have an obvious short-term impact that can be measured and so often tend to be over-used and, as a result, premium price positioning and brand value can be wasted.

Tools, such as advertising or PR, that offer the most valuable long-term effects, such as awareness raising and brand value enhancement are usually more difficult to measure. Internet-based interactive communication is becoming an increasingly important tool that responds quickly to changing consumer attitudes, information search, purchasing behaviour and product and service usage.

Control

Despite some reservations about their inappropriate use a variety of measurement methods shown below are used for decision-making:

- Regular auditing
- Pre-activity research and measurement
- Ongoing research and measurement
- Post-activity research and measurement
- Tracking research
- Benchmarking.

Measurement

The measurements can involve internal staff, customers and other outside agencies and experts. It is worthwhile emphasizing a number of points about decisions on marcomms evaluation.

- o There should be a strong link between measurement and objectives, and in areas such as brand value enhancement this might mean that measurements should relate to the holistic benefit that is gained from integrated communications, rather than the impact of just one tool.
- o The main purpose of evaluation might be considered to be control in order to correct short-term deviations from the intended performance, but, more importantly, it should be to inform strategy development.
- o The most beneficial dimension of evaluation should be to learn from mistakes and good practice, and this should be shared with colleagues through knowledge management processes.

Activity 9.3

Carry out an evaluation of a recent promotion campaign. What lessons can be learned from this and how could the campaign have been improved?

Developing profitable long-term marketing relationships

The key to relationship marketing is developing and maintaining mutual advantageous relationships between supplier and customer. It is particularly relevant for B2B relationships between firms in a supply chain that might use their combined capability and resources to deliver the maximum added value for the ultimate customer. Firms increasingly realize that it is less costly if they can persuade customers to stay loyal rather than lose them to a competitor and face the cost of winning them over again.

Customer retention is particularly important for B2B marketing, where the number of opportunities to bid for and win over new customers may be very limited and the loss of a major customer could have a disastrous effect on the firm. Relationship marketing not only focuses on the lifetime value of the customer to the supplier but also recognizes that the cost of the customer changing to a new supplier can be considerable too. Both supplier and customer have something to gain from the relationship marketing concept which is based on the idea of achieving a 'win–win'.

Throughout the firm the objectives of relationship marketing are to:

- o Maintain and build existing customers by offering more tailored and cost-effective business solutions
- o Use existing relationships to obtain referral to business units and other supply-chain members
- o Increase the revenue from customers by offering solutions that are a combination of products and services
- o Reduce the operational and communications cost of servicing the customers, including the work prior to a trading relationship.

153

System development

Relationship management is usually supported by an IT process that incorporates a database, data analysis (datamining) and a system to manage communications (customer relationship management).

Database
A database is required to manage:

- o Personal and profile data, including contact details
- o Transaction data including purchase quantities, channels, timing and locations
- o Communications data, including response to campaigns.

There is a high initial investment in setting up databases, even when using in-house data, but maintaining data is also costly given that up to 20 per cent of the data will be out of date by the end of a year.

Datamining
Datamining is used to 'discover hidden facts contained in databases'. Identifying relationships between data contained in databases provides a basis for cost-effectively targeting prospective customers, developing co-operative relationships with other companies and better understanding the patterns of customer purchasing behaviour.

Customer relationship management
International consumer markets are characterized by their sheer size and relative anonymity of their customers. Technology has been developed to try to integrate relationship-marketing activity and manage the vast amounts of supporting information. Customer relationship management (CRM) is effectively computer software coupled with defined management processes and procedures to enable staff throughout organizations to capture and use information about their customers in order to maintain and build relationships.

Question 9.5

Explain why relationship marketing is not appropriate for every marketing situation. Why has CRM sometimes failed to live up to expectations?

Challenges to relationship development

Relationship marketing requires a different philosophy in the firm and changes in the marketing and communications strategy objectives, budgets and performance measurements. Chaffey *et al.* (2003) explain that the key objectives are customer retention, customer extension (increasing the depth and range of customers) and customer selection (segmenting and targeting).

However, it is necessary to build relationships not only with the final customers but also with those other stakeholders that might influence the final purchase.

The problems arise when firms see CRM systems as a quick fix to try to manage vast amounts of data. They make broad generalizations about customer segments and are often too insensitive to different consumer cultures and concerns. Too often CRM is not adopted on an organization-wide basis and instead is adopted by individual departments for very specific reasons. It also gets modified because of the need to interface it with existing legacy systems and so becomes fragmented and, rather than reducing cost, actually increases it. The introduction of CRM leads to raised expectations of service levels, amongst customers and staff and if this is not delivered then CRM can have a detrimental effect on the business.

Relationship marketing works if both customer and supplier gain from the relationship but they must also understand their duties. In B2C markets for FMCG, it is questionable whether customers will derive much benefit from relationship marketing and whether the risks outweigh the benefits. Moreover, it is also difficult to measure the long-term benefits of relationship marketing in B2C markets when compared to traditional marketing.

In consumer markets, relationship marketing is becoming more relevant for organizations as one-to-one connections with customers through interactivity and promoting and placing products and services in the appropriate media at just the right moment are likely to become more commonly used. Business relationship marketing is leading to ever-closer relationships and partnerships for essential supply-chain supplies, but at the same time, more transient purchasing relationships for commodity items discussed in Unit 7.

Activity 9.4

Prepare a stakeholder map by listing the organization's stakeholders and their expectations. Evaluate the relationships that the organization has formed and is building with the stakeholders and decide if the investment in relationship marketing is really adding value.

Privacy

It is important to recognize the problems with new communications technologies. There is a conflict between the interests of the firm and customer in developing databases. In order to offer more individually targeted, personalized and relevant communications, the firm requires even more detailed and potentially sensitive information from the customer. However, customers are reluctant to give firms personal information that might be passed on deliberately or accidentally to other firms that will not be so scrupulous in its use. Customers are also concerned about Web security.

Unsolicited e-mail is becoming an increasing problem, not just because of the inconvenience but also because a significant proportion is related to pornography and children are routinely receiving inappropriate messages by e-mail and text.

Case study

Charity innovation at Oxfam

The constant challenge for charities is to overcome donor fatigue and the dilemma is which route to customers will deliver the most benefit. Oxfam is challenging the traditional ways of operating charities. For example, e-mail will soon overtake traditional mail in terms of communications expenditure. Now Oxfam is using the latest information and communications technology to target different groups for different purposes. Students tend to make good activists, young adults have money to donate and older people are willing to work as volunteers.

Oxfam's new approach is obtaining very high response rates. For example, its campaign to persuade Nestle to drop its calls for debt repayment from Ethiopia involved asking people to e-mail the CEO of Nestle: 70–80 per cent of the people contacted/e-mailed the CEO and the debt was cancelled.

By tracking website navigation Oxfam is able to obtain information about the interests, commitment and willingness of people to donate and it has changed its targets for communication as a result. It has been better able to integrate its communications to maximise its impact in collecting donations. Now Oxfam has launched video e-mails using newsreel type footage to complement TV ads and news items. It has described the response to its appeal for donations for Sudan as phenomenal.

Source: Adapted from 'Treating then differently', *Marketing Direct*, February 2005.

Question 9.6

What are the key decisions Oxfam needs to make to further grow its activities to meet demand?

Question 9.7

What are the key implementation issues?

Summary

- Organizations must integrate their communications and ensure that, as far as possible, customers and other stakeholders receive consistent and coherent messages.
- Communications planning must focus on the target audiences and the use of appropriate tools to be most effective.
- Internal staff and staff in the extended organization (distributors, supply chain and partners) must also be part of the communications plan, especially when staff are in remote locations.
- Winning new customers is extremely expensive and it is preferable, particularly in the B2B sector, to use communications to build long-term relationships with stakeholders.
- Relationship marketing involves integrating all aspects of marketing activity and using CRM to build mutually beneficial relationships between customers and suppliers.

Further study

Chaffey, D., Mayer, R., Johnston, K. and Ellis-Chadwick, F. (2003) *Internet Marketing: Strategy, Implementation and Practice*, FT Prentice Hall, provides more insights into electronic marketing communications.

Doole, I. and Lowe, R. (2005) *Strategic Marketing Decisions in Global Markets*, Thomson Learning, Chapter 10.

Fill, C. (1999) *Marketing Communications*, Prentice Hall.

Shimp, T.A. (2003) *Advertising, Promotion and Supplemental Aspects of Integrated Marketing Communications*, Thomson South Western, provide additional reading on communications and relationship development.

Hints and tips

It is useful to have a clear understanding of the advantages and disadvantages of the marketing communications tools, their availability and effectiveness. You could also build up some examples of international marketing communications failures.

Bibliography

Chaffey, D., Mayer, R., Johnston, K. and Ellis-Chadwick, F. (2003) *Internet Marketing: Strategy, Implementation and Practice*, FT Prentice Hall.

Davidson, H. (2002) *Committed Enterprise: How to Make Values and Visions Work*, Butterworth-Heinemann.

Doole, I. and Lowe, R. (2004) *International Marketing Strategy*, Thomson Learning.

Doole, I. and Lowe, R. (2005) *Strategic Marketing Decisions in Global Markets*, Thomson Learning, Chapter 10.

Fill, C. (1999) *Marketing Communications*, Prentice Hall.

Kotler, P. (2003) *Marketing Insights from A to Z*, John Wiley.

Shimp, T.A. (2003) *Advertising, Promotion and Supplemental Aspects of Integrated Marketing Communications*, Thomson South Western.

Wilson, R. and Gilligan, C. (2004) *Strategic Marketing Management, Planning, Implementation and Control*, 3rd edition, Oxford: Elsevier Butterworth-Heinemann.

Sample exam questions and answers for the Strategic Marketing Decisions module as a whole can be found in Appendix 3 at the back of the book.

unit 10
using the extended organization to add portfolio value

Learning objectives

The CIM syllabus for Strategic Marketing Decisions expects you to take a broad perspective that includes creative ways of adding value through the contributions of the extended organization, and the way in which cost, often affected by outsourcing policies, and pricing can affect performance.

In studying this unit you will:

4.7 Examine the role of alliances and the creation of competitive advantage through supply-chain development and marketing partnerships.

4.8 Examine how pricing policies and strategies can be used to build competitive advantage.

4.9 Explain the strategic management of the global portfolio and the expanded marketing mix.

Having completed this unit, you will be able to:

o Identify, compare and contrast strategic options and critically evaluate the implications of strategic marketing decisions in relation to the concept of 'shareholder value'.

o Evaluate the role of brands, innovation, integrated marketing communications, alliances, customer relationships and service in decisions for developing a differentiated positioning to create exceptional value for the customer.

o Demonstrate the ability to develop innovative and creative marketing solutions to enhance an organization's global competitive position in the context of changing product, market, brand and customer life cycles.

o Demonstrate the ability to re-orientate the formulation and control of cost-effective competitive strategies, appropriate for the objectives and context of an organization operating in a dynamic global environment.

This unit relates to the statements of practice

Fd.1   Promote the strategic and creative use of pricing.

Gd.1   Select and monitor channel criteria to meet the organization's needs in a changing environment.

Key definitions

The value chain – is the series of activities that create additional value for customers and comprises the use of materials, tangible and intangible assets.

A strategic alliance – is an informal arrangement between two or more organizations to pursue a common objective.

A joint venture – is a separate enterprise created using assets from two or more companies who share the equity and risk.

Study Guide

This unit is concerned with the ways in which an organization builds value through the extended organization. Distribution channels should add value to the organization and its customers, but with the changes brought about by the Internet, increasing globalization and regionalization, market entry and distribution in international markets strategies must be re-evaluated. Through the supply chain, strategic alliances and partnerships, the organization can further extend the portfolio and increase the impact and influence of the marketing mix and so increase the organization's presence and reach in the global market. We explore partnerships in both the supply and distribution chain.

The success of these partnerships in creating value will ultimately be determined by considerations of costing and pricing. In this unit, the emphasis is placed on taking a strategic view when making pricing decisions.

The value-chain and supply-chain management

The value chain concept

Porter (1985) introduced the concept of the 'value chain' to identify the various strategically relevant activities that contribute to competitive advantage. The activities are of two types: primary and support. The primary activity consists of:

- ○ Inbound logistics
- ○ Operations
- ○ Outbound logistics
- ○ Marketing and sales
- ○ Service.

The support activity consists of:

- o The firm's infrastructure
- o Human resources management
- o Technology development
- o Procurement.

Marketing adds value in a number of areas of the value chain and Doyle (2000) has explained the contributions.

The concept is intended to drive growth, through adding value and improving efficiency in the supply chain and distribution channel. It has helped firms to grow through:

- o Reducing costs through eliminating duplication and unnecessary processes
- o Benefiting from concentrating expertise and complementary activity
- o Exploiting new market opportunities
- o Reducing investment for organizations through outsourcing rather than manufacturing components
- o Enabling small firms to have similar costs to large firms.

It is vital that each part of the value chain maximizes the added value contributions of each member by integrating the activities. A supply chain for a complex product might typically involve design, raw materials supply, manufacture of components, assembly, advertising, logistics and local servicing. The most efficient supplier could be located in different points of the world.

e-Business has provided the mechanism for integrating and further facilitating the contributions of supply-chain members. It has also led to e-procurement and virtual marketplace e-hubs, discussed in Unit 7, which substantially change the basis of competitive advantage particularly in the manufacture and supply of utilities, standard components and services.

The implication of using e-commerce for procurement is that partnerships can be set up and dissolved instantly. Suppliers are in completely open competition with other firms around the world. Of course, suppliers need to have huge flexibility and excellent systems to manage the rapid changes that are necessary to survive in this type of market.

Value chain integration decisions

The key question is how effectively can the individual supply-chain members around the world work in partnership to maximize the effectiveness of their contributions towards improving efficiency and adding value across the entire value chain, so-called 'value chain integration'. The value chain decisions are taken at two levels:

Operational – Assessing the individual contributions of members in the supply chain and making decisions about efficiency, transaction costs, just-in-time, quality management, information transfer and contributions to differentiating the products and services.

Strategic – Assessing the overall effectiveness of the value chain in adding customer value by making dis-intermediation and re-intermediation decisions in the distribution channel and outsourcing decisions (make or buy) in the supply chain.

In other units of this coursebook, we focus upon the organization's direct contribution to the value chain through its internal activities, and here we focus upon the contributions of the extended organization. First, we look at distribution channel management in terms of operational issues before considering the strategic issues. We then extend this further into a re-evaluation of routes to market and the use of strategic alliances, joint ventures and other mechanisms to 'extend' the organization. For a fuller discussion read Doole and Lowe (2005).

Activity 10.1

Using the value chain concept assess the contributions of your organization's value chain and identify three areas where there is scope for cost reduction or value enhancement.

Distribution channel management

Intermediaries often provide the only point of personal contact between the organization and the consumers but they can also fulfil many other roles too. We therefore look at the traditional nature and role of intermediaries before considering the value of their contribution and considering the challenge of channel motivation and management.

The nature and role of intermediaries

The role of intermediaries is changing because of the high cost of physical intermediaries and the increasing acceptance and versatility of the Internet for doing business and carrying out many of these functions and roles more cost-effectively.

Many organizations appear to be reviewing the nature of their partnerships with other members of the supply and distribution chain and either deciding to enhance the relationship through alliances and partnerships, or making the relationships more arm's length and transactional in nature.

There is also a less distinct demarcation between what might be considered to be market entry methods and distribution channels, not only for international markets but also for domestic markets too.

The traditional roles of intermediaries expressed in terms of product distribution are included in Figure 10.1.

o Be part of the organization's push strategy and make products available to customers when and where they want them
o Reduce the cost by efficiently performing distribution functions
o Manage discrepancies between the quantities manufacturers want to supply and the quantities customers want to buy (break bulk)
o Offer a greater range by using products from complementary suppliers
o Standardizing and managing smaller transactions
o Providing customer service and building relationships
o A key consideration is to decide between when the manufacturer and intermediary are best placed to supply the customer and this comparison is made in Table 10.1.

Figure 10.1 The traditional roles of intermediaries

Table 10.1 Best for manufacturer or intermediary to supply the customer

Manufacturer best placed to supply	Intermediaries best placed to supply
Complex products with continuous development	Simple product with basic service levels
Made-to-order products	Standard stocked lines
Where a high level of service and support is required	Large customer base
Where there is a small customer base	Smaller customers
Where the transactions are of high volume or value	Geographically difficult to cover
Easy to cover locations	Small random deliveries from stock
Where shipments are large scale, planned and just-in-time	Low level feedback
High level feedback is required	

Value contributions of intermediaries

The intermediary role typically involves a number of responsibilities that add value:

- Collection of information
- Promotion of the products
- Financing of inventories
- Delivery and physical transfer
- Accept a degree of risk sharing
- An ordering function.

Activity 10.2

List the key decision areas of channel management. Include the issues that relate to member recruitment, replacement, contributions, management and motivation. Assess the effectiveness of the channel management in your own organization and identify measurements that are made to monitor performance.

Channel motivation and management

A major problem for any organization is motivating and managing the intermediaries (Wilson and Gilligan, 2004) as it makes huge demands on management time. The organization must provide channel leadership in order to direct and influence the overall channel performance, build the channel as a competing system by encouraging co-operation between intermediaries that in other circumstances might be competing and manage channel conflicts by identifying and resolving the sources of conflict.

It is necessary to select channel members, evaluate them according to pre-set criteria, such as service levels, drop them if they underperform and replace them with others. Where appropriate, areas and product ranges must be allocated and the role of the intermediaries defined in terms of inventory, selling, marketing, invoicing, support services and so on.

Managing intermediaries in foreign markets is particularly problematic, given the differences in legal frameworks, culture, language, service expectations and communication distances that make motivation, management and development particularly problematic.

Insight

Inchcape

A few years ago, Inchcape was a poorly performing business, part of an earlier era, trading cars, business machines, medical products and bottles around the colonies. Six years ago, CEO Peter Johnson put forward a strategy to exit from many of these disparate business areas and focus on car dealerships. Moreover, he decided to operate in six core countries, unlike other dealers that usually concentrate on just one country. The firm decided to concentrate on premium brands such as BMW and Lexus and aimed to build up a strong presence in an area. The firm would benefit from economies in delivering after-sales service.

Since then, the strategy has delivered double-digit growth in profits and completed the turnaround, achieving a turnover of £4 billion in 2004 and a share price in January 2005 of £19.64 compared to £2.20 in 1999. Now the company is looking to expand into Eastern Europe and China.

Johnson puts the success down to sticking to what the firm is good at and, particularly, its strong partnerships with the key manufacturers. He cites his own 10-year relationships with manufacturers, such as Toyota, who supported Inchcape during its difficult turnaround period.

Other aspects of the strategy have also worked well. The concentration on premium brands has enabled the firm to avoid the worst price wars, and the presence in more than one country could help to avoid the worst effects of a slowdown in the UK car business. Indeed, two-thirds of Inchcape's profits already come from overseas.

Source: Adapted from Davidson, A., 'Sales giant of the motor trade', *Sunday Times*, 16 January 2005.

Dis-intermediation and re-intermediation

Increased competition is putting further pressure on prices and this, coupled with the burden of channel management, makes it obvious why organizations might be tempted to remove intermediaries, shorten the distribution channels and, using technology support, carry out the roles themselves. However, in order to maximize revenue from many products, organizations try to provide as many points as possible for customers to access products and services and in some cases this is leading to re-intermediation. It is the Internet that prompted a channel review for many organizations and an assessment of the potential benefits of new routes to market might prove to be more appealing to customers.

The Internet offers the possibility for an organization to efficiently handle many more transactions than was possible previously. An evaluation of the contribution of the channel has lead to a reassessment of the value of the intermediary and a decision to remove the intermediary. The benefits to the organization are the removal of channel infrastructure costs and intermediary margins and the opportunity to develop a direct relationship with the final customer. 'Cutting out the middleman' is described as 'dis-intermediation'. At the start of the e-business boom, it was expected that there would be widespread dis-intermediation. In some sectors, there has been dis-intermediation, but in others, the results have been disappointing with the organization incurring substantial additional IT, order management and logistics costs. Many organizations have failed to deliver the predicted savings or increase in sales.

'Re-intermediation' is the creation of additional intermediaries in the distribution channel to provide the new Web-based points of access. Whilst many consumer products, financial and travel services lend themselves to online selling, customers want to compare the many offerings from competing companies. The online intermediaries receive a click through commission on sales or enquiries generated.

In many sectors now there are intermediary websites that enable potential customers to compare products for the home, holidays and travel. Of course this means that the Internet marketer must ensure that they are represented on key sites where there are high volumes of potential customers and ensure that they are offering competitive prices. This makes it difficult for firms to differentiate their offering and may not guarantee sales. Instead, some organizations have set up their own intermediary to compete with the existing intermediaries and this is referred to as 'countermediation'. A group of airlines set up www.opodo.com as an alternative to www.expedia.com to offer airline tickets.

Question 10.1

Explain the terms 'dis-intermediation', 're-intermediation' and 'countermediation'; and in what context they are used. Using examples, show their significance and value to customers and organizations.

Routes to market

So far, we have discussed distribution channels but, in practice, organizations have a much wider range of routes to global markets than simply relying on distributors and retailers. Figure 10.2 shows the main alternatives in terms of level of involvement, organizational perceived risk and marketing control. For a fuller discussion of international market entry, read Doole and Lowe (2004, Chapter 7) in order to familiarize yourself with the advantages and disadvantages of each of the methods. E-commerce is not shown as an individual market entry method as it is used to support all of these market entry methods.

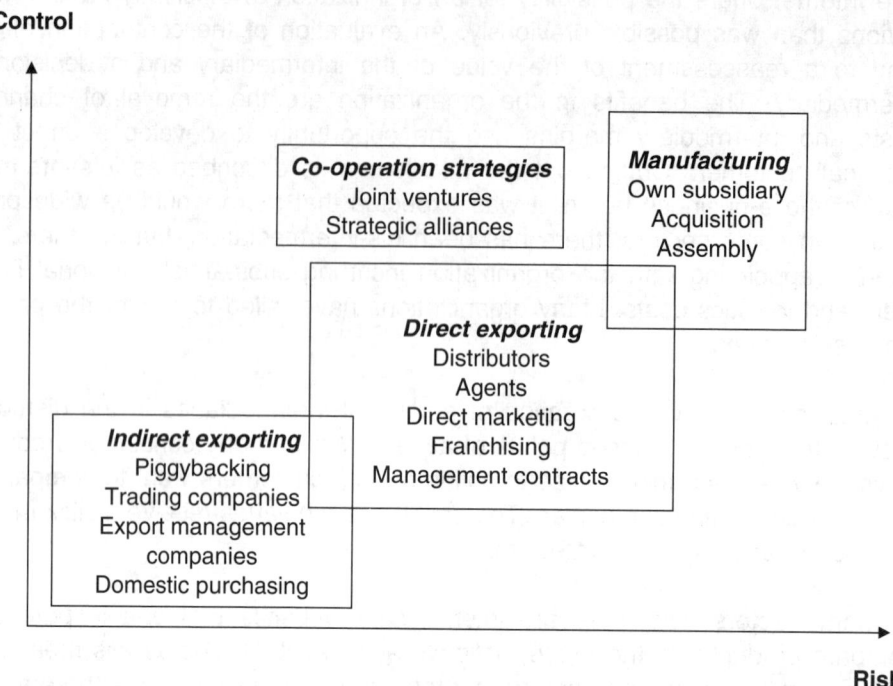

Figure 10.2 Market entry alternatives

The key issue in thinking more broadly about routes to market is to achieve the optimum between the key criteria in order to best add value for the organization and the customer.

- ○ *Level of market involvement* – The level of market involvement is usually determined by the availability of financial resources for investment in operations and direct marketing activity. The greater the involvement, the more market knowledge and influence (as an insider) the company has.
- ○ *Marketing control* – The greater the level of direct involvement in a market the greater the degree of marketing control over how the company and its products are presented. Going through third parties dilutes the degree of control and the customer can be left confused over mixed communication messages. In practice, however, even the most powerful global organizations, such as Coca-Cola and McDonald's, do not have the resources to do everything themselves and use franchising and joint ventures to pursue their objectives.
- ○ *Perceived risk* – The conventional view is that wholly owned operations in foreign markets are the most risky as they involve the greatest financial exposure and in many cases do not benefit from committed local help and support. In practice, the routes to market with the lowest levels of involvement could present the highest risk, as the organization may not be aware of major market changes (and, because of self-interest, partners may not inform them). They may be unable to respond to these major changes quickly enough to save the business.

Firms entering markets and also new emerging markets based on technology change try to reduce their risk exposure, whilst maximizing their market involvement and control by building stronger partnerships with businesses that complement their competencies and assets. A number of traditional and more contemporary partnership mechanisms for achieving this are discussed in the next section.

Question 10.2

When seeking to build an international market, a small- or medium-sized firm must select its methods of market entry carefully. What methods could be used and, using these methods, what would the firm have to do to ensure that its international customers receive a satisfactory product and service?

Extending the organization through alliances and network marketing

Following on from these considerations, it becomes clear that closer collaborative working through a variety of arrangements can provide a solution to a number of problems that arise from the latest environmental trends including:

- ○ Greater unpredictability in the environment and the need for a faster and more effective specific market response
- ○ Increased global competition requiring a global response
- ○ Competition from new competitors attacking markets in new ways with new technology
- ○ The lack of resources of most organizations to cope with the increasing cost of R&D, and marketing to develop distinctive positioning
- ○ Customer expectation of complete solutions, not simply individual products and services
- ○ Changes in supply-chain structures and power.

The main driver of collaboration is the inability of single organizations to be able to produce a complete response:

- ○ Global marketing that is necessary but outside the individual resources of most companies
- ○ The need for composite solutions to meet the diverse nature of customer requirements and the increasing trend to global one-to-one marketing
- ○ The integration of technologies and convergence of industries with the consequence that market boundaries are becoming less defined.

On the one hand, organizations are forced to become more efficient, achieve higher returns from their assets and so focus on core competencies. However, at the same time, they must offer an efficient consumer response on a global basis.

Hooley *et al.* (2004) explain the different types, nature and roles of network marketing and emphasize their role in different types of environment. They also discuss the closeness of the relationships and whether they are likely to be short- or long-lasting.

Outsourcing – tends to be seen as 'arm's length' purchasing, often long term, without any significant commitment or sharing of other than the essential information to complete each transaction. However, with greater interdependence between supplier and customer these arrangements may have to become closer. In times of crisis, for example, it is often recognized that the burden must be shared rather than being simply the responsibility of the other firm.

Partnerships or strategic alliances – involve close relationships but do not involve shared ownership, and examples of marketing alliances can be found in the B2B, B2C and institutional markets.

Vertical and horizontal integration – There are a number of alliances formed to provide customers with better value offers or a package of complementary products or services. This is achieved either through vertical integration of the supply chain or local operators that are carrying out similar tasks by sharing the development and delivery of mutually beneficial products and services. Sometimes this leads to a new jointly owned organization being set up.

Joint ventures – involve shared ownership of a project or operation by two or more organizations with a variety of objectives ranging from international market entry to technological collaboration.

Acquisition and reciprocal share holdings – A number of partnerships and alliances lead to more formal arrangements, such as joint ventures and reciprocal share holdings; and also in some cases, they lead to full acquisition of a partner.

For a fuller discussion of collaborative arrangements read Doole and Lowe (2005, Chapter 11).

Effective collaborations can be a powerful market force, but there are a number of risks. Different studies have suggested that between 50 and 66 per cent of partners in strategic alliances are dissatisfied with their performance.

Question 10.3

Major projects, which involve substantial investment, are often undertaken by two or more firms on a joint venture or strategic alliance basis. Explain why firms undertake partnership projects and outline the major advantages and disadvantages of the approach.

Co-operation and competition

One of the outcomes of developing partnerships is that for the very largest and most complex businesses this means that at an SBU level the organization may be co-operating and competing with another MNE. This poses challenges in deciding which firms to co-operate and compete with, in which markets and for what purpose.

One significant consequence of this is that firms must decide in these circumstances what information to share and what to keep secret. This is particularly problematic given the ease with which information is transferred and the lack of security of IT systems.

Pricing and costing

In this section, we focus on reassessing pricing and costing strategies in the light of the changes in marketing strategy implementation discussed so far. In doing this, we first review the nature and role of pricing and the relationship between pricing and costing, before going on to discuss strategic decisions to cut costs.

We finish the section by considering the factors that affect pricing before discussing the pricing strategies.

The nature and role of pricing

Many organizations believe that pricing is the most flexible, independent and controllable element of the marketing mix and that it plays the pivotal role in strategic marketing decisions. This view is largely based on the fact that pricing changes appear to prompt an immediate response in the market. For example, discounting a price might achieve an immediate attributable sale. However, despite the apparent simplicity of using pricing as a major marketing tool, many managers find pricing decisions difficult to make. This is in part due to the fact that whilst most firms recognize the importance of pricing at a tactical level in stimulating short-term demand, far fewer recognize the importance of the strategic role of pricing.

The nature of costing and its effect on pricing

In most organizations, costing is inextricably linked with pricing, but in practice, the relationship between cost and price has changed considerably over the past few years. There are a number of new factors applying additional pressures on price but there is also now considerably more scope for firms to change the cost base. Inevitably, this changes the relationship between costing and pricing. Some of the most significant trends include:

Pricing transparency – Customers are able to compare prices with increasing ease, mainly due to the Internet, but also in Europe, because of the introduction of the euro. Customers are much more knowledgeable and demanding and more willing to buy from more distant suppliers.

Supply-chain cost considerations – Supply chains must now meet a target market price to compete with other suppliers rather than being able to simply add a margin on top of the total costs. Decisions need to be made about how the chain can optimize customer value whilst reducing costs.

Outsourcing and value chain decisions – Companies must reassess their value chain and decide whether to outsource components, manufacturing and services and evaluate the consequences this might have for customer value and company reputation.

The increase in R&D costs and overheads – The high R&D and marketing costs are unavoidable as firms seek to build competitive advantage but this leads to very high initial investments that need to be recovered and very high fixed costs. This requires very high gross margins to be guaranteed. For example, software volume products can generate over 95 per cent gross margin but still fail to recover marketing and R&D investment.

Actions to reduce costs

A feature of most management is cost reduction and the need to:

- Have a real understanding of what exactly are variable and fixed costs in the organization
- Appreciate the step change nature of fixed costs and the impact on performance
- The opportunity cost of no-hopers and the drain on resources
- The sensitivity of the allocation of overhead and fixed costs across products and product categories
- The precise nature of cost-saving that are claimed through bundling, deals, and so on.

Managers need to be clear about the action that they can take in order to improve profitability by cost reductions, obtaining benefits from the economies of scale and the experience curve effect.

Activity 10.3

> Undertake an audit of one product and service category in your own organization with the aim of making a substantial cost saving – 10 per cent not 1 per cent.

Yield management

The challenge for firms delivering services is to try to balance supply and demand in order to obtain the maximum output for their expensive assets. It is well known that there is not a constant demand from customers for services and so there needs to be some management of demand, wherever possible. One approach is to obtain the best yield for each service delivery occurrence by maximizing the revenue generated. This has been the basis of the business model of low cost airlines, which offer low prices to early bookers and high prices for the 'late comers'. This is the reverse of the traditional airlines, which maintain high published prices but attempt to offload spare tickets close to the time of departure.

Pricing decisions

Reassessment of the pricing strategy within the organization

To make good pricing strategy decisions it is necessary to have a clear understanding of both the uncontrollable factors in the market environment, such as customer expectations and competitor pressures, and the factors that the organization can control, such as the other marketing mix factors.

Price making and price taking

In developing pricing strategies, organizations tend to be either price takers or price makers. Price takers have only limited ability or willingness to control prices and so follow the market leader's pricing strategy and respond reactively to changes in price. Because of their power, size, market leadership or competitive advantage, price makers are able to set prices. For example, powerful organizations are able to temporarily set prices so low that they are able to force a competitor out of business. Over the years, too, there have been many examples of oligopolies illegally running a cartel to fix prices artificially high in order to maximize their profits.

Price makers can add value and, within reason, recover the costs through higher prices. By contrast, a price taker tends to think of making a product that will undercut the market's price by an amount that is attractive to potential purchasers. In order to make the required profit, there will be a limit on the costs allowed in the supply chain.

Pricing objectives

Because of their different current market positions and future business development aspirations, organizations must adopt pricing objectives that will drive their strategic marketing decisions. These alternative pricing objectives are detailed in Table 10.2.

Table 10.2 Pricing objectives

Survival
Return on investment
Market stabilization
Maintenance and improvement of position
Reflecting product differentiation
Market skimming
Market penetration
Early cash recovery
Preventing new entry

Price management

It is worth remembering that pricing is the only mix element that generates revenue – everything else adds cost. Prices are under continual pressure due to more intense competition, similarity of product offers, speed of copying, increasing price transparency because of the Internet search engines, and harmonization of prices within common markets. Customers are less loyal to brands and more willing to switch. B2B customers have worldwide purchasing networks to compare prices, and they can purchase and obtain delivery from the lowest-price producer.

Managing price reductions

Competitive actions, often unexpected, can threaten short-term revenue and performance and managers are often under great pressure to make an instant response. It is too tempting, quick and easy to cut prices in order to deal with an immediate shortfall in sales volume. It often prompts a price war and it becomes much more difficult and takes much more time and effort to secure price increases to restore profit margins. Quite often, the task proves impossible, and so price cutting intended to be a short-term tactic usually ends up either as a routine feature of the sector or as a step towards establishing a long-term lower pricing point.

Decisions are often made very quickly with no time to assess or test the implications but they usually have a major impact on profits. Quite often, the reason for short-term underperformance is the impact of extraneous variables that the organization fails to fully understand or take into account, and so quite often, nothing is learned from the price change, and the organization is no better informed when a similar situation occurs later.

Mistakes in pricing occur because they are too often based on costs, not market conditions; set independently of the mix and so do not reflect superior quality; because of brand value; and price changes make no attempt to reflect the product and service differentiation and so organizations fail to recover the additional cost of adding value.

Prices are inflated by extended distribution channels, where mark-ups and margins are applied even when the intermediaries are adding little value. In this situation managers find it easier to simply maintain status quo and not upset intermediaries with whom they have had a long-term relationship, even though the organization and its distributors both might be priced out of the market by more aggressive competitors with shorter routes to market.

A number of factors should be considered, therefore, in assessing the company's capability to deal with competition:

○ Whether they are a leader, follower or me-too?
○ Whether they can prevent new entry?
○ Do their cost levels offer scope for price cutting?
○ Have they the level of resources to fight a war?
○ Are they dependent on the product?
○ Are they committed to the market sector?
○ The potential returns from price cutting
○ The distinctiveness of the product and brand loyalty.

International pricing problems and decisions

In international marketing, there are a number of additional factors that should be taken into account in decision-making:

○ The greater scope of the international organization should allow it to benefit from the economies of scale and the experience effect, provided that it is committed to achieving these gains through standardization of some of the marketing programmes or management processes.
○ Markets can be cross-subsidized.
○ Different market segments that are based on different cultures or countries are likely to require adaptations to the marketing mix in a similar way to different segments in a domestic market but on a much larger scale. The cost of adaptation can be very significant if not managed carefully.
○ Many domestic organizations have some experience of costs varying because of fluctuating exchange rates as a result of buying components and services from different countries. For international organizations, fluctuating exchange rates can become a major problem because of the scale and scope of both purchasing and selling products in foreign markets.
○ When competing globally there is a continuous need to source products, components and services at ever-lower costs from anywhere in the world.
○ When compared to domestic marketing, however, the key difference is that international marketers not only set and agree prices with foreign customers but in emerging countries quite frequently must also arrange the financing for the deal.

International pricing problems are discussed in greater detail in Doole and Lowe (2004).

Question 10.4

The Internet is increasing price transparency across international markets. Fully evaluate the problems and opportunities this brings to a company trying to build a global competitive advantage.

Portfolio integration decisions

In Units 8 and 9 and in this unit we have discussed a number of decision areas relating to the marketing mix. We have emphasized throughout the need to add customer value with the intention of increasing prices and revenue and making cost reductions in order to increase profitability. In practice, these activities should not be undertaken in isolation and need to be integrated. Table 10.3 provides the starting point.

Table 10.3 Portfolio integration

	Providing opportunity to increase prices (or revenue)	**Making cost reductions to increase revenue or profitability**
Product portfolio		Better sourcing
		Better plant utilization
		Better use of raw materials and labour
		Design or specification changes
Service enhancement		Better use of labour and processes
		Better use of assets (yield management)
Promotion		Better choice of communication methods from mix elements
		More targeted, less mass communications
Channel		More value from channel
	Re-intermediation	Dis-intermediation
Relationship		Cost-effective one-to-one marketing
	Value chain contribution	Supply-chain efficiency

Case study

TESCO attacks a new sector

TESCO is the world's third largest retailer with 2318 stores in Europe and Asia. In the UK it is the leading food retailer and accounts for £1 of every £8 spent on the UK's high streets. However, it is becoming increasingly difficult to obtain planning permission for supermarkets in the UK. Its response is to target the non-food sector by planning to open stores on out-of-town retail parks selling clothes, electrical goods, CDs and DVDs.

One rival, ASDA, which is owned by Wal-mart, has already opened a non-food outlet in Walsall, built around its highly successful clothing brand, George.

Source: Adapted from Fletcher, R., 'Tesco targets rivals with new non-food store', *Sunday Times*, 16 January 2005.

Question 10.5

Identify the choices and key decisions for TESCO in pursuing this opportunity.

 ## Activity 10.4

What factors affect your organization's pricing strategy? What scope is there for the organization to adopt a more offensive approach to pricing?

Summary

○ Analysis of the value contributions of the supply chain should lead to development work to increase customer value and reduce unnecessary costs.
○ Evaluation of channel effectiveness and new channel opportunities leads to dis-intermediation and re-intermediation decisions.
○ The choice of route to market in international markets will be determined by the organization's desire for market involvement and control, set against the perceived risk.
○ Organizations can extend their reach and influence in markets by developing closer partnerships.
○ Costing and pricing decisions are often made with short-term objectives in mind but the consequences can be long term.
○ It is essential to fully integrate the marketing mix decisions with the costing and pricing strategy.

Case study

Online music

During the dot-com era at the end of the last millennium, Napster, followed by other pirate websites, sent shock waves through the music industry by allowing people to illegally download music to their computer from the Internet at free of cost. The pirate websites still remain, but the business has now gone legitimate with dozens of companies opening up online music stores in the expectation that millions of consumers would download music legally, as a result of high-speed Internet access and intensive marketing. However, an analyst with Forrester research claims that there are three times as many stores as there need to be and profits are slim.

In reality, these sites were the forerunners in an industry breakthrough and the creation of a new business model, arguably more radical than Amazon and e-Bay, because it changed the whole process of the purchase, delivery and usage of music for consumers.

Napster was shut down in July 2001 but now it has reinvented itself as a legitimate business to capitalize on its well-known brand. Napster operates two marketing formats: selling permanent downloads, which in the UK sell typically for 79p but can be as low as 39p, and by monthly subscription, where users can rent the downloads for £9.95 per month. Napster's current competitors include Virgin Digital at £9.99 per month and HMV at £14.99 per month for the subscription service. iTunes only sells permanent downloads.

It appears to be that all the computer hardware and software manufacturers, home entertainment suppliers and music companies are involved in alliances in the sector, as well as many major retailers. The interesting question is going to be who will be the winners when the inevitable shakeout occurs?

Question 10.6

What do you consider to be the main factors and the key strategic marketing decisions that will determine success or failure in marketing online music?

Question 10.7

Who are likely to be the winners in this market and why?

Further study

Doole, I. and Lowe, R. (2004) *International Marketing Strategy*, 4th edition, Thomson Learning, Chapters 7, 10, 11 and 12 for the international dimension to market entry, channels, pricing and value chain.

Doole, I. and Lowe, R. (2005) *Strategic Marketing Decisions in Global Markets*, Thomson Learning, Chapters 9 and 11.

Wilson, R.M.S. and Gilligan, C. (2004) *Strategic Marketing Management*, Butterworth-Heinemann for further discussion on pricing, value chain and distribution strategies.

Bibliography

Doole, I. and Lowe, R. (2004) *International Marketing Strategy*, 4th edition, Thomson learning, Chapter 7.

Doole, I. and Lowe, R. (2005) *Strategic Marketing Decisions in Global Markets*, Thomson learning, Chapter 11.

Doyle, P. (2000) *Value Based Marketing*, Wiley (ISBN 0471877271).

Hooley, G., Saunders, J. and Piercy, N. (2004) *Marketing Strategy and Competitive Positioning*, FT Prentice Hall, Chapter 15.

Porter, M.E. (1985) *Competitive Advantage: Creating and Sustaining Superior Performance*, FreePress.

Wilson, R.M.S. and Gilligan, C. (1997) *Strategic Marketing Management*, Butterworth-Heinemann.

Sample exam question and answers for the Strategic Marketing Decisions module as a whole can be found in Appendix 3 at the back of the book.

unit 11 financial appraisal for strategic marketing decisions

Learning objectives

The CIM Postgraduate Diploma in Marketing requires candidates to show they have the financial skills to demonstrate the contribution marketing strategies made to the business, to financially justify the budgets needed in their strategic marketing decisions and to financially evaluate potential investment decisions so they are able to focus on those marketing activities that offer the best returns.

In this unit you will:

5.1 Examine the implications of strategic marketing decisions for implementation and control.

5.3 Apply investment appraisal techniques to marketing investment decisions.

5.4 Examine alternative approaches to modelling potential investment decisions in the deployment of marketing resources.

5.6 Define budgetary and planning control techniques for use in the control of marketing plans and explain the pitfalls of control systems and how they may be overcome.

Having completed this unit, you will be able to:

o Identify, compare and contrast strategic options and critically evaluate the implications of strategic marketing decisions in relation to the concept of 'shareholder value'.

o Define and contribute to investment decisions concerning the marketing assets of an organization.

o Demonstrate the ability to re-orientate the formulation and control of cost-effective competitive strategies, appropriate for the objectives and context of an organization operating in a dynamic global environment.

This unit relates to the statements of practice

Bd.1 Promote a strong market orientation and influence/contribute to strategy formulation and investment decisions

Fd.1 Promote the strategic and creative use of pricing.

Key definitions

Return on capital employed – is a measure commonly used by companies to assess the added value to shareholders resulting from the capital invested.

Payback – measures the number of years it will take to recover the original investment from the net cash flows resulting from a project. The method is based on being able to estimate a future flow of funds.

Cost/Volume/Profit (CVP) analysis – is used to help a company understand the relationship between volume, costs and profits and used to budget and forecast the break-even point.

A ratio – takes two variables (e.g. profit/sales) and compares them with other measures of the same variable in another time period or in another company in order to assess the performance of the company and the efficiency of its operations.

Study Guide

Examination candidates of Strategic Marketing Decisions will be expected to demonstrate an understanding of the financial implications of the decisions you make. Finance is the common language of business enabling the costs and benefits of the different strategic options you may be considering to be quantified, evaluated and compared. Thus in studying this unit you need to develop the skills to understand the impact of the decisions you make on the financial health of the company and be able to use financial techniques to assess the decisions you make.

Assessing owner/shareholder value

The main objective of a business is to maximize the shareholders'/owners' wealth. Much has been said in previous units about the importance of value-based marketing and the need for marketing managers to be able to quantify the economic benefits to the company of the strategic marketing decisions taken and contribute to shareholder/owner added value. However, the question we need to ask in this unit is how added value to the company is measured. The share price as an indicator of improvements in shareholder value has major shortcomings in that it is essentially a *second hand market* trading in stocks and shares, the market certainly determines a price for a company's shares, but it is questionable whether this is a true assessment of the value. Doyle (2000) suggests two approaches to assess shareholder value: the cash flow valuation method and the calculation of economic profit or what Stern, Stewart & Co. branded 'economic value added' (EVA). In this section, we also include Return Capital Employed (ROCE) as a method for calculating added value.

Economic value added

Economic value added is used to assess ongoing performance and help managers to determine whether the current policies are creating value. It is used in the development of a position appraisal by the company; in other words, assessing what the position is now in terms of the creation of value by the past and current marketing strategies being employed. Basically, if a company achieves a positive Economic Value Added then the investment will have generated a surplus greater than the firm's weighted average cost of capital and therefore created value for the owners/shareholders. The calculation of Economic Value Added is:

EVA = adjusted profits after tax − (adjusted invested capital × weighted average cost of capital)

Cash flow valuation

The cash flow valuation approach is useful in assessing how investment decisions contribute to the building of shareholder value and so is useful in the financial evaluation of strategic options. Essentially, the principle of this method is that a strategy creates value when it produces returns that exceed the cost of capital and therefore generates a positive net present value. However, in using cash flow valuation for shareholder added value measuring the long-term value may be difficult as the investment input may be creating long-term value but in any 1-year show a negative or declining cash flow. Thus, the measure used in assessing the cash flow is the continuing value of cash flow.

Doyle (2000) splits the calculation of the continuing value of cash flow into two parts: the value created in the initial forecast period and the present value created after the explicit forecast period.

Continuing value = present value of cash flow during the forecast period + present value of cash flow after the forecast period.

Return on capital employed (ROCE)

This is a measure commonly used by companies to assess the added value to companies resulting from the capital invested. It is criticized as a technique for measuring shareholder value by Doyle (2000), as it is difficult to take into account the fact that returns today may be the results of a gradual investment built over many years and not just a result of the most recent injection of capital. ROCE is used to evaluate the efficient use of capital. A company may make a profit of $100 000, however, that is only meaningful if we know how much capital was invested to achieve that profit.

ROCE is the amount of profit expressed as a percentage of the capital employed. It is calculated as follows:

ROCE = Estimated profit before interest and tax/capital employed.

Activity 11.1

For a company known to you calculate the ROCE and the profit margin.

Question 11.1

A company operates in three distinct market segments. For each segment, calculate the profit on sales turnover.

	Sales ($k)	Profit ($k)
segment A	600	36
segment B	1000	200
segment C	3000	450

Financial analysis for long-term decision-making

 ## Activity 11.2

For a company of your choice investigate the criteria used in financially evaluating the feasibility of a new product being developed.

There are many financial approaches to investment appraisal in the context of this workbook, we will consider two – *payback* and *discounted cash flow.*

Chinese quotas removed

Prior to 2005 Chinese clothing imports faced strict quotas. This all changed when clothing quotas ended on 1 January 2005. This could mean huge price reductions for retailers who source predominantly from China, such as H&M and Next. Analysts suggest this could mean as price competition hots up the retailers who have strong Far East sourcing capability and flexible supply chains, are in a much better position to sustain their competitive advantage. It will also mean consumers will able to buy clothing more cheaply.

Next and H&M are viewed as being two retailers who are in strong competitive position to benefit from the changing quota regulations. OCC, a leading firm of retail analysts, predict that these two retailers could achieve at least 5 per cent higher growth over the next 3 years even as their customers enjoy lower prices and equal or higher product quality.

By contrast, the losers to the ending of the Chinese quotas will tend to be more traditional, smaller and typically UK-focused retailers that have failed to develop Far East sourcing capabilities. For instance Zara, with its own European factories, could lose out. They are viewed as having a less flexible supply chain which is too UK and Europe focused.

Source: Adapted from *The Retail Bulletin*, 28 January 2005.

Question 11.2

What options are there for the smaller players with less flexible supply chains? How would you construct a business case for investing in a more globally flexible supply chain in order to sustain a competitive advantage in the longer term?

Payback

Payback simply measures the number of years it will take to recover the original investment from the net cash flows resulting from a project. The method is based on being able to estimate a future flow of funds. Thus, a marketing manager evaluating two strategic options both requiring $100K investment would estimate net cash in-flows for each project and for the life of the projects. If payback was the sole evaluation criterion, the company would choose the option which resulted in the shortest payback period. The advantage of using payback is that the calculations are simple and it focuses on the company's liquidity position and minimizing cash flow risk. However, the overall profitability is not considered and no account is taken of the long-term value of the strategic options being evaluated.

Question 11.3

The following information relates to an enterprise producing and selling one product:

Selling price per unit	£60
Variable costs per unit	£42
Total fixed expenses	£900

Find:

(a) Contribution per unit
(b) Break-even sales (in units)
(c) Sales (in units) which will produce a net profit of £360
(d) Sales (in units) which will produce a net profit margin of 20 per cent of sales
(e) Net profit if 80 units are sold
(f) The break-even sales (in units) if variable expenses are increased by £4 per unit and if fixed expenses are reduced by £340
(g) If the company requires a net profit of £700 on a sales volume of 200 units, what must the selling price per unit be, assuming no changes in the variable expenses of £42 per unit or in the fixed expenses of £900?

Net present value (NPV) and discounted cash flow

Discounted cash flow (DCF) is based on the principle that money received today is worth more than money received next year because of the opportunity to invest and consequently earn a return. THUS, DCF concentrates on cash flows rather than profits.

An investment appraisal using DCF would involve the following steps:

- o identifying the cash flows that would result from the investment in the project
- o identifying when the cash flows will take place
- o applying the appropriate discount factor to the cash flows
- o calculating NPV by aggregating the discounted cash flows
- o comparing the NPV of one project with another.

In calculating NPV, there are three possible outcomes to the analysis:

1.	NPV = 0	In which case you would be indifferent to the investment
2.	NPV = Negative	In this case, the project would fail to generate sufficient funds to cover the cost of capital. Thus it would destroy shareholder value
3.	NPV = Positive	In this case, the project would most likely generate a return greater than the cost of capital and so would be considered. Only if there is a positive NPV is there any possibility of increasing shareholder value

The following illustration is given in Chapter 4 of Doole and Lowe (2005) *Strategic Marketing Decisions in Global Markets* where a more detailed treatment of the concepts introduced in this unit can be found.

A company has a choice of two projects A or B, the firm's cost of capital is 10 per cent. Both projects involve an investment of £800 and have the following profits and cash flows.

Projects	Year	A (£)	B (£)
Initial sum invested	0	800	800
Cash flow generated by the project	1	100	900
	2	900	100

Discounted cash flows (DCF) – using a 10 per cent discount rate

	A			B		
	CF	DR	DCF	CF	DR	DCF
	(£)		(£)	(£)		(£)
Year 1	100 ×	.909 =	90	900 ×	.909 =	818
Year 2	900 ×	.826 =	743	100 ×	.826 =	83
			834			901
Initial investment		(800)			(800)	
Net present value		34			101	

Using the NPV of the cash flows, the enterprise would select project B. For project B, NPV is greater because the bulk of the cash flow from the project occurs in year 1.

Financial analysis for short-term decision-making

Activity 11.3

Consider a decision to change the price of a product/service in your company. What financial analysis did the company undertake in making the appropriate decision.

Insight

Sales and marketing managers who are busy making sales often assume that they are also making a profit. Yet, this is not always the case, particularly in smaller businesses whose owners are technically competent but who are not familiar with the basic accounting methods used to determine whether a profit is being generated by the organization. If a company's cost structure is too high, the organization will be unlikely to generate a profit because any increase in volume also generates a high increase in costs. Understanding the relationship among costs, volume and profit is critical if a company is going to be able to make strategic marketing decisions to develop strategies which will promote long-term growth.

Cost/Volume/Profit analysis

Cost/Volume/Profit (CVP) analysis provides a company with a decision support system for managers that allow management to test out the implications of their plans without committing the company to expensive experiments. CVP analysis incorporates break-even analysis; the reason for this is that one of the main functions of the CVP analysis is to predict the volume of sales that must be achieved for the company to make neither a profit nor a loss (i.e. break-even). Understanding the relationship between volume, costs and profits is essential for any marketing manager. In high fixed costs businesses volume is the key to success! CVP analysis evaluates:

- o The impact of volume on costs and profits
- o The volume of sales required to achieve a target profit
- o The required break-even volume for the range of products being assessed.

CVP analysis is based on the assumption that costs can be accurately divided into their fixed and variable elements. A fixed cost does not change with the volume of production, a variable cost will change directly with the volume of production. The profits are calculated on a variable cost basis, this means they will reflect the firm's cash flow.

Thus, the contribution is sales revenue, less variable costs.

The break-even point will occur where the contribution exceeds fixed costs.

CVP analysis enables the manager to calculate the break-even level of activity for the company using the following formula:

$$\text{Break-even volume} = \frac{\text{Total fixed costs}}{\text{Contribution per unit}}$$

Thus if fixed costs are £10 000 and the contribution is £20, the company would need to sell 500 units to break-even.

If the company wished to make a profit of £5000 then the volume required can be calculated by treating the target profit as an additional fixed cost.

$$\text{Required sales units would need to be sold} = \frac{\text{Fixed costs} + \text{Profit}}{\text{Contribution per unit}}$$
$$= (10000 + 5000)/20 = 750 \text{ units}$$

A break-even chart for the above example would look as in Figure 11.1.

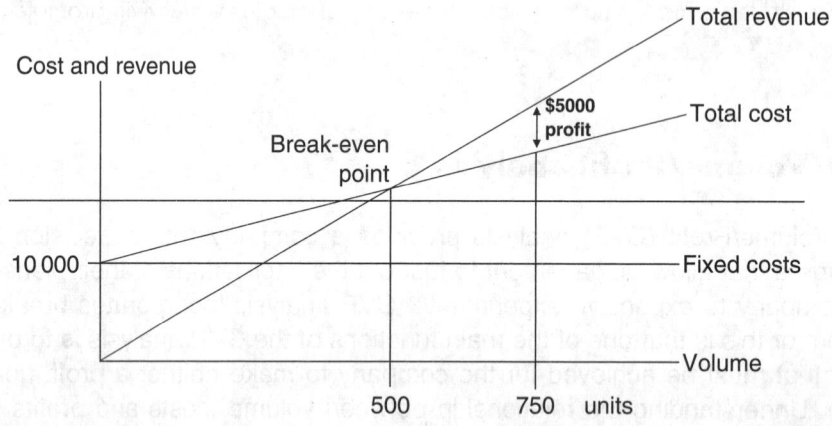

Figure 11.1 Break-even analysis

There are several assumptions applied in CVP analysis:

- ○ the sales price is constant over the relevant range of products
- ○ production outputs and sales outputs are the same
- ○ variable costs do not change in the short run
- ○ fixed costs are constant.

CVP ratios

CVP analysis also provides a number of ratios for the analysis of the performance of a product.

- ○ The margin of safety ratio (MOS) indicates by how much sales may fall before a company will suffer a loss.

$$\text{per cent margin of safety} = \frac{(\text{expected sales} - \text{break-even sales}) \times 100}{\text{expected sales}}$$

The margin of safety is an indicator of the risk profile of a product, the smaller the margin of safety the greater is the risk that the enterprise's level of activity may fall below the break-even point.

$$\circ \quad \text{Contribution sales ratio (CSR)} = \frac{\text{Selling price} - \text{Variable cost}}{\text{Selling price}}$$

$$\circ \quad \text{Profit volume ratio (PVR)} = \frac{\text{Sales revenue} - \text{Total variable cost}}{\text{Sales revenue}}$$

CSR and PVR are simply different ways of calculating the same ratio. The ratio tells us what per cent from an additional £1 of sale will go towards covering the fixed costs and providing profit.

The CSR/PVR ratio can be used to calculate the break-even level of sales revenue for an enterprise.

$$\text{Break-even sales revenue} = \frac{\text{Fixed costs}}{\text{CSR}}$$

Question 11.4

Last year, the trading company Nig Yabmob achieved sales of £100 000 and a profit of £6000 on a capital employed of £18 000. The company wishes to increase their profit margin by 10 per cent and believe if they raise prices and inject £50 000 extra capital they could increase sales turnover to $150 000.

Evaluate the decision in terms of profit margin and ROCE.

Control in a low cost airline

Ryanair claims to have more cash and lower costs than its competitors.

In the past 6 months passenger numbers rose 45 per cent to 11.3 million and interim profits rose 12 per cent. However, it is also adding to its costs. It is adding capacity to its network and the number of seats is forecast to increase 60 per cent this year.

As a result, the load factor – a measure of seats sold as a proportion of seats available on each flight – is coming under pressure. In the first half of this year, it fell almost 5 percentage points, from 82 to 77 per cent. Average fares, or yields, fell 12 per cent, partly because of currency movements but also owing to a number of special promotions to sell tickets and its staff costs have risen by 32 per cent.

By 2009 they will have introduced 125 new Boeing 737s, about two thirds of its fleet will be owned and one third leased. If it had stuck with a wholly owned fleet, it would not have turned free-cash-flow-positive until about 2006.

Analysts forecast full-year net profits will grow by about 10 per cent, which, although good compared to competitors, is much lower than Ryanair's compound average over the past 4 years of about 40 per cent.

Question 11.5

What performance ratios could Ryanair use to enable it to take further control of its costs?

Source: Adapted from Done, K. (2003) *Financial Times*, 4 November..

See CIM SMD Examination December 2004, Question 5

Financial appraisal techniques are central to the SMD syllabus and so questions such as this one are important to practice. You need to ensure you understand the differences between short- and long-term decision-making and that in each area you understand which financial appraisal techniques are most relevant.

Financial techniques for evaluating performance

 Activity 11.4

> For a company of your choice find out what financial ratios are calculated in assessing performance. Which ratios does the company view as the most critical as indicators of performance?

All of the above techniques explored in the previous sections, whilst discussed in the context of making strategic marketing decisions, can also be used for assessing performance. In addition to the techniques identified in previous sections, the use of ratios is the common financial technique for evaluating performance. Ratios measure the interrelationships of various measures in a company and are used to assess corporate performance and the effectiveness of marketing programmes as well as other operational activities. The calculations of certain ratios enable the performance of an activity to be compared year on year so that trends or potential problems can be identified. It also allows for comparing actual performance against the budgeted performance forecasted as well as enabling businesses to compare their performance with others in their industry. Any variance from the expected norm can then be investigated and decisions as to the relevant corrective action taken. A fuller discussion of control and evaluation techniques is given in Unit 12. In this section, we will focus on identifying some of the main ratios used by companies to assess and evaluate marketing performance.

Ratios fall into three main groups: profit ratios, sales ratios and operational ratios.

Profit ratios

The main profit ratio is the profit margin: the ratio of profit before interest + tax (PBIT) over sales turnover.

Other profit ratios include profit/net assets, gross profit/sales, net profit/sales.

Related to profit expectations is share price/earnings (P/E) ratio, which reflects the investor's view of the future prosperity of the company as the share price is seen to reflect the view as to the expectations of future earnings. The P/E ratio is the share price/earnings per share.

Sales ratios

The main sales ratio is asset turnover = sales/net assets; other sales ratios used by firms involve sales turnover being calculated as a ratio of fixed assets, working capital, selling costs, or perhaps such things as admin costs, overheads, and so on. All these ratios either tracked over time or compared against competitors or the standards set can give a company a measure of the efficiency of their performance in these areas.

Operational ratios

Operational ratios help a company assess to generate cash on which to run the business. Without cash, a company cannot operate its business; therefore, the liquidity of the company and its amount of working capital will be regularly monitored. In these ratios, the turnover periods in which cash will be generated are calculated usually and are expressed in terms of days of how many times the business is exchanging cash. The main liquidity ratios are:

Debt collection period – level of debt/sales turnover
Stock turnover period – average stock level/total cost of goods sold
Creditors turnover period – average trade credit/cost of sales
Current ratio – current assets/current liabilities.

Any increase in any of these ratios will warn the company that cash is being tied up in funding the work in progress. As stated previously any of these ratios alone is not terribly meaningful, it is by tracking these measures over time and with other metrics that trends and changes can be identified.

See CIM SMD Examination June 2005 Question, 5

This non-numerical finance question allows you to test your knowledge of the financial criteria used to assess strategic options. Invariably, in all SMD examinations, there will be some type of question testing your skills to assess the financial viability of marketing plans. The more you practice these questions, the better prepared you will be.

Question 11.6

Fully explain how variance analysis can be used in the assessment of marketing performance.

Summary

- Three approaches assess shareholder value: the cash flow valuation method, the calculation of economic value added and ROCE.
- The two financial approaches to investment appraisal considered in this unit were payback and discounted cash flow (DCF).
- Discounted cash flow is based on the principle that money received today is worth more than money received next year because of the opportunity to invest and consequently earn a return. THUS, DCF concentrates on cash flows rather than profits.
- Understanding the relationship between volume, costs and profits is essential for any marketing manager and used in evaluating the options available particularly in short-term decision-making.
- Ratios measure the interrelationships of various input and output factors in a company and are used to assess corporate performance and the effectiveness of marketing programmes as well as other operational activities.

Further study

Doole, I. and Lowe, R. (2005) *Strategic Marketing Decisions in Global Markets*, Thomson Learning.

Doyle, P. (2000) *Value Based Marketing: Marketing Strategies for Corporate Growth and Shareholder Value*, Wiley & Sons Ltd, Chapter 2.

Hints and tips

In preparing for the Postgraduate CIM Diploma, it is important for you to learn how the concepts examined in this unit would be used in the strategic marketing decision process. The three major areas are the appraisal of investment decisions, short-term decision dilemmas and dilemmas in assessing and tracking the performance of the programmes, resulting from the decisions made. However, in the Strategic Marketing Decision examination, it is unlikely you will be expected to have to make any complex calculations. What is important is that you can show the examiner that you have the knowledge and understanding to apply the relevant approaches to the specific situation you may be given in an exam. However, you will certainly be expected to use and apply, in appropriate manner, a number of the approaches identified in this unit in strategic marketing in practise. Thus, it is important you practise using these techniques and develop the ability to use them in the analysis of the case study on which the examination for strategic marketing in practice is based.

Bibliography

Doole, I. and Lowe, R. (2005) *Strategic Marketing Decisions in Global Markets*, Thomson Learning.

Doyle, P. (2000) *Value Based Marketing: Marketing Strategies for Corporate Growth and Shareholder Value*, Wiley & Sons Ltd.

Sample exam question and answers for the Strategic Marketing Decisions module as a whole can be found in Appendix 3 at the back of the book, for this unit you may want to try the December 2004 paper question 5.

unit 12
achieving a sustainable competitive advantage

Learning objectives

In this unit, we examine the decisions a company has to make in its approaches to its evaluation of marketing performance. We also explore the wider dimensions of strategic marketing decision-making and discuss the goals and expectations of its stakeholders and the impact they have on strategic marketing decisions and the achievement of a sustainable competitive advantage.

In this unit you will:

4.10 Assess the issues of corporate and social responsibility (CSR), sustainability and ethics in achieving competitive advantage, enhancing corporate reputation and creating stakeholder value.

5.2 Explain the concept of, and evaluate methods such as Balanced Scorecard for, stakeholder value measurement.

5.5 Define performance measurement systems for the deployment of marketing assets and the implementation of marketing plans.

5.6 Define budgetary and planning control techniques for use in the control of marketing plans and explain the pitfalls of control systems and how they may be overcome.

Having completed this unit, you will be able to:

o Identify, compare and contrast strategic options and critically evaluate the implications of strategic marketing decisions in relation to the concept of 'shareholder value'

o Demonstrate the ability to re-orientate the formulation and control of cost-effective competitive strategies, appropriate for the objectives and context of an organization operating in a dynamic global environment

This unit relates to the statements of practice

o Bd.1 Promote a strong market orientation and influence/contribute to strategy formulation and investment decisions.

Key definitions

Evaluation and control mechanisms – set standards to which marketing strategies should aspire, measure performance and take corrective action when the measurement varies from the level of performance required.

The Balanced Scorecard – is a management system to measure current performance and to set priorities for future performance. It incorporates four perspectives: financial perspective, the customer perspective, the internal business perspective and the innovation and learning perspective.

Corporate social responsibility – is the term used to describe the level of awareness shown by companies of their social responsibility and the values exhibited with regard to the societal impact of strategic marketing decisions.

Study Guide

In this final unit, we examine the issues in establishing evaluation and control mechanisms in strategic marketing decision-making and discuss the wider implications of assessing added value for all stakeholders in the company. Increasingly the CIM examinations are expecting candidates to show they have an appreciation of the wider dimensions of a company's efforts to achieve a sustainable competitive advantage over the longer term. In studying this unit, therefore, you need to consider how issues discussed would impact on the evaluation of strategic options and the marketing decisions you make as a marketing manager. A fundamental value underpinning all the subjects at the Postgraduate CIM Diploma is the belief that in order to drive business success, the marketing decision process has to be a disciplined process, which achieves demonstrable added value for all stakeholders and is supported in its application by robust marketing metrics. In studying this unit, you need to consider how you can, therefore, incorporate such values into your own strategic marketing decisions.

Approaches to measuring performance

Companies are continually striving to find relevant and appropriate measures by which to measure and control the complexity of marketing programmes and show how they contribute to the economic value of a company and in turn shareholder/owner added value. If marketing managers are to take a more strategic role in marketing at board level, they need to talk the language of the CEO. This means there has to be a demonstrable link between marketing expenditure and its contribution to the profitability of the company. In the past marketing has been accused of regarding marketing activities as beyond measurement. Examiners of the CIM Diploma are constantly bemoaning the fact that examination candidates recommend marketing strategies without taking any regard of the resource implications or how their proposals will be controlled and evaluated. It is therefore important that you ensure you have an understanding of the implications of the strategic marketing decisions you take in examinations and how the resultant programmes will be controlled and evaluated.

Control systems have four primary objectives:

1. To set standards to which marketing strategies should aspire
2. To measure performance in a meaningful way
3. To assess areas of strengths and weaknesses in marketing programmes
4. To establish mechanisms for taking corrective action when required.

If standards are to be set, it presupposes that there is a marketing plan which has targeted budgeted outcomes. The standards set are essentially the guidelines towards which all the personnel involved in the implementation of the marketing programme are aiming. Performance against those standards will then be measured by comparing actual performance against the predetermined standards. Variance from the standards set will be analysed to identify the reasons for the shortfall and to identify the strengths and weaknesses in the programme. Therefore, a feedback mechanism is an essential component if the control system is to be effective. The results need to be fed back to management, to enable decisions to be taken as to what corrective action is needed to control the planned outputs of the marketing programme. The results also need to be fed back to the strategic marketing decision-makers as the variance identified could well have implications for the marketing strategy itself. If the variance is due to a change in environmental factors then to maintain a competitive advantage, decisions as to what strategic changes are necessary need to be made. For a much fuller treatment of this subject, the reader is directed to Chapter 12 of the accompanying textbook, Doole and Lowe (2005).

 ## Activity 12.1

Identify six critical success factors which you consider drive the marketing performance of your company.

Performance metrics

In establishing a performance evaluation process there are some basic but fundamental questions which managers need to ask.

- What are they going to measure?
- What are the organizational mechanisms for the measuring activities?
- How to ensure performance is measured against a balanced range of goals and objectives?

What are we going to measure?

In choosing the metrics to apply, the CIM (2003) suggests, metrics need to be robust and reliable and have the following characteristics:

- Be clearly linked to business objectives of economic added value.
- Be focused on measuring the key indicators in a clear way so they are easily understood.
- Encompass broad and balanced factors and incorporate a range of marketing measures.
- Be able to track performance reliably over time and so visibly signal changes in performance.
- Be cost-effective in that the financial and staff time resources required to collect and analyse the data should not outweigh the benefits.

The type of metrics that can be used in performance measurement can be either non-financial or financial. Table 12.1 gives an indication of some of the more common metrics used by companies.

Table 12.1 Financial and non-financial metrics

Financial	Non-Financial
Shareholder added value	External rankings
Economic added value	Market share
Return on capital employed	Sales volume/growth
Return on investment	Unfulfilled orders
Return on net assets	Meeting delivery schedules
Cost/revenue/profit ratios	Market penetration levels
Profits and profitability	Customer commitment/loyalty
Cash flow/liquidity	Number of customer complaints
Return on sales	Market image and awareness levels
Production costs	Employee motivation
Unit costs of marketing activities	Employee turnover

In deciding the particular metrics to measure, companies need to consider what they view as the critical success factors that drive performance in their market/industry. The metrics chosen need to assess performance in these areas. Thus if a critical success factor is superior customer value, then level of customer satisfaction and level of customer loyalty may be key measures. If the source of competitive advantage is of lower relative costs to a competitor, then production capacity utilization, quality standards, CVP ratios will be key measures.

What are the organizational mechanisms for the measuring activities?
Benchmarking
Benchmarks can be set against key competitors or in a large multinational against performance in other subsidiaries. If, however, competitor benchmarks were to be the main organizational mechanism for measuring performance, then marketing research and competitor intelligence would be needed. There are two main type of competitor benchmarking processes:

- *Industry-based benchmarking* – In this case the company is comparing their performance against the average known performance in the industry. In industry-based benchmarking data is exchanged between companies, usually by an independent industry or trade association so that companies can benchmark their activities whilst maintaining confidentiality of information.
- *Competitor benchmarking* – In this case the company is identifying key competitors and acquiring information on their performance on specific measures. Targets are then set of either matching or perhaps outperforming them in particular measures.

The annual budgeting procedures
In the implementation programmes of marketing strategies, the goals and objectives set will be translated into annual budgeted targets for the operational performance of the marketing programme. These targets will usually comprise targets for the achievement of the overall financial objective for each of the planning periods, as well as budgeted financial targets for marketing activities. These budgets will then be broken down to specific activities within the marketing programme (e.g. sales budget, advertising budget etc.). Budgeted performance targets will also be set for product/brand strategies as well as performance targets for each element of the marketing mix. Performance will then be evaluated and the marketing programme controlled by measuring actual results against the target for each period. The advantage of using the annual budgeting procedures to control marketing strategies is that it facilitates the coordination of a different range of activities by setting either financial or numerical targets, which have a common language across functional activities. Furthermore, if managers are involved in the budget-setting process, then it can act also as a key motivational

device. Most budgets are prepared over a 1-year period, which enables managers to plan and control activities in line with the process of preparing the annual accounts of the company.

The major problem with using the budgeting process, however, is that the very first task of the budgeting process is the sales forecast on which all subsidiary budgets and targets will be based. The accuracy in forecasting future sales therefore is critical to the meaningfulness of any budgets set to control activities. If this forecast is wrong, for whatever reason, using the budgeting process can become a dispiriting exercise for marketing managers.

Auditing as a control mechanism

As we have said in previous units, strategic marketing decision-making is an iterative and continuous process. Marketing auditing is also a continuous process and an integral part of evaluating the current position as well as controlling the activities of the company. The auditing process is intertwined with the decision-making process, which itself is intertwined with the control and evaluation process. Thus, the auditing processes established by a company are important for signalling likely changes and problems in the marketplace in the strategy development process and ensuring performance standards are met. Auditing processes need to be established to monitor the marketing environment, the marketing strategy, the organization and systems set up to deliver the strategy as well as the functions and profitability of different aspects of the marketing programme. In setting up control and evaluation procedures all the above areas will be regularly monitored and performance assessed against the objectives and standards articulated in the marketing strategy.

Question 12.1

Identify the barriers to measuring and evaluating performance that marketing managers may encounter. Suggest how these barriers might be reduced.

How to ensure performance is measured against a balanced range of stakeholder goals and objectives?

Kaplan and Norton (1992) suggested the use of the Balanced Scorecard (Figure 12.1) to ensure a balanced range of metrics to measure the added value of a company to all stakeholders. The Balanced Scorecard is essentially a management system to measure current performance and to set priorities for future performance. It takes companies beyond the conventional metrics of sales, profit and cash flow, and incorporates the many vital goals and measures against which a company can evaluate their performance rather than simply relying on one measure alone. It addresses four elements:

1. The financial perspective – what is our added value to shareholders/owners?
2. The customer perspective – what is our added value to customers?
3. The internal business perspective – what must we excel at to create value?
4. The innovation and learning perspective – how can we create and improve added value?

The Balanced Scorecard can be used by companies to measure stakeholder value and so assess company performance against their goals and expectations. If used in the manner suggested in Figure 12.2, for each component, standards will be set and then measures established by which the company can evaluate the performance in each area against the goals set.

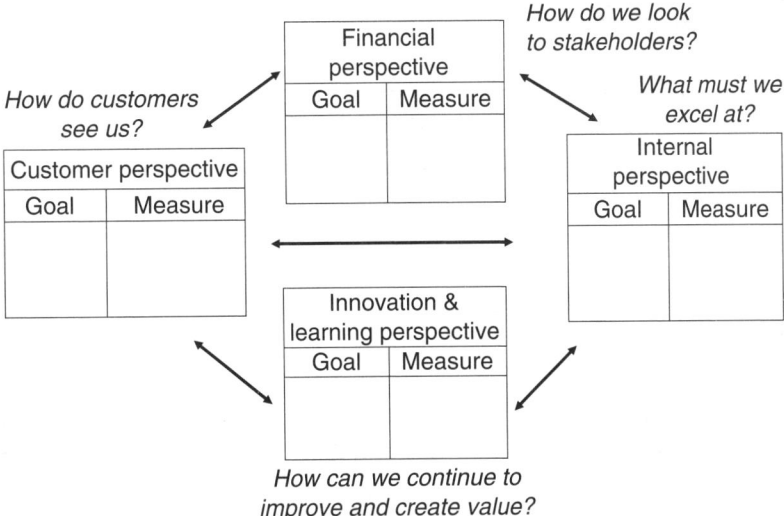

Figure 12.1 The Balanced Scorecard
Source: CIM Professional Postgraduate Diploma in Marketing Tutor pack: Adapted from Kaplan and Norton (1992) 'The Balanced Scorecard – measures that drive performance', *Harvard Business Review*, January–February

Case study

Does the Royal Mail have a healthy Balanced Scorecard?

The Royal Mail made a profit of £220 million in 2004 compared to a loss of £200 million in 2003. The turnaround reflects tough cost-cutting measures, including large-scale job losses and a programme of post office closures.

But, the financial recovery was marred by the fact that it missed all 15 delivery targets as late deliveries increased. Royal Mail aims to deliver 92.5 per cent of first class letters on the day after they were posted, but has undershot the target. As a result, Royal Mail is now due to make compensation payments of about £80 million.

Such a lacklustre performance on non-financial targets poses a huge competitive threat to Royal Mail. Overseas competitors will soon enter the market who will have much more cash to plough into their operations. The company is still only making returns of 2 per cent while the Dutch and Germans who are intending to move into the UK market are making 20 per cent plus. Chief executive Adam Crozier warns that they still need to radically change the company if they are to deliver the necessary profits over the longer term and fight off overseas competition.

Question 12.2

What performance measures would you recommend the Royal Mail should use to develop a Balanced Scorecard that would allow the company to more effectively assess its competitive performance?

Activity 12.2

How does your company ensure a balanced and integrated approach to its system of performance measurement?

Question 12.3

For a company of your choice, develop a Balanced Scorecard that would allow the company to effectively and efficiently manage the marketing process. Justify the performance measures you have selected.

Managing stakeholder expectations

A stakeholder is anyone who has an interest in, or an impact on, the organization. In making marketing decisions managers need to appreciate that different stakeholders have different perceptions of the value they expect to receive from the strategic marketing decisions made. Shareholders/owners will perceive value in terms of the financial benefit they hope to receive, whilst customers will perceive value in terms of the benefits consumption of the product or service will give them. Employees' perception of value, on the other hand, will be couched in terms of the rewards they receive due to their efforts.

 Activity 12.3

Using Figure 12.2, the stakeholder framework, draw up a diagram of the stakeholders of an organization known to you.

According to Doyle (2000) stakeholders fall into a number of major groups:

Shareholders/owners – From the perspective of shareholder/owner value, the first priority of any strategic marketing decision is that they result in activities which create economic benefits which in turn translate into economic value.

Employees – The knowledge and skills that employees have are the intangible assets of an organization that can help a company create and deliver superior value to the customer.

Managers – Managers may well have priorities relating to how they are paid, promotion prospects as well as their political motivations for status and power within an organization, which may sometimes conflict with the interests of other stakeholders.

Customers – The sustainable competitive advantage that will deliver economic value added has to be achieved by maximizing customer value at a cost that generates cash for the company. Customers are interested in obtaining value. If the company fails to meet their value expectations then they will switch suppliers.

Suppliers – A totally integrated marketing effort requires the co-operation and commitment of all the partners involved in the route to market of the products and services being offered by the company.

Community and society – Companies today are seen to have a social responsibility to ensure that their actions are in line with the expectations of the society and in keeping with the public interest and the regulations set down by governments.

The typical stakeholders of a company are depicted in Figure 12.2.

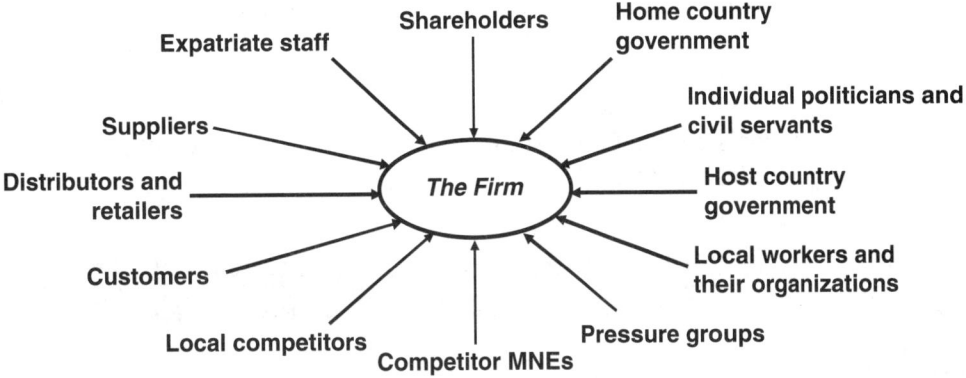

Figure 12.2 Typical stakeholders of a company

In making strategic marketing decisions a company has to assess the varying interests of their stakeholders and evaluate the risks that the different strategic options they are considering in terms of the potential reaction of the different stakeholder groups. The risk that a stakeholder group may react in an adverse way may make the proposed marketing decisions less attractive. Thus, to ensure the effective implementation of its marketing programmes, managers have to manage their relationships with their stakeholders and ensure they meet their expectations. If a company has a high retention rate amongst employees, it is much more likely to be able to retain customers and deliver superior value. If it has a continuous and stable relationship with its suppliers, the government and the wider community, it will be more able to develop appropriate responses to challenges in the marketplace.

Question 12.4

Show how a multinational enterprise can incorporate a consideration of its stakeholders into its strategic marketing decision-making process.

Issues of corporate social responsibility

Activity 12.4

Discuss with a senior manager within your organization how corporate social responsibility is managed within your organization and how it influences the marketing decision-making process.

If a company is to manage the varying demands of its stakeholders then it has to be seen as a company that exhibits a strong sense of corporate social responsibility. Fundamental to achieving this are the shared values between the company and its stakeholders. This is the heart of the societal marketing concept which proposes that in determining the needs and wants of target markets, the strategic marketing decisions made must enhance the well-being of the society as well as that of the consumer. Thus in order to sustain a long-term competitive advantage the decisions made must take into account the social impact of these decisions on the well-being of the society.

Insight

Is CSR really at the top of the agenda?

The challenge of global poverty is now on the agenda of the world's top companies. Whereas the Indian Ocean Tsunami has focused recent attention on philanthropy, there has been a quieter change of tide in the opinion of key marketing strategists who now see poorer regions of the world as potential markets to be developed whilst at the same time helping the local populations combat poverty. Many companies have seized opportunities by designing products and services that can be consumed by the world's poor.

However, how far is this evidence of CSR or, is it just another form of relationship marketing? There are some suggestions that much of the profitable business with lower-income markets involves products such as mobile phones, not the provision of basic nutrition, sanitation, education and shelter, so the current expansion of profitable business in the global South does not necessarily imply poverty reduction. The type of 'development' that is promoted by marketing consumer products to the poor is also questioned. The environmental impacts of changing consumption patterns need to be looked at, as well as the potential displacement of local companies and increasing resource drain from local economies, as larger foreign corporations become more active.

Society increasingly expects companies to show an ethical responsibility in the decisions they take and share their social responsibility with their stakeholders. Thus, it is becoming increasingly apparent that to sustain a long-term competitive advantage companies need to show at a corporate level they have a strong awareness of their social responsibility and that it is a key component of the values on which they build their marketing strategies and an integral consideration in the decisions they make. This means that companies have to consciously engender a culture of shared responsibility amongst all their stakeholders: shareholders, employees, customers, suppliers as well as the wider community. This involves developing in the strategic marketing decision process an ethic of collective good which is marked by a voluntarily accepted solidarity amongst stakeholders that the company, with them, hold a common interest in achieving a sustainable future.

Question 12.5

To what extent should marketing managers recognize the social responsibility of their marketing decisions beyond the boundaries of their organization?

Ethical implications of decision-making

 ## Activity 12.5

Draw up an ethical code of conduct with the aim of instilling ethical values for your company sales personnel.

The ethical dimensions of strategic marketing decision-making have become more visibly important due to the increased sense of corporate social responsibility. In response to this, companies have introduced codes of ethical conduct to guide decision-making and also invite independent auditors to review their ethical performance, which is increasingly used to help companies differentiate themselves from competitors. The prevalence of consumer watchdogs, industry ombudsmen, consumer TV programmes have all encouraged companies to take a positive stance on these issues so they can defend themselves publicly on such issues if a controversy does arise.

Insight

The Dilemma of the long supply chain

Whitline sell a range of premium kitchen accessories. Their principal international markets are the US, Australia and Northern Europe. They have become aware that a number of their competitors, particularly in the US have become enthusiastic members of the ethical trading initiative (ETI). Whitline's own, company research has shown indications that a growing number of consumers across their priority international markets are concerned about the ethical origins of the goods they purchase. However, to become a member of the ETI would require a comprehensive and costly series of verification visits to suppliers with repeat visits at regular intervals. Over 60 per cent of the products sold by Whitline are sourced in China and East Asia. Often their products are bought through intermediaries and so they have little contact with the original manufacturers. The process then, of verifying the ethical practices of the original supplier, could involve the company in considerable cost and effort.

The questions to be considered are how such ethical issues impact on a company when trying to build a global brand image and should Whitline make the necessary investment.

Source: Adapted from Doole and Lowe (2004) *International Marketing Strategy*, Thomson Learning, 4th edition.

In today's markets, a number of the ethical dimensions of marketing decisions are backed by law, both domestic and international. However, ultimately ethics really comes down to the moral behaviour of managers within a company and the importance they place on acting and behaving in an ethical manner. Managers need to form a view as to what constitutes ethical decision-making within an organization. In taking such a view mangers need to reflect on how their views on what constitutes ethical behaviour reflects changing societal views of acceptable behaviour, how decisions will be viewed by stakeholders and the perceived and real impact upon the organization of making those decisions. Central to their concerns is the importance the company places on the need for an ethically responsible approach to their operations on the global markets. However, interwoven within this are the commercial concerns of the business and how they meet the expectations of their stakeholders with regard to their ethical behaviour whilst delivering added value to their shareholders/owners and their customers.

Question 12.6

A large household furniture retailer recently received criticism for its policy of sourcing its rugs and carpets from unregulated sources of supply in India. Suggestions have been made that the rug manufacturers pay very low wages and are guilty of exploitative employment practices. The furniture retailer defended their ethical integrity.

How should the company deal with such criticism?

Case study

Aveda conserving the nuts

For Peru, Brazil nut processing is an important economic activity reliant on the demand from major international companies, who effectively carry out domestic purchasing from local people. In the past, many community enterprises of this type have been exploited by unscrupulous buyers.

Aveda, the personal care product company has formed a partnership with Conservation International (CI) to add sustainability to the activity by taking a nut by-product and using it in a hair care product. Aveda's interest is to source plant-based ingredients for its developing product range. The unique ingredient for Aveda is the protein Morikue. CI's objective is to help local communities create sustainable, environmentally friendly businesses and avoid damaging the natural resources upon which they depend. Activities of this type add value to the nut processing operation.

The enterprise is based in the Tambopata-Candamo reserve zone, an area rich in biodiversity and claiming the highest single site species diversity records for woody plants, birds, butterflies, mammals and dragonflies. The nut collection and processing activities directly affect conservation and natural resource management, and so Aveda supports training activities for Brazil nut collectors and has run enterprise development workshops to show how sourcing guidelines can be used to establish reliable supply chains and improve product quality, necessary for enterprises aiming to develop new markets.

Aveda has also helped to fund Profores, a business founded in 2000 to produce and market sustainable forest products such as fruit nectars. The funding has been used to improve the quality of manufacturing and establish the systems, necessary for quality recognition that will enable the company to develop new markets.

Source: Adapted from Corporate partnerships at Conservation International at www.conservation.org.

Question 12.7

What benefits do partnerships of this type offer to Conservation International?

Question 12.8

Evaluate the marketing benefits of this example of CSR at Aveda and the impact on its marketing activity?

Summary

- o Managers have to ensure a demonstrable link between marketing expenditure and its contribution to the profitability of the company.
- o In establishing a control and evaluation process managers need to decide what they are going to measure and how they are going to measure activities and ensure performance against a balanced range of goals and objectives.
- o In making marketing decisions managers need to appreciate that different stakeholders have different perceptions of the value they expect to receive from the strategic marketing decisions made and these varying expectations have to be managed.
- o If a company is to manage the varying demands of its stakeholders then it has to be seen as a company that exhibits a strong sense of corporate social responsibility.
- o Managers' views on what constitutes ethical behaviour need to reflect the changing societal views of what is acceptable ethical behaviour.

Further study

Doole, I. and Lowe, R. (2005) *Strategic Marketing Decisions in Global Markets*, Thomson Learning, Chapter 12.

Doole, P. (2000) Value Based Marketing: *Marketing Strategies for Corporate Growth and Shareholder Value*, Wiley & Sons Ltd, Chapter 2.

Wilson, R.M.S. and Gilligan, C.T. (2004) *Strategic Marketing Management: Planning Implementation & Control*, 3rd edition, Butterworth-Heinemann, Chapter 19.

Hints and tips

Any marketing decisions you are asked to make in the examination are incomplete without consideration of how those decisions can be evaluated. In the Strategic Marketing Decision examination, it is the process and the approaches that you would recommend that are important. In the examination, it is unlikely there will be a detailed financial question on the setting up and implementation of a control system. Such questions are more likely in Managing Marketing Performance and the Marketing in Practice paper. However, you will be expected to consider the implications of your strategic marketing decisions for control and evaluation. In the evaluation of those decisions, it is also important for the wider perspective and to consider how you would measure the added value to stakeholders as well as shareholders/owners.

Bibliography

CIM (2003) *Shape the Agenda: Hard Edged Marketing, Chartered Institute of Marketing*, September.

Doole, I. and Lowe, R. (2005) *Strategic Marketing Decisions in Global Markets*, Thomson Learning.

Doyle, P. (2000) *Value Based Marketing: Marketing Strategies for Corporate Growth and Shareholder Value*, Wiley & Sons Ltd.

Kaplan, R.S. and Norton, D.P. (1992) 'The Balanced Scorecard – Measures that Drive Performance', *Harvard Business Review*, January–February.

Sample exam question and answers for the Strategic Marketing Decisions module as a whole can be found in Appendix 3 at the back of the book.

appendix 1

guidance on examination preparation

Preparing for your examination

You are now nearing the final phase of your studies and it is time to start the hard work of exam preparation.

During your period of study you will have become used to absorbing large amounts of information. You will have tried to understand and apply aspects of knowledge that may have been very new to you, while some of the information provided may have been more familiar. You may even have undertaken many of the activities that are positioned frequently throughout your coursebook, which will have enabled you to apply your learning in practical situations. But whatever the state of your knowledge and understanding, do not allow yourself to fall into the trap of thinking that you know enough, you understand enough, or even worse, that you can just take it as it comes on the day.

Never underestimate the pressure of the CIM examination.

The whole point of preparing this text for you is to ensure that you never take the examination for granted, and that you do not go into the exam unprepared for what might come your way for three hours at a time.

One thing's for sure: there is no quick fix, no easy route, no waving a magic wand and finding you know it all.

Whether you have studied alone, in a CIM study centre or through distance learning, you now need to ensure that this final phase of your learning process is tightly managed, highly structured and objective.

As a candidate in the examination, your role will be to convince the Senior Examiner for this subject that you have credibility. You need to demonstrate to the examiner that you can be trusted to undertake a range of challenges in the context of marketing, that you are able to capitalize on opportunities and manage your way through threats.

You should prove to the Senior Examiner that you are able to apply knowledge, make decisions, respond to situations and solve problems. Essentially you will be expected to demonstrate an ability to:

- Analyse
- Critically evaluate
- Understand models and techniques

203

- o Draw implications
- o Develop scenarios
- o Develop implementation plans.

Very shortly we are going to look at a range of revision and exam preparation techniques, and at time management issues, and encourage you towards developing and implementing your own revision plan, but before that, let's look at the role of the Senior Examiner.

A bit about the Senior Examiners!

You might be quite shocked to read this, but while it might appear that the examiners are 'relentless question masters' they actually want you to be able to answer the questions and pass the exams! In fact, they would derive no satisfaction or benefits from failing candidates; quite the contrary, they develop the syllabus and exam papers in order that you can learn and then apply that learning effectively so as to pass your examinations. Many of the examiners have said in the past that it is indeed psychologically more difficult to fail students than pass them.

Many of the hints and tips you find within this Appendix have been suggested by the Senior Examiners and authors of the Coursebook series. Therefore you should consider them carefully and resolve to undertake as many of the elements suggested as possible.

The Chartered Institute of Marketing has a range of processes and systems in place within the Examinations Division to ensure that fairness and consistency prevail across the team of examiners, and that the academic and vocational standards that are set and defined are indeed maintained. In doing this, CIM ensures that those who gain the CIM Professional Certificate, Professional Diploma and Professional Postgraduate Diploma are worthy of the qualification and perceived as such in the view of employers, actual and potential.

Part of what you will need to do within the examination is be 'examiner friendly' – that means you have to make sure they get what they ask for. This will make life easier for you and for them.

Hints and tips for 'examiner friendly' actions are as follows:

- o Show them that you understand the basis of the question, by answering *precisely* the question asked, and not including just about everything you can remember about the subject area.
- o Read their needs – how many points is the question asking you to address?
- o Respond to the question appropriately. Is the question asking you to take on a role? If so, take on the role and answer the question in respect of the role. For example, you could be positioned as follows:

  - – 'You are working as a Marketing Assistant at Nike UK' or 'You are a Marketing Manager for an Engineering Company' or 'As Marketing Manager write a report to the Managing Partner'.
  - – These examples of role-playing requirements are taken from questions in past papers.

- o Deliver the answer in the format requested. If the examiner asks for a memo, then provide a memo; likewise, if the examiner asks for a report, then write a report. If you do not do this, in some instances you will fail to gain the necessary marks required to pass.
- o Take a business-like approach to your answers. This enhances your credibility. Badly ordered work, untidy work, lack of structure, headings and subheadings can be off-putting. This would be unacceptable in the work situation, likewise it will be unacceptable in the eyes of the Senior Examiners and their marking teams.

- o Ensure the examiner has something to mark: give them substance, relevance, definitions, illustration and demonstration of your knowledge and understanding of the subject area.
- o See the examiner as your potential employer or ultimate consumer/customer. The whole purpose and culture of marketing is about meeting customers' needs. Try this approach – it works wonders.
- o Provide a strong sense of enthusiasm and professionalism in your answers; support it with relevant up-to-date examples and apply them where appropriate.
- o Try to do something that will make your exam paper a little bit different – make it stand out in the crowd.

All of these points might seem quite logical to you, but often in the panic of the examination they 'go out of the window'. Therefore it is beneficial to remind ourselves of the importance of the examiner. He/she is the 'ultimate customer' – and we all know customers hate to be disappointed.

As we move on, some of these points will be revisited and developed further.

About the examination

In all examinations, with the exception of Marketing in Practice at Professional Certificate level, Marketing Management in Practice at Professional Diploma level, and Strategic Marketing in Practice at Professional Postgraduate Diploma level, the paper is divided into two parts.

- o Part A – Mini-case study = 50 per cent of the marks
- o Part B – Option choice questions (choice of two questions from four) = 50 per cent of the marks.

Let's look at the basis of each element.

The mini-case study

This is based on a mini-case or scenario with one question, possibly subdivided into between two and four points, but totalling 50 per cent of marks overall.

In essence, you, the candidate, are placed in a problem-solving role through the medium of a short scenario. On occasions, the scenario may consist of an article from a journal in relation to a well-known organization: for example, in the past, Interflora, EasyJet and Philips, among others, have been used as the basis of the mini-case.

Alternatively, it will be based upon a fictional company, and the examiner will have prepared it in order that the right balance of knowledge, understanding, application and skills is used.

Approaches to the mini-case study

When undertaking the mini-case study there are a number of key areas you should consider.

Structure/content

The mini-case that you will be presented with will vary slightly from paper to paper, and of course from one examination to the next. Normally the scenario presented will be 250–500 words long and will centre on a particular organization and its problems or may even relate to a specific industry.

The length of the mini-case study means that usually only a brief outline is provided of the situation, the organization and its marketing problems, and you must therefore learn to cope with analysing information and preparing your answer on the basis of a very limited amount of detail.

Time management

There are many differing views on time management and the approaches you can take to managing your time within the examination. You must find an approach to suit your way of working, but always remember, whatever you do, you must ensure that you allow enough time to complete the examination. Unfinished exams mean lost marks.

A typical example of managing time is as follows:

Your paper is designed to assess you over a three-hour period. With 50 per cent of the marks being allocated to the mini-case, it means that you should dedicate somewhere around half of your time to both read and write-up the answer on this mini-case.

Do not forget that while there is only one question within the mini-case, it can have a number of components. You must answer all the components in that question which is where the balance of times comes into play.

Knowledge/skills tested

Throughout all the CIM papers, your knowledge, skills and ability to apply those skills will be tested. However, the mini-cases are used particularly to test application, that is your ability to take your knowledge and apply it in a structured way to a given scenario. The examiners will be looking at your decision-making ability, your analytical and communication skills and, depending on the level, your ability as a manager to solve particular marketing problems.

When the examiner is marking your paper, he/she will be looking to see how you differentiate yourself, looking at your own individual 'unique selling points'. The examiner will also want to see if you can personally apply the knowledge or whether you are only able to repeat the textbook materials.

Format of answers

On many occasions, and within all examinations, you will most likely be given a particular communication method to use. If this is the case, you must ensure that you adhere to the requirements of the examiner. This is all part of meeting customer needs.

The likely communication tools you will be expected to use are as follows:

- Memorandum
- Memorandum/report
- Report
- Briefing notes
- Presentation
- Press release
- Advertisement
- Plan.

Make sure that you familiarize yourself with these particular communication tools and practise using them to ensure that, on the day, you will be able to respond confidently to the communication requests of the examiner.

By the same token, while communication methods are important, so is meeting the specific requirements of the question. This means you must understand what is meant by the precise instruction given. *Note the following terms carefully*:

- o *Identify* – Select key issues, point out key learning points, establish clearly what the examiner expects you to identify.
- o *Illustrate* – The examiner expects you to provide examples, scenarios and key concepts that illustrate your learning.
- o *Compare and contrast* – Look at the range of similarities between the two situations, contexts or even organizations. Then compare them, that is ascertain and list how activities, features, and so on agree or disagree. Contrasting means highlighting the differences between the two.
- o *Discuss* – Questions that have 'discuss' in them offer a tremendous opportunity for you to debate, argue, justify your approach or understanding of the subject area – *caution*: it is not an opportunity to waffle.
- o *Briefly explain* – This means being succinct, structured and concise in your explanation, within the answer. Make your points clear, transparent and relevant.
- o *State* – Present in a clear, brief format.
- o *Interpret* – Expound the meaning of, make clear and explicit, what it is you see and understand within the data provided.
- o *Outline* – Provide the examiner with the main concepts and features being asked for and avoid minor technical details. Structure will be critical here, or else you could find it difficult to contain your answer.
- o *Relate* – Show how different aspects of the syllabus connect together.
- o *Evaluate* – Review and reflect upon an area of the syllabus, a particular practice, an article, and so on, and consider its overall worth in respect of its use as a tool or a model and its overall effectiveness in the role it plays.

Source: Worsam, Mike, *How to Pass Marketing*, Croner, 1989.

Your approach to mini-cases

There is no one right way to approach and tackle a mini-case study, indeed it will be down to each individual to use their own creativity in tackling the tasks presented. You will have to use your initiative and discretion about how best to approach the mini-case. Having said this, however, there are some basic steps you can take.

- o Ensure that you read through the case study at least twice before making any judgements, starting to analyse the information provided or indeed writing the answers.
- o On the third occasion read through the mini-case and, using a highlighter, start marking the essential and relevant information critical to the content and context. Then turn your attention to the question again, this time reading slowly and carefully to assess what it is you are expected to do. Note any instructions that the examiner gives you, and then start to plan how you might answer the question. Whatever the question, ensure the answer has a structure: a beginning, a structured central part of the answer and, finally, always a conclusion.
- o Keep the context of the question continually in mind: that is, the specifics of the case and the role which you might be performing.
- o Because there is limited material available, you will sometimes need to make assumptions. Don't be afraid to do this, it will show initiative on your part. Assumptions are an important part of dealing with case studies and can help you to be quite creative with

your answer. However, do explain the basis of your assumptions within your answer so that the examiner understands the nature of them, and why you have arrived at your particular outcome. *Always ensure that your assumptions are realistic.*

o Only now are you approaching the stage where it is time to start writing your answer to the question, tackling the problems, making decisions and recommendations on the case scenario set before you. As mentioned previously, your points will often be best set out in a report or memo-type format, particularly if the examiner does not specify a communication method.

o Ensure that your writing is succinct, avoids waffle and responds directly to the questions asked.

Part B

Part B is also worth 50 per cent of the marks. You will be asked to answer two questions from four, each of the two being worth 25 marks each.

Realistically, the same principles apply for these questions as in the case study. Communication formats, reading through the questions, structure, role-play, context, and so on – everything is the same.

Part B will cover a number of broader issues from within the syllabus and will be taken from any element of it. The examiner makes the choice, and no prior direction is given to students or tutors on what that might be. Something you should consider is that each of these questions will not singularly assess one area of the syllabus, but will be more if you complex and assess a number of different areas from within the syllabus, namely two or more.

As regards time management in this area, you should have used half your time for the mini-case you should have around half the time remaining. This provides you with around 45 minutes to plan and write a question review and revise your answers. Keep practising – use a cooker timer, alarm clock or mobile phone alarm as your timer and work hard at answering questions within the timeframe given.

Specimen examination papers and answers

To help you prepare and understand the nature of the paper, go to www.cim.co.uk/learningzone/ to access Specimen Answers and Senior Examiner's advice for these exam questions. During your study, the author of your Coursebook may have on occasions asked you to refer to these papers and answer the questions. You should undertake these exercises and utilize every opportunity to practise meeting examination requirements.

The specimen answers are vital learning tools. They are not always perfect, as they are answers written by students and annotated by the Senior Examiners, but they will give you a good indication of the approaches you could take, and the examiners' annotations suggest how these answers might be improved. Please use them.

The CIM learning zone website provides you with links to many useful case studies, which will help you to put your learning into context when you are revising.

Key elements of preparation

One Senior Examiner suggests the three elements involved in preparing for your examination can be summarized thus:

- Learning
- Memory
- Revision.

Let's look at each point in turn.

Learning

Quite often students find it difficult to learn properly. You can passively read books, look at some of the materials, perhaps revise a little and regurgitate it all in the examination. In the main, however, this is rather an unsatisfactory method of learning. It is meaningless, shallow and ultimately of little use in practice. Additionally, it leads to likely problems in the examination.

For learning to be truly effective it must be active and applied. You must involve yourself in the learning process by thinking about what you have read, testing it against your experience by reflecting on how you use particular aspects of marketing, and how you could perhaps improve your own performance by implementing particular aspects of your learning into your everyday life. You should adopt the old adage of 'learning by doing'. If you do, you will find that passive learning has no place in your study life.

Below are some suggestions that have been prepared to assist you with the learning pathway throughout your revision.

- Always make your own notes, in words you understand, and ensure that you combine all the sources of information and activities within them.
- Always try to relate your learning back to your own organization.
- Make sure you define key terms concisely, wherever possible.
- Do not try to memorize your ideas, but work on the basis of understanding and, most important, applying them.
- Think about the relevant and topical questions that might be set – use the questions and answers in your Coursebooks to identify typical questions that might be asked in the future.
- Attempt all of the questions within each of your Coursebooks since these are vital tests of your active learning and understanding.

Memory

If you are prepared to undertake an active learning programme then your knowledge will be considerably enhanced, as understanding and application of knowledge does tend to stay in your 'long-term' memory. It is likely that passive learning will only stay in your 'short-term' memory.

Do not try to memorize parrot fashion; it is not helpful and, even more important, examiners are experienced in identifying various memorizing techniques and therefore will spot them as such.

Having said this, it is quite useful to memorize various acronyms such as SWOT, PEST, PESTLE, STEEPLE, or indeed various models such as Ansoff, GE Matrix, Shell Directional, and so on, as in some of the questions you may be required to use illustrations of these to assist your answer.

Additionally, with the new syllabus there is also a requirement not just to use the models and acronyms but also to show you understand how to use the models and various techniques. Therefore ensure your understanding is very thorough and developed.

Revision

The third and final stage to consider is 'revision', which is what we will concentrate on in detail below. Here just a few key tips are offered.

Revision should be an ongoing process rather than a panic measure that you decide to undertake just before the examination. You should be preparing notes *throughout* your course, with the view to using them as part of your revision process. Therefore ensure that your notes are sufficiently comprehensive that you can reuse them successfully.

For each concept you learn about, you should identify, through your reading and your own personal experience, at least two or three examples that you could use; this then gives you some scope to broaden your perspective during the examination. It will, of course, help you gain some points for initiative with the examiners.

Knowledge is not something you will gain overnight – as we saw earlier, it is not a quick fix; it involves a process of learning that enables you to lay solid foundations upon which to build your long-term understanding and application. This will benefit you significantly in the future, not just in the examination.

In essence, you should ensure that you do the following in the period before the real intensive revision process begins.

- o   Keep your study file well organized, updated and full of newspaper and journal cuttings that may help you formulate examples in your mind for use during the examination.
- o   Practise defining key terms and acronyms from memory.
- o   Prepare topic outlines and draft answers, perhaps in report format as opposed to essay style questions. Even think about developing discussion documents and so on, to enhance your approach.
- o   When you start your intensive revision, ensure it is planned and structured in the way described below. And then finally, read your concentrated notes the night before the examination.

Revision planning

You are now on a critical path – although hopefully not too critical at this time – with somewhere in the region of between 4 and 6 weeks to go to the examination. The following hints and tips will help you plan out your revision study.

- o   You will, as already explained, need to be very organized. Therefore, before doing anything else, put your files, examples, reading material, and so on in good order, so that you are able to work with them in the future and, of course, make sense of them.
- o   Ensure that you have a quiet area within which to work. It is very easy to get distracted when preparing for an examination.

o   Take out your file along with your syllabus and make a list of key topic areas that you have studied and which you now need to revise. You could use the basis of this book to do that, by taking each unit a step at a time.

o   Plan the use of your time carefully. Ideally you should start your revision at least six weeks prior to the exam, so therefore work out how many spare hours you could give to the revision process and then start to allocate time in your diary, and do not double-book with anything else.

o   Give up your social life for a short period of time. As the saying goes 'no pain – no gain'.

o   Looking at each of the subject areas in turn, identify which are your strengths and which are your weaknesses. Which areas have you grasped and understood, and which are the areas that you have really struggled with? Split your page into two and make a list on each side. For example:

Analysis and evaluation	
Strengths	**Weaknesses**
Audit – PEST, SWOT, Models	Ratio analysis
Portfolio analysis	Market sensing
	Productivity analysis
	Trend extrapolation
	Forecasting

o   Break down your list again and divide the points of weakness, giving priority in the first instance to your weakest areas and even prioritizing them by giving them a number. This will enable you to master the more difficult areas. Up to 60 per cent of your remaining revision time should be given over to that, as you may find you have to undertake a range of additional reading and also perhaps seeking tutor support, if you are studying at a CIM Accredited Study Centre.

o   The rest of the time should be spent reinforcing your knowledge and understanding of the stronger areas, spending time testing yourself on how much you really know.

o   Should you be taking two examinations or more at any one time, then the breakdown and managing of your time will be critical.

o   Taking a subject at a time, work through your notes and start breaking them down into subsections of learning, and ultimately into key learning points, items that you can refer to time and time again, that are meaningful and that your mind will absorb. You yourself will know how best you remember key points. Some people try to develop acronyms, or flowcharts or matrices, mind maps, fishbone diagrams, and so on, or various connection diagrams that help them recall certain aspects of models. You could also develop processes that enable you to remember approaches to various options. (But do remember what we said earlier about regurgitating stuff, parrot fashion.)

Figure A1.1 is just a brief example of how you could use a 'bomb-burst' diagram (which, in this case, highlights the uses of advertising) as a very helpful approach to memorizing key elements of learning.

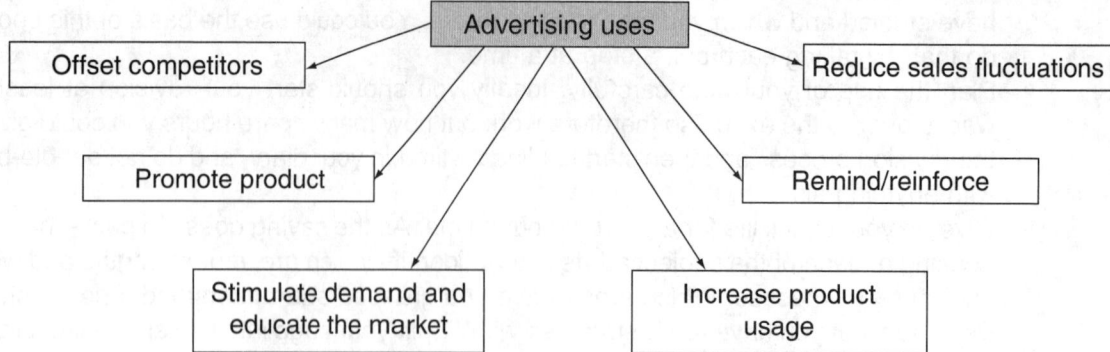

Figure A1.1 Use of a diagram to summarize key components of a concept
Source: Adapted from Dibb, Simkin, Pride and Ferrell, *Marketing Concepts and Strategies,* 4th edition, Houghton Mifflin, 2001

o Eventually you should reduce your key learning to bullet points. For example: imagine you were looking at the concept of Time Management – you could eventually reduce your key learning to a bullet list containing the following points in relation to 'Effective Prioritization':

  – Organize
  – Take time
  – Delegate
  – Review.

Each of these headings would then remind you of the elements you need to discuss associated with the subject area.

Time management has been highlighted as a key issue with the new examinations, and the new Senior Examiners are keen that students understand the limitations of the examination and the depth of answers required. Therefore getting as much practice as possible would be extremely invaluable to your examination success.

o Avoid getting involved in reading too many textbooks at this stage, as you may start to find that you are getting confused overall.

o Look at examination questions on previous papers, and start to observe closely the various roles and tasks they expect you to undertake, and importantly, the context in which they are set.

o *Use the specimen exam papers and specimen answers* to support your learning and see how you could actually improve upon them.

o Without exception, find an associated examination question for the areas that you have studied and revised and undertake it (more than once if necessary).

o Without referring to notes or books, try to draft an answer plan with the key concepts, knowledge, models and information that are needed to successfully complete the answer. Then refer to the specimen answer to see how close you are to the actual outline presented. Planning your answer, and ensuring that key components are included, and that the question has a meaningful structure, is one of the most beneficial activities that you can undertake.

o Now write the answer out in full, time-constrained and written by hand, not with the use of IT. (At this stage, you are still expected to be the scribe for the examination and present handwritten work. Many of us find this increasingly difficult as we spend more and more time using our computers to present information. Do your best to be neat. Spidery handwriting is often offputting to the examiner.)

o When writing answers as part of your revision process, also be sure to practise the following essential examinations techniques:

  – *Identify and use the communication method* requested by the examiner.
  – *Always have three key parts to the answer* – an introduction, middle section that develops your answer in full, and a conclusion. Where appropriate, ensure that you have an introduction, main section, summary/conclusion and, if requested or helpful, recommendations.
  – *Always answer the question in the context or role set.*
  – *Always comply with the nature and terms of the question.*
  – *Leave white space.* Do not overcrowd your page; Leave space between paragraphs, and make sure your sentences do not merge into one blur. (Don't worry – there is always plenty of paper available to use in the examination.)
  – *Count* how many actions the question asks you to undertake and double-check at the end that you have met the full range of demands of the question.
  – *Use examples* to demonstrate your knowledge and understanding of the particular syllabus area. These can be from journals, the Internet, the press or your own experience.
  – *Display your vigour and enthusiasm for marketing.* Remember to think of the Senior Examiner as your customer, or future employer, and do your best to deliver what is wanted to satisfy their needs. Impress them and show them how you are a 'cut above the rest'.
  – Review all your practice answers critically, with the above points in mind.

Practical actions

The critical path is becoming even more critical now as the examination looms. The following are vital points.

o Have you registered with CIM?
o Do you know where you are taking your examination? CIM should let you know approximately one month in advance.
o Do you know where your examination centre is? If not find out, take a drive, time it – whatever you do don't be late!
o Make sure you have all the tools of the examination ready. A dictionary, calculator, pens, pencils, ruler, etc. Try not to use multiple shades of pens, but at the same time make your work look professional. *Avoid using red and green as these are the colours that will be used for marking.*

In the words of one Senior Examiner, this is how you should pass brilliantly:

o Show you can critically analyse and evaluate a range of information and situations
o Be creative and innovative in providing marketing solutions
o Present your work in a professional style
o Ensure your recommendations are well argued and justified.

Summary

Above all you must remember that you personally have invested a tremendous amount of time, effort and money in studying for this programme and it is therefore imperative that you consider the suggestions given here as they will help to maximize your return on your investment.

Many of the hints and tips offered here are generic and will work across most of the CIM courses. We have tried to select those that will help you most in taking a sensible, planned approach to your study and revision.

The key to your success is being prepared to put in the time and effort required, planning your revision, and equally important, planning and answering your questions in a way that will ensure that you pass your examination on the day.

The advice offered here aims to guide you from a practical perspective. Guidance on syllabus content and developments associated with your learning will become clear to you as you work through this Coursebook. The authors of each Coursebook have given subject-specific guidance on the approach to the examination and on how to ensure that you meet the content requirements of the kind of question you will face. These considerations are in addition to the structuring issues we have been discussing throughout this Appendix.

Each of the authors and Senior Examiners will guide you on their preferred approach to questions and answers as they go. Therefore where you are presented with an opportunity to be involved in some activity or undertake an examination question either during or at the end of your study units, do take it. It not only prepares you for the examination, but helps you learn in the applied way we discussed above.

Here, then, is a last reminder:

- Ensure you make the most of your learning process throughout.
- Keep structured and orderly notes from which to revise.
- Plan your revision – don't let it just happen.
- Provide examples to enhance your answers.
- Practise your writing skills in order that you present your work well and your writing is readable.
- Take as many opportunities to test your knowledge and measure your progress as possible.
- Plan and structure your answers.
- Always do as the question asks you, especially with regard to context and communication method.
- *Do not leave it until the last minute!*

The writers would like to take this opportunity to wish you every success in your endeavours to study, to revise and to pass your examinations.

Karen Beamish
Academic Development Advisor

appendix 2
answers and debriefings

Unit 1

Debriefing Question 1.1

This is meant as an introductory general question to help you think about some of the issues you will be studying in this module. Use your learning from Professional Diploma in Marketing of the CIM syllabus and your learning in the previous modules you have studied at Professional Postgraduate Diploma in Marketing to consider some of the capabilities you consider important if a company is to make effective strategic decisions. You may want to reflect on the stages of the strategy development process and consider the capabilities in the companies you have studied in case studies. Some of the capabilities you may consider are such things as.

- o Knowledge management capabilities
- o Innovative and open culture in an organization
- o Appropriate performance metrics
- o The flexibility to be responsive to environmental changes.

Debriefing Question 1.2

This is an open question to allow you to think further about the context in which strategic marketing decisions are made and the changing dimensions in the environment that are influencing the way in which companies build a competitive advantage. You need to consider such factors as increasing customer sophistication, increasing turbulence in global markets, the fast pace of change in some markets and the increasing inter-dependency of economies across the globe. You could also discuss the impact of shrinking communications and the impact of the Internet on the way a company's competitive advantage is achieved in the marketplace.

Debriefing Activity 1.1

Consider the basis of your company's competitive advantage and ask yourself whether it is based on the actual transaction, whether it has been built by achieving brand leadership or has it been built through the relationships the company has formed with its customers or members of the supply chain. The concept of value-based marketing is discussed in Unit 2, but at this stage perhaps you might want to consider how successful your company is in offering superior value to its customers and does it differentiate itself from its competitors through the integration of its total marketing effort or one aspect, perhaps either the product or service attributes it offers.

Debriefing Question 1.3

Innovative and creative thinking requires managers to develop the mindset where they can reflect on the information presented, re-orientate their thinking in the light of the analysis and then use their learning of the new situation to reinvent the basis on which they develop their competitive advantage. Such thinking, therefore, means managers have to step outside the formal strictures of the traditional rational linear planning models and approach their strategic marketing decisions from an entirely new angle. In view of the changing dimensions of competitive advantage discussed previously, it is becoming ever harder to achieve a sustainable competitive advantage. There are some schools of thought that propose the only sustainable basis for competitive advantage is innovative leadership in the market, be this through the product or services offered, the route to market or in the way a company builds and uses its relationships with customers to offer superior value.

Debriefing Activity 1.2

In completing this activity, you need to first consider what the important elements of hard-edged strategic marketing decisions are. In considering how hard edged your company is perhaps you may want to think about:

- The process in which marketing decisions are made
- The different management functions that are involved in making those decisions
- Whether marketing decisions are made at board level
- Whether creative and innovative thinking are encouraged in the organization
- How far do the marketing decisions create superior value for customers
- Whether marketing decisions are financially appraised prior to the decision being taken
- Whether marketing metrics are used to assess the performance of decisions.

Debriefing Activity 1.3

The shape of the life cycle will vary enormously depending on the industry or market chosen. If this activity is carried out in a classroom situation, it would be interesting to note the varying shapes of the life cycles identified and reflect on the similarities and differences between the industries where the differences in shape are most pronounced. Likewise, in some industries, it will be possible to discern quite clear stages that have existed for considerable time periods, whereas in high-tech markets, stages of the life cycle are more difficult to discern and the time periods at each stage are more difficult to isolate. In carrying out this activity, the easiest way is to consider the competitive activity at each stage and the way the market structure has developed in the period of time being observed.

Debriefing Question 1.4

In answering this question, you need to consider the changing competitive landscape of British supermarkets. The decision seems to imply that Sainsbury's believe that an important area in which they have lost market share is in the everyday basic shopping basket. The appropriateness of the decision will depend on how far you think this is true or whether there are other important factors causing the fall in market share. You perhaps also need to think of other options for Sainsbury's and the decision areas you think are important to consider.

Debriefing Question 1.5

The life cycle concept, for many scholars, is useful in explaining the past structure of the market/competitive/demand/product life cycle. However, given all that has been said with regard to the changing dimensions of competitive advantage, it may well be that just because a certain cycle has been followed in the past it will follow the same pattern in the future. Managers making decisions for future time horizons need to do more than simply extrapolate what has happened in the past. A large number of companies operate in global markets and so there is not necessarily one life cycle but a multitude of cycles to understand. It is thought, therefore, that the life cycle concept is a two-dimensional one that has little value in explaining a market structure which is multidimensional and complex. In managing life cycles in global markets, managers need to recognize that life cycles do not always follow such a set pattern. Competition today in many markets is global rather than domestic for many products and services. Consequently, there is a reduced time lag between product research, development and production, leading to the simultaneous appearance of a standardized product in major world markets. Nor does the model go very far in explaining the rapid development of transnational companies networking production and marketing facilities across many countries and targeting transnational consumer segments. Such developments impact on the shape and characteristics of all life cycles, be they market/competitive/demand/product life cycle.

Debriefing Activity 1.4

This may be quite a difficult activity to complete if you do not have access to the required information. In that case, try to talk to a manager of another company who operates in global markets, and discuss the life cycle concept with them. See if you can identify the different stages each of the various countries is at and justify why you think you would plot them in that particular position. In other words, consider the characteristics you are identifying as being relevant to the particular stages of the global product life cycle.

Debriefing Question 1.6

Operational excellence – This is about efficiency, not necessarily about effectiveness, and so can only be a basis of obtaining customer preference if it is geared to a strategy, which delivers superior value to the customer. Operational excellence is usually a major strategic thrust in markets where it is difficult to differentiate on product benefits and so competitive advantage has to be built on being cheaper, faster and more efficient. The problem is how to sustain such an advantage over time.

Customer intimacy – Can be extremely effective not only in the service sector but also in industries that have the capability to build detailed individual profiles on customers through datamining. This allows for a mass customization strategy which, if effective, can almost deliver a one-to-one–targeted personalized strategy. Supermarket retailers and online retailers such as Amazon are examples of companies that have such a capability.

Brand leadership – Companies basing their strategic positioning on brand leadership need to work actively to deliver an extra value proposition which is valued by the customer in order to sustain brand leadership over a period of time. Price transparency, the growth of Internet marketing and the growth of grey marketing has led in some markets to the deteriorating perception of the value of some designer brands.

Debriefing Question 1.7

The high-tech market is a fast-moving and changing market where the cost of R&D is constantly spiralling and technical progress is at such a pace that it is difficult for companies in such markets to resource and build the capability to develop a sufficiently robust R&D programme on their own. In answering this question, you need to consider the synergies that both partners brought to the relationship and how these can be exploited in the market. However, it would also be good to consider the potential difficulties in forming such a joint venture across two very disparate cultures could bring and consider some of the strategies and techniques the joint-venture company could exercise to minimize such difficulties.

Debriefing Activity 1.5

Consider the relationships, if any, your company has with companies that it may be in direct or indirect competition with. If your company does not have any relationships, see if you can ascertain why and what the senior management view is of such relationships. If you work for a large company, it could well be that you have a complex web of such relationships. If this is the case, it would be interesting to categorize the relationships and examine the purpose and objectives of them, the time span of the relationship and whether it is a simple bilateral or a complex multilateral relationship.

Unit 2

Debriefing Activity 2.1

The reader should consider changes in competitor activity that has rendered a firm's strategy obsolete or perhaps changes in the market that have impacted on the competitive landscape. This activity builds upon Question 1.2 in Unit 1 but here the emphasis is on drivers that you anticipate are affecting the company in its future direction and should be specific to the market or industry you have specified.

Debriefing Question 2.1

P&G believes they can build a sustainable competitive advantage globally through this merger and that they will be in a much stronger position to maintain shareholder value in the light of the increasing pressure on margins being brought by the globalization of retailer power. Some of the drivers the reader may wish to consider are such things as increasing global retailer power, the opening of new markets, high growth in emerging markets and increasing homogeneity of the global consumer.

Debriefing Question 2.2

The Internet for many companies has broken down barriers of access to markets and enabled them to redefine the geographical boundaries of their market. It is now considerably more easy for companies to access disparate and fragmented markets across the world through the Internet. It has meant that they are able to build knowledge on individual customers, which has given them the ability to develop mass customization strategies, changing the way many companies approach their marketing strategy. However, it has become much harder for companies to identify and track competitors, as in the virtual competitive landscape of e-marketing, it is much more difficult to identify and locate competitors and keep track of their movements. Thus, the way in which a differentiated position is built and maintained has required considerable rethinking for many companies operating Web-based marketing strategies.

Debriefing Question 2.3

Companies in their off-line marketing activities have had to consider the changes in consumer behaviour that the impact of the Internet has brought. However, marketing, whether it be online or off-line, is about how a company achieves the competitive advantage and sustains that advantage over time. Thus, the principles of marketing remain the same, in that it is about anticipating and satisfying customer needs and building a value-added proposition in the market. However, in many markets, the Internet has changed the expectations of consumers, and changed the way they seek information and evaluate the options available. Such changes have, in some markets, therefore, led to companies reconsidering their off-line marketing strategies.

Debriefing Activity 2.2

The breakpoints themselves may be easy to identify and for any company you may in fact be able to identify several. However, what may be more difficult to ascertain are the decisions and actions the company took to overcome the breakpoints. It may be that the company did nothing. If this is the case, then consider what the consequences of their inaction were? Did the company survive or was it ultimately forced to realign its strategic thinking? You may also want to consider the strategic marketing decision process in the company and whether this facilitated or inhibited the company's ability to react to the breakpoint.

Debriefing Question 2.4

A totally integrated marketing effort reflects the ability to take a long-term perspective to its strategic marketing decisions and ensure that the customer proposition in the marketplace is clear, that it has an explicit positioning strategy and a high level of resource coordination in the delivery of that strategy to the market. To achieve this, there needs to be a good understanding within the organization of the needs, wants and behaviour patterns of the customers. There also needs to be a clear direction from senior management that is understood by all the employees of the company. In this way all the company will understand what is required of the marketing effort and they will be able to work to the same goal. Of course, to achieve this, the company has to be effectively organized, have a good knowledge management system and strong marketing orientation.

Debriefing Question 2.5

The shareholder value principle asserts that marketing strategies should be judged by the economic returns they generate for shareholders and company owners. It is important for marketing managers in their drive to gain more representation at board level of companies. There is a strong view that marketing is not adequately represented at senior management level as what the value-added marketing brings to an organization has been difficult to quantify in financial terms. Value-based marketing offers a way for managers to show how marketing strategies increase the value of the firm as well as providing a framework and language for integrating marketing more effectively with other functions of the business.

Debriefing Question 2.6

In high-tech markets the pricing dilemma facing companies is how to maximize revenues when they have gone through a highly expensive R&D programme and the cost of producing one product is incredibly high. In high-tech markets it is highly expensive to produce one product but the marginal cost of producing large numbers is incrementally very low, hence the pressure to reduce process quickly. The reader needs to consider in such a market how the company can best employ strategies that will maintain long-term shareholder value whilst maintaining competitiveness in the market.

Debriefing Activity 2.3

Obstacles to applying the economic value-added principle are:

o   Absence of clear objectives from senior management
o   No clear lines of responsibility for the accountability of marketing decisions taken
o   Lack of integration between departments
o   No effective knowledge management system
o   The lack of performance metrics within the organization.

Debriefing Question 2.7

The main components of value-based marketing are:

o   A deep understanding of customer needs, operating procedures and decision-making processes
o   Value propositions that meet the needs of customers and create a differential advantage
o   Long-term relationships with customers so a level of loyalty and trust is built based on satisfaction and confidence in the supplier
o   The delivery of superior value to customers requires superior knowledge, skills, systems and marketing assets.

Debriefing Activity 2.4

Some companies clearly articulate their value disciplines and ensure they are known and understood by all employees. If this is the case then it gives clear criteria against which strategic options can be evaluated when companies are making strategic decisions and helps them to clarify which decision is in line with their values. However, a company where such values are not evident does not have the same strategic steer. This means in making strategic decisions in difficult and complex circumstances it is much harder to clarify a clear path forward and so harder to judge the appropriateness of decisions.

Debriefing Question 2.8

Both the approaches outlined have validity and the approach taken may well be determined by the core ideology expressed by the senior management of the company as well as the competitive and market situation. However, all approaches have to have inbuilt flexibility to respond to challenges in the marketing environment. Thus, in the view of Mintzberg, strategy development processes need to be an iterative process allowing a company to reflect and respond to challenges, so the company has to be proactive in seeking knowledge to anticipate future developments and also have the ability to react and change the strategic basis should the market demands it.

Debriefing Activity 2.5

In many SMEs, the managing director may have the sole responsibility for all marketing decisions. One of the problems they have in making decisions is that unlike in a large firm they do not have the capacity to generate ideas, assess options and clarify the best route forward by bringing together teams of experts and professionals within the organization. Thus, the responsibility of making strategic decisions can be a lonely and onerous one. This is why SMEs build an almost virtual organization through a network of relationships with external partners who play a huge part in not only advising on any decision to be made but also the provision of information on which to base decisions and helping to validate any decisions that are made as appropriate to the market conditions.

Unit 3

Debriefing Activity 3.1

To complete this activity, draw a grid with the names of the five companies along the top and then down the side the components of a customer value-based philosophy, that is marketing orientation, continuous learning and a commitment to innovation. For each of these components assess what evidence there is that the company gives priority to these components and in what way do you see these three activities being implemented by each of the companies identified.

Firms with positive marketing-oriented values have the capacity to understand the needs of the customer in a manner that allows superior value to be provided. As the firm is geared towards the market, it is aware of both existing and potential competitor activities and so able to identify potential opportunities and threats. As they are organized with the emphasis on achieving competitive advantage, they are able to marshal the firm's resources towards creating superior value for customers. Thus marketing-oriented firms are seen to be innovative, have a strong customer focus, make decisions with reference to competitor activities, have an integrated marketing approach and most of all are able to deliver a high level of economic added value. It is essential therefore that the organization develops and reflects a market-oriented culture and reinforces this with a commitment to learning.

Debriefing Question 3.1

In order to create a learning environment a company needs to:

- Remove the barriers to learning that may exist between departments
- Have a top-management commitment to the process of learning
- Define widely the scope of their learning activities
- Develop mechanisms for leveraging the learning by the company to gain competitive advantage
- Be flexible and be prepared to respond to the learning gained.

Debriefing Activity 3.2

The key indicators identified will vary depending on the characteristics of the market and the type of product/service being offered in that market. They will also vary depending on whether the company is operating in the B2B market or the B2C market and the route to market used by the company. Generally speaking, however, the indicators may include such factors as:

- ○ Macro environmental changes
- ○ Changes in legislation
- ○ Changes in industry/competitive structures
- ○ Changing consumer demographics
- ○ Market segment changes
- ○ Level of customer satisfaction
- ○ Operational efficiency measures
- ○ Level of repeat purchase.

Debriefing Question 3.2

3R learning is an important component of strategic marketing decision-making in that it helps companies to develop the capability to:

- ○ Develop advance knowledge of key events in markets
- ○ Build the flexibility to quickly reconfigure operations and reallocate resources
- ○ Focus on an emergent opportunity
- ○ Identify threats in the environment
- ○ Achieve a rapid response to competitive challenges.

However, in evaluating the role of 3R learning you need to consider the time, resources and expertise required to carry out the role and the possible cost/benefits to an organization. It may be that in a firm with limited financial resources, the role of 3R learning in strategic decision-making takes on a very different character to a much larger organization.

Debriefing Question 3.3

The starting point in answering this question is to reflect on the nature of political decision-making and the possibility that a decision is taken to give the appearance of doing something to respond to criticism from the public and employees in the public sector. Consequently a more up-to-date approach, accompanied by a lot of publicity and speed of action can give the appearance of dynamism. This should be set against a more considered approach which would take into account the various factors affecting the decision. Both signal and 3R learning should be used.

It is essential that the cost of a new initiative is set against its potential stakeholder benefits and value. An assessment needs to be made of the gaps in provision , which the new service aims to fill, and the reductions in costs compared to the existing provision. The delivery of services to those that may not be well-served by the existing services is particularly important. You should evaluate whether this service is useful for the various patient segments, for example, the elderly, those from ethnic minorities and the articulate middle classes.

Debriefing Question 3.4

You should begin by explaining why an understanding of customers and competitors is so important. You should distinguish between direct, indirect and potential competitors; and for each of the different types of competitors, consider the factors that should be considered in your analysis. However, in carrying out such an analysis, it is important to consider that:

- Identification of competitors is closely related to the definition of market boundaries.
- In a global market, it is difficult to ascertain who competitors are and where the future competitive threat is coming from.
- Collecting reliable information on competitor activity is notoriously difficult.
- It is the direction of future competitive activity that it is important to try and anticipate, not past behaviour.

Debriefing Question 3.5

What is happening in the mobile phone industry is not dissimilar to what happened previously in the car industry. To gain cost-efficiencies, companies outsourced a number of operations which brought them huge benefits in terms of their access to markets and the speed of bringing new innovations to market. However, the barriers to enter into the mobile phone market are somewhat less than that of the car industry. As a fashion market, the mobile phone market moves very quickly and it has become increasingly fragmented. Thus, the emerging specialists which have grown up as a result of the outsourcing policies are now looking for ways to grow by themselves and are able to cherry-pick segments in which to compete. Motorola, who outsource 35 per cent of their production, is particularly vulnerable.

Debriefing Activity 3.3

To start this activity you may want to draw up a grid detailing

- Your organization's products and services
- The principal competitors for each of them
- Your own organization's position
- The intensity and the basis of the competitor activity
- The likely new entrants
- The level of similarity between competitors.

Then draw the matrix as illustrated in Figure 3.2 and plot the competitors as to the degree of their resource similarity and market commonality to assess whether they are direct, indirect or potential competitors.

Debriefing Activity 3.4

In completing this activity it may be better if you choose a purchase that involved you in making a number of decisions and where you had a choice of alternatives. Consider when it was that you recognized you had a buying need or a problem that required a solution. Ask yourself how you searched for the relevant information, where you searched for it and what media did you use. Did you search the Internet? Once you had the information, what specific criteria did you use to help you decide amongst the alternatives on offer? Did you rank the alternatives and arrive at a final shortlist? Did you seek advice from other people? If so what sort of people did you consult? How did you reduce the risk of making a wrong decision? Did you seek reassurance after the purchase that the decision made was the correct one?

Debriefing Question 3.6

The major barriers to the integration of knowledge management and learning activities are:

- Lack of involvement of marketing decision-makers in the development of a knowledge management system
- The inability to access relevant information required for decision-making
- Lack of co-operation between departments as to the inputting of relevant information
- Lack of commitment from top management to the integration of knowledge management into decision-making
- The time and resources required to allow integration of the two activities to develop
- Inadequate expertise within the company.

In considering how these may be overcome you may want to refer to the obstacles you have identified and consider possible solutions for each of them.

Debriefing Activity 3.5

For some companies the growth of Internet-based strategies has played a significant role in the way they compete on the marketplace and has impacted on all aspects of the marketing process and the way decisions are made. Other companies simply view the Internet as a medium for them to advertise their products and services. Consider which category your company falls into and think about how this has, or has not, changed their approach to marketing decision-making. You could also consider how the Internet has added value to the various stages of the marketing process and what changes this has brought in the company. You could also consider how the use of the Internet has impacted on the way your customers behave and whether it has meant new and changing demands have been made on the company.

Debriefing Question 3.7

Disintermediation is one of the latest buzzwords. It describes the process by which middlemen in the supply chain are progressively being cut out as companies more and more deal directly with their customers. This is not a trend necessarily started by the Internet but it is a process that has been further stimulated by its growth. By giving companies the capacity to deal direct with customers across geographical boundaries, the need for agents and distributors with local market knowledge has for some industries become much less important. Thus for intermediaries in the supply chain the Internet has been a breakpoint which has meant the traditional basis on which they compete has been made obsolete. Many of these companies, therefore, to survive, have had to reinvent their competitive strategies. In this question you need to discuss the new services being offered by intermediaries and explore the way they have tried to reposition themselves in the market so they can still offer value-added services to traditional customers.

Debriefing Question 3.8

Here is a good example of business failure acting as a catalyst for David Charlton to identify the barriers to escaping the past and building for the future (Hamel and Prahalad), and to recognize that a new set of rules for the game were emerging. He adopted the 3R learning approach and you should explain how this, rather than signal learning, can be used in this situation to identify the new set of rules. The new game rules are needed in response to the drivers from the macro- and microenvironment and particularly the change in customer value and competitive actions.

Debriefing Question 3.9

The key to answering this question is to identify the main elements of the discount retailing model that will indicate when further changes are needed. You should explain how signal learning can contribute to monitoring progress and development and how 3R learning might be used to identify potentially significant changes that may lead to further re-invention of the model.

Unit 4

Debriefing Question 4.1

The starting point is to define technological discontinuities and industry breakpoints, and explain the effect they have on the competitive offerings within a market. You should explain the nature of incremental change in technology and markets, and then discuss the nature and effect of visionary leaps forward. There are a number of reasons for the breakpoints and you should explain how they occur. You should emphasize that many of the reasons for the change in the sector originate from the external environment. Even the breakpoints that are driven by individual companies may be initiated by environmental change, as discussed above.

The marketing strategy of firms in any market should include environmental scanning, and customer and competitive analysis that will anticipate breakpoints and either take advantage of them or prepare a response when competitive products enter the market. The challenge for the firms is to develop the characteristics of a market pioneer or concentrate on being rapidly responsive in order to benefit from opportunities that breakpoints generate.

Debriefing Activity 4.1

You should assess the dimensions of innovation capability including:

- o How generally proactive the firm is, in innovation
- o Whether the firm tends to introduce more, or less, innovations than its competitors
- o An approximate ratio of innovations that succeed compared to those that fail
- o The nature of innovation and whether it tends to create breakthroughs or is continuous incremental change
- o How long it takes to get innovations to market and whether the firm is typically first to the market with new ideas
- o How successfully the organization is able to anticipate customer needs, launch and market the innovation.

You should also make some assessment of where the capability (or lack of) resides: whether it is technologically or marketing based.

Debriefing Activity 4.2

If you are unable to think of an organization or market sector, you may wish to use the case study below.

You should begin by listing the various techniques for opportunity identification and identify some of the sources of innovation that have been discussed. Then go on to assess their advantages and disadvantages in the market and company that you are studying. It is important to distinguish between the types of opportunity because the way that each might be identified and exploited will require a different technique.

Most managers have tried brainstorming, researching customer needs and evaluating complaints, so it might be useful to try the exercise in generating a 'quantum leap in customer benefits'. At first, most managers find this difficult, as the whole basis of the technique is overcoming the industry assumptions and challenging preconceived ideas that familiarity with the industry brings. For this reason you might start by carrying out the technique on a quite different organization first.

Debriefing Activity 4.3

The starting point is to list the stages in the innovation process discussed earlier and then objectively assess the effectiveness of the organization at each stage, for example:

o   Are sufficient ideas encouraged and generated?
o   Is there an effective process for acknowledging ideas and reporting progress back to the initiator?
o   Is there an objective process for assessing ideas?
o   Does the business case contain a realistic assessment of the potential market or is it based purely on (largely hypothetical) financial calculations?

You should then consider whether the whole process is overly bureaucratic and time-consuming and whether or not this is simply a reflection of the culture of the organization. Once you have been through the process, it should then be possible to identify areas where the process could be better managed.

Debriefing Question 4.3

Clearly, the critical factor is achieving fast diffusion of the product or service into the market. But this starts with knowing who the innovators of the diffusion curve in the market are, and what will make them adopt the product right at the start of the innovation process. The same questions can then be applied to the other groups of the diffusion curve. Answers are needed to the following questions:

o   Who are the customers?
o   How many of them can you switch?
o   How quickly (the diffusion curve)?
o   Who needs to be influenced (the customers or the distribution channel)?
o   What are the best routes to market?
o   What are the barriers to introduction that must be overcome?
o   How will competitors react? Will they be a threat?

Debriefing Activity 4.4

Your organization might fall into this category in which case the evidence of a poor record is probably easily obtained but the solutions are more difficult. You should then consider whether the whole process is overly bureaucratic and time-consuming and whether this is simply a reflection of the culture of the organization that needs to be addressed. The actions that you would propose taking should include:

- o The nature and effectiveness of the process
- o The innovation culture within the organization and the absence of a 'blame' culture
- o Developing the firm's capability, for example, in marketing research, technical expertise (where appropriate), project management and marketing promotion.

Debriefing Question 4.4

In answering this question, it is important to start by explaining the market context and whether it is a fast-growth sector, before going on to explain the nature of the company and how it gained success in the market. You should analyse where the innovations come from, how they are supported within the company and the extent to which the drive for innovation comes from the owner or chief executive.

In thinking about the future, you must decide whether the factors that have generated success to date will be the same ones that will deliver success in the future.

Debriefing Question 4.5

The diffusion curve provides the basic concept of spreading new products into the market through persuading successive segments of the market that a product and service solves a problem and fulfils a need. It seems to be quite clear that third generation phones seemed to be a technology looking for an application that would appeal and be useful to customers. It has taken some time and substantial discounting for the mass of the market to be prepared to purchase the product. There was a lack of services that were needed to provide the customer solutions and this should be explained.

In the case of the Internet consumer purchasing, the marketers appear not to have fully educated customers about the benefits and reassured them about the risks of buying in this way. There is considerable interest amongst the computer literate consumers and this has led to the success of companies such as e-Bay.

Debriefing Question 4.6

The marketing aims reflect the vision of the Eden project and particularly the personal vision of Tim Smit. This requires some discussion before the objectives and then be articulated in terms of meeting a number of different criteria, including financial requirements, value for visitors, organization sustainability, continued employment and business for local suppliers, as well as the environmental sustainability and education issues.

Debriefing Question 4.7

At Eden, there are some conflicting stakeholder expectations and these can be spelled out by evaluating the stakeholder in turn. It is necessary to explain how, in these circumstances, decisions might be taken but, more importantly, implemented with some sensitivity to individual stakeholders so as to manage stakeholders rather than alienate them. The criteria for decision-making need to be explained in such a way that the stakeholders that are adversely affected might at least understand the reasoning behind the decisions.

Debriefing Question 4.8

Some creativity is needed to suggest ways in which the lessons and good practice might be exploited. In part 1 of the answer (within Cornwall), some explanation of the benefit of network marketing, the use of 'exemplar projects' and 'spin off' benefits to the wider community might be discussed. In part 2, some discussion of exploiting the capability, expertise and knowledge being built could provide some structure to the answer. Refer to the resource-based view of marketing.

Unit 5

Debriefing Question 5.1

You should decide if the management's claims that the reasons were unexpected and outside their control were correct, or if the reasons given were a change in customer demand or the emergence of new competition. If this is the case then you should decide if the management should have foreseen the changes and reacted to them.

Use the factors discussed above as a checklist in making your judgement. What should the management have done to protect themselves? For example, was the cause ultimately a weakness in their marketing information system and poor environmental scanning?

Debriefing Activity 5.1

The factors that are discussed at the start of this unit provide a checklist for carrying out the evaluation. You should then prioritize the factors in terms of the level of probability and the likely effect they would have on the firm's performance. You should think about the external factors, such as the potential changes to the market sector, and decide whether the organization is capable of responding to changes and managing the new situation.

In assessing risk, again, there are external factors, such as customers move elsewhere, competitors become much more powerful or the structure of the market changes to exclude the business, and these will have an effect on every aspect of the marketing strategy but there are also internal management issues, such as the inability of the organization to respond to external factors as fast as competitors.

Debriefing Question 5.2

For IBM a main benefit is realizing financial and management resources from an underperforming area of business so that they can be focused on the new direction and opportunities. The challenge is to demonstrate the wisdom of this move by showing improvements in profitability and Return of Capital Employed (ROCE) and so on. There are a number of threats including narrowing the customer base from the consumer into the business market, reducing the portfolio and the loss of synergy between the PC division and the remainder of the business.

For Lenovo this is an opportunity to establish a strong global presence and improve its financial and marketing performance. The threats include the market not proving to be as buoyant as it has been, competition forcing prices down further or new innovations changing the balance between suppliers. A specific challenge for Lenovo is to effectively integrate the two parts of the business and benefit from the potential synergies.

Debriefing Activity 5.2

The strategy definitions and criteria for success provide a checklist for answering this question. However, it is important to try to take an objective view of the situation in order to focus future actions more effectively and so consider the checklist in the light of the competitive market situation. In thinking what action can be taken to achieve future success, you need to consider not only the strategy itself but also the implications for communication of the strategy internally as well as externally, and you might obtain some additional ideas from Unit 9.

Debriefing Activity 5.3

It is easy to simply jump to conclusions about whether the strategy is a cost, focus or differentiation strategy, but you need to decide first what the intended generic strategy is and then how well it is being implemented. You should list the criteria that characterize the generic strategies and then look for evidence from the organization's actions as to which is being followed. Today most firms will claim to be following a cost containment strategy, in addition to clear focus or differentiation. You should use the evidence to decide what is correct.

Debriefing Question 5.3

The introduction should start by explaining that segmentation is a concept that underpins the marketing strategy; and that to be effective, it requires a deep understanding of customers. Using the appropriate bases of segmentation it is possible to develop a targeting and positioning strategy that enables the marketing mix to be developed, which is distinctive from competitor offerings. By developing a hierarchy of segmentation, an international marketing strategy can be developed that achieves economies of scale and experience. You might contrast a transnational segmentation approach with the deficiencies of a country-by-country approach.

Debriefing Question 5.4

The introduction should begin with an explanation of the traditional approaches to segmentation in the B2B markets and an explanation of the typical bases used. Strategies are changing in the B2B market and you should take into account the factors that are affecting them to explain more innovative ways of market segmentation before explaining the implications for targeting and positioning. In the case of B2B markets, which are driven by Internet developments, the segmentation might also drive the business model used, or the business model might self select the target segments.

Debriefing Question 5.5

You should explain the characteristics of the different marketing approaches, expanding upon the material detailed above and provide examples from different sectors, including not-for-profit and international marketing examples. It is necessary to provide some insights into the types of organizations that adopt these approaches and the examples should help in the identification of competitive advantage. It is important to provide a clear explanation of the resource-based view of firms, focusing on assets and competencies.

Debriefing Question 5.6

Both of these developments are incremental changes intended to maintain revenue growth for Apple between the industry breakpoints (such as after the introduction of iPod and iTunes, the music download service). More importantly, however, Apple is aiming to target another segment of customers that want Apple products but are unwilling or unable to pay the price of the existing products.

Clearly, there are dangers of cannibalization, brand and price erosion of the Apple products but the potential benefit of widening the number of Apple users outweighs this. Moreover, continuing to build the 'added value' product range will ensure that the firm is seen to be introducing products at the leading edge of technology, rather than simply 'dumbing down' a successful product.

Debriefing Activity 5.4

Using the additional reading, you should assess the organization in terms of one of these categories. In practice, you might find that different strategic business units are in different positions in the market. You should decide if the organization is proactive and has made a conscious decision to adopt a particular stance (even to be a follower), in which case you will see plenty of evidence of one of the categories. You may find that the picture is confusing with evidence of inconsistencies in the company's stance. You should then try to work out which competitive marketing strategy (attacking and defensive) it is pursuing and again you might find inconsistencies in the strategy, in which case you might decide if this is an intended or an emergent strategy.

Debriefing Question 5.7

Given the nature of the process and the importance of convincing the voting committee members, it is important in your answer to address the factors that will influence their decision. This will include rational factors, such as financial arrangement, security, transport, completion on time, attractiveness of the venue. It also includes very subjective factors too, such as relationships, influences – even meeting celebrities! You might then go on to discuss in detail the balance between areas in the bid for innovation – to create excitement and interest for spectators and a lasting Olympic legacy, and the rather more mundane elements that will demonstrate the ability to deliver on time and on budget.

Debriefing Question 5.8

To answer this question, it is necessary to separate clearly between the two elements. There is a need to create a vision that will attract and mobilize the innovators in the diffusion curve. Often they have to use marketing processes and integrated communications to respond to those that doubt the wisdom or the country's capacity for taking on such a project. It is necessary to promote the message and also build up a marketing network of stakeholders that supports and is committed to the project. Of course, the individual members of the network need to be convinced of the benefits they will receive.

A discussion of planning will highlight the systematic approach that is necessary for managing a project of this size. The process should be explained and examples of the activities and their timing discussed. Following the experiences of recent Olympics an explanation should be included of how marketing can help in risk management and control.

Unit 6

Debriefing Activity 6.1

You should decide to what degree the organization is already exploiting the opportunities that globalization offers and protecting itself from the threats. Is the organization robust against global competitors and what might it do to better exploit the opportunities and deal with the threats?

Debriefing Question 6.1

This requires a presentation of the arguments for standardization, including:

- o Economies of scale
- o The experience curve effect
- o The increase in customer value of a consistent image and brand
- o The advantages of a simpler planning process.

And then, an explanation of the reasons why products are adapted to local needs, including:

- o Legislation, such as health and safety and promotion
- o Cultural and usage factors
- o The lack of 'buy in' to the standard product by local managers.

Debriefing Question 6.2

Start off by listing the methods and outline the characteristics then explain how the following criteria will affect the choice at each stage:

- o Existing company operations and resources
- o Existing foreign market involvement
- o Management expertise and attitudes to internationalization
- o Nature and size of competition
- o Legal, tariff and non-tariff
- o The nature of the market and the products and services.

You should also give some thought to any scope for more innovative (e.g. e-commerce) approaches and explain the reasons for including them.

Debriefing Activity 6.2

There will be fairly obvious reasons why the majority of the elements are adapted but you should pick two or three examples where you think that the arguments for adaptation are less clear and try to determine whether the justification was really market based or whether it was a fairly arbitrary management decision. In the areas of standardization, check whether there is market 'logic' for it or whether it is a head office dictating!

Debriefing Question 6.3

Markets are changing ever faster because of:

- ○ Rapid changes in fashion, consumer attitudes
- ○ Changes in the environment: technology, the economic situation and legislation
- ○ Shorter product life cycles and faster copying by competitors
- ○ More rapid innovations and new product introductions.

The implications are that the traditional systems are:

- ○ Too slow, as the environment has changed by the time the plan is ready for implementation
- ○ Too many activities and people are involved in the process
- ○ Unresponsive as too much data is collected
- ○ General and unresponsive to specific situations
- ○ Ineffective in their feedback and control mechanisms.

Improve the process by better use of:

- ○ Marketing information systems
- ○ Environmental scanning and expert knowledge
- ○ Benchmarking and best practice
- ○ Emergent strategies facilitated by a 'top-down' strategy and 'bottom-up' local action.

Debriefing Question 6.4

It is important to explain the various global strategy options: multi-domestic, regional and global; and then how these strategies can be used in a complementary way in a transnational firm. You should focus on the segmentation approaches, which are quite different between the approaches. You should then go on to explain the competencies in terms of global efficiency and competitiveness, local sensitivity and global learning.

Debriefing Question 6.5

At the moment, many universities and colleges are operating a simplistic product-push strategy (see Unit 5). Others are more service oriented and are attempting to move on from that into a more customer-led marketing strategy. However, both these strategies are short term and fail to address the changing nature of the environment, competition and customer expectation in the market.

A more fundamental review is required to decide a longer-term sustainable international marketing strategy. For different institutions in various different situations resource-based, entrepreneurial and network marketing approaches may offer more substantial benefits, particularly in terms of identifying the most appropriate market entry strategies and marketing mix offer to potential students. You should reflect on where students are expecting to gain value from the experience, including the living in a new location, gaining exposure to a new culture, mixing with others from different nationalities, the quality of the learning experience, the course content, the possibility and experience of working in the host country, and overall value for money from the expenditure incurred.

Debriefing Activity 6.3

You should regard the model as a continuum between exporting and niche international marketing, and assess the overall pattern that emerges, as this is a reflection of the company's attitude to international marketing as well as strategy.

It is likely that some functions or business units within the organization will operate rather differently from others. Probably what would be more revealing is assessing the organization on a periodic basis to see how it is progressing.

Debriefing Activity 6.4

What is important to remember is that informal learning through reflection on practice, good or bad and using informal information networks can be extremely powerful for more entrepreneurial firms. They are quite willing to experiment on the basis of new information and adapt if things do not go exactly right.

Equally important if the firm is at an early stage of internationalization is whether the firm is progressing quickly to the next level of internationalization and becoming more proactive.

Unit 7

Debriefing Activity 7.1

You should base your assessment on evidence rather than an instinctive feel. You should see what pattern emerges from the evidence as it may show that an organization behaves differently in different market sectors (or it may behave exactly the same). You might find that certain competitors are becoming more proactive and the evidence of this that you identify may well provide a strong indication of their future priorities, intentions and even what their future strategies are likely to be.

You might also consider whether the proactive competitors show the characteristics of fast growth, which now follow, and whether they will be able to sustain any potential lead they might gain.

Debriefing Activity 7.2

Remember that the organization should be seeking to deliver a memorable customer experience that will ensure that that organization is the first choice for future purchases. You should begin by drawing a flow chart of the various interactions between customers and the organization throughout the purchasing and consumption process. At each interaction, you should examine the criteria that will determine whether the customer is disappointed or entirely satisfied. You should think about what pattern emerges from this and decide what should be the focus for improvements. You could make a start by thinking about the three service Ps, any gaps between the customer expectations set and the quality of delivery through staff–customer interactions, and the process that customers are taken through.

You should then decide if the organization has a customer service strategy. To check whether a strategy is being enthusiastically implemented use an assessment based on Table 7.1.

Debriefing Question 7.1

A number of characteristics of fast growth are included in this unit and it is useful to group them under a number of headings such as:

- o Market awareness
- o Speed and focus in new opportunity identification and exploitation
- o Recognition of the nature and source of competitive advantage and a recognition of the importance of marketing innovation
- o A focus on creating customer value
- o The attitude and ambition of the organization.

Using some examples from fast-growth organizations will help to identify the key factors.

You should then consider each of the factors and explain the difficulty each presents for larger, more administratively (rather than entrepreneurially) managed organizations.

Debriefing Question 7.2

You should begin by explaining the nature of fast growth and draw a distinction between early stage development and then maintaining growth as the organization matures. Figures 7.4 and 7.5 provide the basis for a discussion of the early stages of fast growth development. You should then go on to explain how organizations can generate fast growth in sectors that have reached the mature phase of the life cycle. Clearly there may or may not be the opportunity for a breakthrough, discussed in Unit 4. If there is no possibility of visionary leaps forward, then the approaches discussed earlier in this unit and particularly improving the customer management process to provide exceptional customer value can be the competitive advantage driver and lead to fast growth. Again, you should think of organizations in a mature market that have increased market share at the expense of the competition.

Debriefing Question 7.3

Clearly, the timing of Sony's entry was right, but the main factor was achieving a breakpoint in the industry by adopting a strategy that makes the product desirable for a new customer segment and then building further incremental growth through targeting new segments and supplying new innovative designs for games.

To achieve fast growth, it is essential to create a 'cool brand' that becomes part of popular culture and serve the market with interesting, challenging and technically innovative products.

Debriefing Activity 7.3

You should avoid undertaking this activity in a relatively superficial way unless the organization has already reflected on its position and already carried out a full re-evaluation of its products and services and defined its future source of competitive advantage. If this has not been done then you should think about the way you have classified the products and services. You should take a market perspective (customer and competitive viewpoints) and not fall into the trap of focusing on products and services alone (and especially products that are easy to make). You should focus on what customers will want in the future – solutions that they value, not simply products and services. You can then identify the types of knowledge, competencies and assets that will be needed to exploit future opportunities, without defining them precisely in terms of specific products.

For example, your markets may become more volatile, in which case the ability to respond to new opportunities and withdraw from yesterday's successes may be critical. In this case, the organization must become more flexible, adaptable and responsive.

Debriefing Question 7.4

A number of the previous activities provide the background to answering this question and you should list the good practice lessons that you have already identified from companies that have succeeded in the past and are succeeding now, and you should add some examples. You should then think about the sources of competitive advantage that have been highlighted before deciding which of these will be important in the future. You should then use the list of possible areas of knowledge for competitive advantage discussed above to identify what will be important in the industry that you have selected.

Debriefing Activity 7.4

It is essential to critically analyse the reasons for visiting the sites, think about exactly what the customer is looking for and whether this can be better obtained from other websites or alternative information sources. It is useful to assess other sites before concentrating on your organization's site. The use of the customer management process characteristics provides a checklist to assess satisfaction. In thinking about innovation, you should decide whether the improvements are genuinely innovative, enhancing the application of existing good practice or simply applying technology for no real customer or company benefit.

Debriefing Question 7.5

This is a straightforward question that requires the advantages and disadvantages to be listed from different viewpoints, including the buyer, seller and supply-chain leader. You should comment on the different situations, such as using hubs for core and peripheral components and services, simple and complex purchasing situations and the consequences of successful suppliers putting out of business less successful companies.

In explaining the characteristics of the companies that are likely to be successful you should focus on both the 'hard' issues, such as systems, organizations and operational efficiency and then discuss the importance of 'soft' issues, such as organizational skills, knowledge and capability, management style and the overall culture, given the need to be quicker to respond to new opportunities and challenges.

Debriefing Question 7.6

Should Perez go for consolidation or are innovative marketing strategies needed again?

- o Set the trends with a new product
- o Further build the 'cult' following
- o Public relations to build brand awareness
- o Seek out new sub-segments
- o Attack the London market.

Also Perez might decide what size of business it should be, but whatever happens he should maintain the lean, tight organization.

Unit 8

Debriefing Question 8.1

The answer requires an explanation of the role that branding plays in the purchasing decision for customers and the value proposition made to customers by organizations. It is important to discuss the nature of intangible benefit and the contribution of attribute branding to this, especially in areas where customers are unable to assess the quality and specification of products and services themselves and have to rely on the brand to provide the assurance. Aspirational and experience branding also deliver benefits in other customer situations and these should be explained. Examples should be provided to reinforce the points made.

It might be useful to refer to research (de Chernatony, 2001) amongst consultants that highlighted different interpretations of 'brand':

- The input perspectives: logo, legal instrument, company, shorthand, risk reducer, positioning, personality, cluster of values, vision, adding value and identity
- The output perspectives: image and relationship
- The time perspective: the evolving identity.

Debriefing Activity 8.1

Question 8.1 provides the starting point for this activity but you should then move on to the list above entitled 'specific benefits to the organization' and use these criteria to assess the brands.

From the research quoted, the atomic model of the brand is proposed by de Chernatony (2001) as a planning approach to branding. In that he suggests that the brand essence consists of a distinctive name, sign of ownership, functional capabilities, service component, risk reducer, legal protection, shorthand notation and symbolic feature and these might be used for evaluating the organization's brands.

Debriefing Activity 8.2

You should start by contrasting the customer's view of the brand with the organization's view (by asking them) and decide whether or not the organization is 'milking' the brand and stretching it inappropriately over too many dissimilar products or investing and building the brand through effective portfolio and communications management.

Debriefing Question 8.2

In addressing the purpose of rationalization, it is important to explain the need to use scarce resources effectively and provide the contrasting arguments that might be offered for and against rationalization. It is necessary to use the portfolio analysis tools referred to earlier to make the case for retaining or rationalizing products but you should also refer to other parts of the marketing mix and portfolio dependencies. For example, we have listed some reasons why loss-making products might be retained and these include: the potential damage to communications; more effective use of distribution channels; and recovery of overheads.

Debriefing Activity 8.3

Use your answers to Activity 8.2 and Question 8.2 as a basis for evaluation based on value addition.

Debriefing Question 8.3

The introduction to the answer should include an explanation of the management of the service elements in the banking situation and how services differ in different markets. Against the background of the difficulties of managing services and, for example, the need to provide tangible evidence it is necessary to explain the standardization and adaptation issues.

- o Physical evidence such as corporate identity, branches, Internet capability
- o People such as staff, advisers, and so on and different response to and expectations of service
- o Processes such as how customers are managed, their experience in dealing with the bank and the supporting 'back office' processes
- o You should also refer to any relevant 4P issues such as advertising and promotion campaigns and the range of products.

You should then go on to explain how competitive advantage can be built through an understanding of the various markets and routes to market, the different products and processes that are needed, interest rates and the knowledge and capabilities of the staff.

Debriefing Question 8.4

The starting point with new product development is to identify clear benefits and additional customer value that can be offered by the new products. At launch, this must be followed through with clear and distinctive positioning that is understandable for customers. In the example given in the case, it seems that the new C2 product was not sufficiently distinctive and was confused with promotions of the regular product.

It is essential too to have real customer insights and understand customer motivations. The Dasani launch in the UK failed because of differences between the US and UK culture relating to the concept of 'pure', which is interpreted in the US as chemically pure rather than in the UK where pure is interpreted as natural. Of course, the apparent contamination simply exacerbated the problem.

In large organizations, there can be corporate arrogance, and the idea that the senior managers know best and can make any new innovations work.

Debriefing Activity 8.4

You should start by taking a period of, say the previous 2 years, and list the projects that have been started, been launched and achieved commercial success. You should think about not just the major products but also the line extensions and product upgrades. If you were able to do it, it would be useful to compare at least the number of successes of your competitors too.

You should think about what pattern emerges from this, particularly in the light of the investment that is made, and think about what aspect of the process is being done well and what not so well. For example, you may wish to think about the effectiveness of outsourced services as well as in-house activity.

Debriefing Question 8.5

You should use the section headings in this unit to provide a checklist for your work on the portfolio, but you should supplement this with additional areas outside this unit including, for example, customer requirements, branding, communications, supply chain and distribution.

Debriefing Question 8.6

The introduction might start by explaining the concepts behind Unilever's strategy and comparing it with other strategies in the industry, for example that of Nestle and Heinz.

One way to answer this question is to carry out a brief situation analysis, including environmental analysis (PEST), changes in customers, competition and the market structure. This might include the globalization drivers and focus on converging customer needs. You should then consider the internal management issues and particularly opportunity cost of management of local brands against global brands.

Debriefing Question 8.7

This is a classic example of whether the strategy has been given enough time to work, so one option is to do nothing.

Other options include focusing returns and shareholder value, further acquisitions and further rationalization of underperforming products. You might add some more. In assessing the advantages and disadvantages of each strategy, you should identify the criteria that you might use to make the decision.

Unit 9

Debriefing Activity 9.1

You should take the viewpoint of the customer and list all the messages received, including the direct and indirect communications, then again compare what you think the customer might be expecting and what they receive. Where appropriate you might undertake a survey to find out exactly what their impressions are. You should particularly take notice to see if the communications are integrated or sent out separately.

Debriefing Activity 9.2

In carrying out this activity, consider the intended and unintended messages, the formal and informal communications, process, people and content problems, the controllable and uncontrollable elements. Think particularly about the physical aspects, appearances and locations that made an impression on you (good or bad).

Think about how many of the negative communications would require better discipline and management, better training or more substantial changes that require significant investment.

Debriefing Question 9.1

The introduction should start with a definition of integrated marketing communications that emphasizes the need to put the customer at the heart of the communications, and to assess the communications from the customer perspective.

The communications come from all parts of the marketing mix and include every intended and unintended interaction. Using examples, the communication problems and failures can then be explained. Methods to improve the integration can be discussed, including customer relationship management.

Debriefing Question 9.2

The important thing to note here is that a plan is not needed, but a planning framework would be useful, as this would highlight the areas where decisions would be needed. Whilst decisions would be needed for each section of the plan, you may decide that certain factors will be critical in the decision such as the available budget, location and competition. It would also be important to know which customer segment should be targeted and by which media.

Debriefing Question 9.3

The first question for the Soil Association must be what kind of organization it wants to be. To increase membership by the numbers suggested, it needs to take a more proactive approach to marketing and, through integrated communications, explain the short- and long-term benefits for its members and the community in general. The individual (short-term) campaigns will then mutually reinforce a broader-based long-term strategy.

In doing this, the Soil Association must question whether its name provides the right fit with its objectives and consider establishing a new brand, if necessary. The key task will be to fully understand the perceptions and expectations of its various stakeholders and ensure that its brand and future communications fit with them.

Debriefing Question 9.4

The important thing with this question is to explain the importance of setting clear objectives for the use of any communications tool and how it might be used within an integrated communications strategy. Explain the advantages and disadvantages, and where its use might be inappropriate. Finally, identify the generic criteria for communications evaluation and explain how the tools deliver against these criteria.

Debriefing Activity 9.3

The following checklist might start your evaluation:

- Communication objectives delivered
- Contribution to marketing strategy (integration)
- Efficiency and value for money
- Message effectiveness
- Success with the target audience
- Impact on other audiences
- Communication tool/media effectiveness
- Was success quantified?

     o Was process effective and efficient?
     o Could it have been done a different/better way?

Then you should decide what was learned from the campaign. Finally you should think about what would have been lost if the communication had not been used and whether this could be justified as an investment, rather than an expenditure.

Debriefing Question 9.5

The concept of relationship marketing is based on the idea that both sides, customer and supplier, benefit from the relationship, but it is often the supplier that pushes the 'relationship'. You should explain when relationship marketing works well (e.g. B2B and certain types of retailing) and when it works less well (e.g. FMCG). The critical success factors can then be listed and an explanation given of how CRM might deliver these. There are a number of reasons why CRM has not always worked. Often CRM installations are technology-led rather than customer-led and, because relationship marketing demands a different philosophy, organizations have not developed and implemented suitable strategies to make it work.

Debriefing Activity 9.4

It is important to assess the level of resource put into each relationship and decide if it is appropriate to the value the relationship is expected to deliver. Very often, organizations put considerable effort into developing close relationships with stakeholders that are not influential or have little power and fail to invest in more important relationships. Because it is difficult, they fail to develop the most important relationships. Moreover, you might question whether some of your relationships are one sided and therefore are not relationships according to the definition.

Debriefing Question 9.6

Oxfam has to focus on delivering its mission and objectives as effectively as possible so that it is recognized for giving value to its stakeholders. You should consider the strategic marketing decisions that are needed to manage the expectations and contributions of each of its key stakeholders. You should particularly focus on the types of innovation that are required to secure support, and financial and human resources to enable it to carry out its work. In doing this, you should think about how it can embrace the latest marketing and operations processes to add value and become more efficient in the use of resources. The greater use of the Internet and collaborative working are two obvious areas.

Debriefing Question 9.7

The demands on Oxfam continue to increase as the consequences of war and natural disasters require ever-greater resources to put right. Oxfam also works in an increasing glare of publicity that surrounds war and disasters with the media seeking sensational news stories rather than sticking to reporting tragedies. To continue to be able to carry out its essential work Oxfam has to operate in an exemplary and professional manner throughout its operations. This includes effective management of its marketing and communications activity and the challenges that are posed in doing this, including providing examples of the ethical issues that need to be addressed.

Unit 10

Debriefing Activity 10.1

First, list in detail the value chain contributions and the role of your own organization within it. Define the activities or interfaces carefully as they are now and specify exactly what value is obtained and at what relative cost. Think carefully about whether this offers value for money and consider whether the contributions are both appropriate now and relevant in the future market. Think particularly of issues such as response time, constraints, duplication, flexibility, complaints and feedback of information.

Debriefing Activity 10.2

The key decision areas in setting up or reassessing the channel include the (re)formulation of the channel strategy, designing the channel structure after considering the options, selecting channel members, motivating and managing the channel members, coordinating the channel strategy with the marketing mix and evaluating channel member performance. Measurement should include comparative costs and sales of different channels, qualitative and quantitative assessment of channel members and customer satisfaction.

Debriefing Question 10.1

The answer should build on the explanation earlier in the text and list the key drivers of the three approaches as well as the advantages and disadvantages. By using examples, it is possible to provide detailed explanation of the different strategies and challenges posed in each sector. Consider B2B, B2C and different market sectors. To do this, you should refer to other units and the additional reading.

Debriefing Question 10.2

The answer should start with an explanation of the limitations of SMEs in international markets, and the problems of entering markets, including their lack of resources, market knowledge and expertise. It is then necessary to outline the concepts of the market entry alternatives in relation to SMEs and the criteria that might be used to choose between the options.

The alternatives are direct entry methods, including e-commerce, or indirect including the use of intermediaries (agents and distributors), the use of partnerships or licensing. The specific advantages and disadvantages for SMEs should be explained.

In ensuring that customers receive a satisfactory offer, firms should recognize the importance of adapting to local needs, cultural sensitivity if using these methods, in adapting the product/ service mix.

Debriefing Question 10.3

The introduction should include a definition of different forms of partnership and their use in the global market. Typically for a major project no single partner has the necessary technology, marketing and financial capability. Moreover, the risk of failure is often too great for a single organization.

Advantages include:

o Reduction through sharing of market/product risk
o Synergy of combined skills and capabilities
o Delivery of complex project with different requirements
o Complementary marketing, technological and financial assets and competencies
o Filling resource and skills gaps.

Disadvantages include:

o Conflict of interests
o Cultural differences
o Different and changing levels of interest of the partners
o Difficulties of management and lack of clear decision-making
o Giving away competitive advantage and secrets.

Debriefing Activity 10.3

This level of cost reduction requires the elimination of some activities, possibly by outsourcing, and benefiting from economies of scale and the experience effect. It might be possible to take an entirely radical approach, such as yield management:

o Greater labour efficiency
o Work specialization and methods improvement
o New production processes
o Better performance from existing equipment
o Changes to resource mix
o Greater product standardization
o Faster product redesigns
o Process standardization.

Debriefing Question 10.4

The problems include:

o Difficulties in keeping international markets separate
o Grey marketing/parallel importing
o Commoditization of brands
o Sustaining a competitive advantage
o Low entry barriers
o Monitoring fragmented competition.

The opportunities include:

o Huge cost savings through removing intermediaries
o The ease of response to random requests
o The ease of processing orders
o JIT and reduced stockholding.

Achieving global competitive advantages are through:

o Transnational segments
o Low-cost market entry opportunities

- o Closer and cost-effective global communications through supply chain
- o Intranets for tendering and global sourcing
- o Development of integrated supply chain
- o Competing the supply chain
- o Creating worldwide call centres
- o Impact on the time element in logistics.

Debriefing Question 10.5

An analysis of TESCO's competitive advantage should provide the basis on which to build in the new sector. The firm has been exceptionally successful in adding customer value and managing its costs, so offering customers attractive prices. Customers are satisfied with the quality of food products and increasingly with non-food items which account for £7 billion sales across the group. Profitability has doubled to £2.1 billion in the last 5 years demonstrating the efficiency of its logistics and retailing operation.

There are a number of decision areas, including the branding strategy, range of products to be stocked, locations and market entry strategy. After a downturn in customer demand, a number of competitors in the non-food sector are performing poorly and may be suitable acquisition targets for TESCO.

Debriefing Activity 10.4

This activity is either going to be very quick or rather slow. The organization might adopt a very simple cost-plus or competitor matching approach, so ignoring most of the factors, or the approach is more considered.

The more offensive approach can be considered in two stages, first, the market considerations of customer and competitor factors. You should then consider the portfolio integration issues (Table 10.3) as potential sources of additional customer value and the possibility to increase prices.

Debriefing Question 10.6

The starting point is to consider the environmental factors that will affect the business. Then it is necessary work out whether one of the two business models will be preferred and whether this will quickly become a 'commodity' business in which the lowest price supplier will always win or whether there will be other factors that might add customer value. You should therefore consider the package of benefits for the consumer. Once this has been completed then the extended organization should be considered and, particularly, the value that could be created in the supply chain (both tangible, such as combining hardware and software, and intangible, such as brand associations) through the co-operation of one or more partners.

Debriefing Question 10.7

You should first identify some key issues here before discussing the players. A brief environmental and market analysis would be useful in explaining the history of pirate websites and the legal situation before explaining the changing customer needs and expectations. You should then explore the marketing mix factors (branding, technology and access) and some partnership issues as there are some interdependencies here that may or may not be critical. Finally you should discuss pricing in more detail before making your own judgement about the potential winners and why (innovation, power, influence, 'cool brand' etc.).

Unit 11

Debriefing Activity 11.1

To start this activity you will need to find out the operating profit, the total capital employed and the sales turnover.

Then:

- profit margin = profit/sales
- ROCE = Estimated profit before interest and tax/capital employed.

Debriefing Question 11.1

You need to calculate profit/sales turnover in percentage

A 6 per cent

B 20 per cent

C 25 per cent

Debriefing Activity 11.2

The company could perhaps use a range of techniques: break-even analysis, Discounted cash flow projections and the calculation of the projected ROCE.

Before an investment project in marketing is undertaken, the company must attempt to establish the financial viability of the project. This means estimating the probable return from the investment, the potential increase in profits or for that matter the potential reduction in costs. Any investment must create value: The purpose of investment appraisal is to assess the likely value by:

- Forecasting the results of potential projects
- Financially evaluating potential projects
- Financially controlling the development of the project
- Carrying out a post-decision audit, to assess performance against the estimates made.

Debriefing Question 11.2

Smaller players need to consider how they are going to compete in what is forecast to be a deflationary pricing cycle. They perhaps need to consider developing a more flexible supply-chain sourcing on a more global scale. In building a business case you need to consider the tools and techniques you would use to evaluate the options you identify. In this, you will also need to consider the pricing architecture the company has and how they can use their pricing strategy to deliver economic added value.

Debriefing Question 11.3

(a) Contribution per unit = Selling price − Variable cost

$$= £60 - 42$$
$$= £18$$

(b) Break-even in units $= \dfrac{\text{Fixed costs}}{\text{Contribution}}$

$$= \dfrac{£900}{£18} = 50 \text{ units}$$

(c) Break-even + profit $= \dfrac{£900 + £360}{£18} = 70 \text{ units}$

(d) Volume of sales to give a net profit of 20 per cent
£60 Selling price ×.20 = £12 per unit profit
Contribution per unit to fixed overheads = Contribution − profit margin

$$= £18 - £12$$
$$= £6$$

Break-even with 20 per cent profit $= \dfrac{£900}{£6} = 150 \text{ units}$

(e) Net profit if 80 units sold = (Expected sales − Break-even volume) × Contribution

$$= (80 - 15 \text{ units}) \times £18$$
$$= £540 \text{ profit}$$

(f) Increase in variable costs £42 + £4 = £46

Reduction in fixed costs £900 − £340 $= \dfrac{£560}{£46}$

Break-even $= 40 \text{ units}$

(g) Selling price per unit for sales of 200 units to give a £700 profit
Variable cost = £900 ÷ 200 units = £42.00
Fixedcosts = £900 ÷ 200 units = £4.50
Profit = £700 ÷ 200 units = £3.50
Selling price = £50.00

Debriefing Activity 11.3

You need to ask what cash flow forecasting took place. Did the company use break-even analysis? What financial ratios were calculated? You also could investigate the ways they evaluated the impact of the change. What method of costing was used, marginal or absorption?

Debriefing Question 11.4

The current situation is that the company has a profit margin of 6 per cent and the capital employed is £18K. This means their current ROCE is 6/18 × 100 = 33 per cent.

In making the changes the profit would be 10 per cent × £150K = £15K. The increased capital figure is now 18K + 50K, therefore the ROCE is 15/68 × 100 = 22 per cent.

Debriefing Question 11.5

A range of ratios could be used by Ryanair. Consider the ratios outlined in this unit for evaluating profit, sales and operations. Which of these can be applied to the airline industry? You should also be able to think of other ratios that have particular relevance to the airline industry. Further detailed information on performance ratios can be found in Chapter 4, Doole and Lowe, *Strategic Marketing Decisions in Global Markets*, Thomson Learning.

Debriefing Activity 11.4

A ratio takes two variables (e.g. profit/sales) and compares them with other measures for the same variable. In assessing marketing performance a variety of financial ratios may be used, such as profitability, ROCE, revenue/sales personnel, revenue/advertising budget, contribution per sales call, average mileage per sales, contribution by customer/market segment. Essentially, the ratios used will vary from firm to firm depending on the critical success factors identified and the key operational performance measures the company wishes to assess.

Debriefing Question 11.6

Variance analysis is a control device used to assess performance against budgets and standards set. For instance, if the forecasted sales budget is $500K but the actual sales turnover achieved is $460K, the sales variance is $40K. On its own, this gives little information and so the actual price achieved, and the volume achieved will also be examined. The variance to the budgeted forecasts will help to identify the reasons for the sales variance.

Unit 12

Debriefing Activity 12.1

The critical success factors identified may well be financial as well as non-financial measures and capable of giving the company key insights to the important measures indicating their level of performance in key areas. Identifying such factors will enable the company to develop an efficient and effective methodology to control and evaluate marketing programmes.

Debriefing Question 12.1

There are many barriers a company may face in measuring and evaluating performance. The most significant are:

- The environment in which the company operated is too complex to monitor efficiently
- The set up costs, in terms of finance and time, are difficult resources
- Internal departmental resistance
- Lack of appropriate information system to facilitate the monitoring and evaluation.

You need then to suggest ways in which companies can overcome such barriers. The discussion should include such factors as, commitment from the top, wide participative discussions with departments, identification of critical success factors, relating the mechanism for measuring performance to the reward system in the company and so on.

Debriefing Question 12.2

You need to start by considering the specific measures you see as appropriate for a service company such as the Royal Mail. As you can see from the text, a Balanced Scorecard incorporates four perspectives. Construct a scorecard which will give the company a balanced view of the four perspectives. You need to consider how far this will allow the company to evaluate the factors that will be important in beating overseas competition.

Debriefing Activity 12.2

Does your company use a Balanced Scorecard approach? You could look at what measures they use in each of the categories and where they place highest priority. Is it in the financial or non-financial measures? Perhaps you could make a judgement as to whether you think the system used by your company enables it to obtain a balanced view of the organization or are there particular problems they face in the collection of the data for the analysis?

Debriefing Question 12.3

You would need to start the answer to such a question by introducing the specific company on which you are going to base the Balanced Scorecard to enable the examiner to understand the context of your answer. The Balanced Scorecard consists of four parts, the financial perspective, the customer perspective, the internal business perspective and the learning perspective. However, within each of those parts the specific measure you choose to use is up to you. They must, however, be relevant to the context and you must show the examiner why you think they are appropriate to the company you have specified. Thus, the application of the techniques in this question is critical.

Debriefing Activity 12.3

Think widely when considering the stakeholders and if the organization operates internationally, it is important you consider the stakeholders from a global perspective.

Debriefing Question 12.4

The problem for a global MNE is that across the varying cultures within which it operates there will also be highly different views as to what business practices constitute ethical behaviour, what the priorities are in terms of corporate social responsibility, as well as a huge number of different political priorities. How to incorporate these into decision-making on a global basis is indeed a challenge. To a certain extent, it will depend on whether the company follows a decentralized approach to marketing decision-making or a centralized approach. In a centralized approach, the company may well have an ethnocentric view of the world and work to instil the values and priorities of the stakeholders in the country of the HQ on the rest of its subsidiaries. A more decentralized company will have a much more polycentric view and be more concerned with achieving a harmony of values than dictating a global corporate policy.

Debriefing Activity 12.4

In tackling this activity, consider the expectations different managers have within the organization and their relationship to the marketing decision-making process. You may in your interview ask how the company manages the expectations of different stakeholders and whether or not such consideration is formally integrated into the marketing decision-making process. There are also issues of how the policy of corporate social responsibility is managed, resources allocated and decisions made as to where the priorities lie. It may also be interesting to assess how the policy contributes to the long-term reputation and image of the company.

Debriefing Question 12.5

Strategic marketing decisions impact on a whole range of parties who may not be a constituent part of the organization but have an interest in the outcome of the strategic decisions made. Such bodies constitute the stakeholders of a company comprising of employees and managers within the organization; but external to the organization comprise customers, shareholders, suppliers, as well as the local community, government and wide members of society who have an interest in the organization. To sustain a competitive advantage over time, the company may well have to consider how its policy of corporate social responsibility is aligned to the goals and aspirations of its stakeholders. A good answer will recognize the varying demands of the different stakeholders and the conflict their varying aspirations of corporate social responsibility may cause the company in its decision-making.

Debriefing Activity 12.5

In completing this activity, you need to consider the feasibility of implementing your proposed code of conduct and the market situation your sales staff have to compete in. You would also need to ensure the code does not demotivate sales staff and act as a barrier to them achieving company objectives. You would also need to consider how you would introduce such a code and what changes it would require to the ways in which sales personnel were controlled and evaluated.

Debriefing Question 12.6

There is never a simple approach to the handling of ethical issues of this nature. If the company has a code of ethical conduct and is clear that it is in full compliance with this then a proactive and positive policy to handling the publicity surrounding such criticism is vital. The inclusion of the senior management and a constructive attitude to the dissemination of information would also be important. Often, however, such issues are not as clear-cut as they may appear and the retailer may feel they have been judged unfairly and harshly. Such a situation can be difficult for companies. Defending their position may appear callous and show they lack an acceptance of their responsibilities. Even if the criticism is unfounded, the company needs to protect the long-term reputation and image of the company and so be proactive in dealing with such issues.

Debriefing Question 12.7

The starting point should be to reflect on the aims and objectives of CI and then systematically identify their stakeholders and their expectations. It is then necessary to consider the different roles and influence that the stakeholders can bring to implementing the CI strategy. For example, CI is unlikely to have sufficient finances to both carry out its intervention work in individual projects as well as gaining wider publicity for its work that will lead to further companies and individuals becoming involved. Partners of this kind also provide complementary skills knowledge and resources, for example, maintaining the commercial focus, necessary to maximize the revenue from projects, which in turn helps CI to achieve the greatest impact locally.

The starting point here is to address the issue of how Aveda can add stakeholder value and set it against the incurred costs. A substantial and growing customer segment is more aware of sustainability issues and will seek to buy products that are produced by companies with an ethical stance. A far larger segment is emerging that regards sustainability as a 'hygiene factor' in that these customers do not preferentially select products that are produced using environmentally sound process, but will expect all producers to produce products using ethical processes. Organizations will need to invest in developing the appropriate processes in the supply chain as they target new customer segments, develop and promote new and existing products and services and communicate with their stakeholders.

A further consideration is internal marketing. It is necessary to explain the aims and objectives to internal stakeholders but this can also be a benefit. For example, demonstrating an ethical approach can be important in recruitment as well as motivating existing staff.

appendix 3

sample exam questions and answers

Unit 1

Exam question 1.1

Taking the role of the marketing director of a global consumer electronics manufacturer addressing a world conference of marketing executives, outline the major factors and difficulties to be considered when making strategic marketing decisions in a global market.

Answer

In answering this question the candidate should give a brief synopsis of the issues facing a consumer electronics manufacturer operating in global markets. It may be helpful in setting the context to use an example of a consumer electronics industry, for example telecommunications, semi-conductors, computing and so on to apply the concepts being discussed. A good answer would show for the industry chosen an awareness that decisions would have to be made in the context of a highly competitive environment where there is a fast pace of technological change. Innovation and product leadership is the key to achieving a global competitive advantage. The competitive landscape is highly rationalized and global in nature. Furthermore the market will be highly segmented and so achieving a differentiated position through an effective targeting and positioning strategy will also be of paramount importance.

The major factors to be considered therefore in making strategic marketing decisions would relate to:

- ○ The nature of the competitive landscape and the nature of the challenges that require a response.
- ○ The alternative approaches to strategic decision-making.
- ○ The requirements of effective decision-making.
- ○ The basis on which the market is segmented.
- ○ The nature of the market/competitive/demand and technology life cycles.

The major difficulties for the company in making strategic marketing decisions would incorporate such factors as:

- ○ Are the decisions to be centralized globally or decentralized?
- ○ The relationship between HQ and its subsidiaries.
- ○ Cultural sensitivities across the global market.

- o The different competitive strengths the company may have in different markets.
- o The variations in the product life cycle across the globe.
- o How they should achieve competitive leverage in disparate markets.

Exam question 1.2

Competitive relationships are increasingly becoming more important in achieving a global competitive advantage. Why is this so? What are the implications for the making of strategic marketing decisions in a global market?

Answer

The candidate should give an assessment as to why co-operation strategies are becoming more evident in global markets and give examples of industries in which companies have formed relationships in order to achieve a sustainable competitive advantage. They should then discuss the drivers for this trend. Factors such as:

- o The rising cost of R&D.
- o Fast pace of change across market life cycles.
- o Markets reaching maturity in their life cycles and so firms need to compete on cost and build economies of scale.
- o In some markets it is politically more acceptable.
- o Firms often do not have the resources on their own to keep abreast of technological changes in the marketplace.
- o Developments in the market require specialist expertise to which the firm gains access quickly.

The types of competitor relationships that companies enter into could then be outlined. Relationships are usually for specific purposes and for a set duration of time and may cover a number of different areas such as distribution, R&D, technology swaps, joint agencies, product development and market sector relationships.

The implications for strategic marketing decision-making would revolve around the problems and difficulties in the strategic marketing decision process that may arise in the relationship. The discussion therefore would incorporate such issues as:

- o How will the decision-making process be managed and controlled, who makes the decisions and who carries responsibility?
- o How will such issues as quality, geographical, coverage, culture problems be dealt with?
- o Potential conflict in decision-making because of lack of perception of the mutuality of benefits of the agreement or perhaps conflict because the agreement on which the relationship is based is too rigid.
- o Problems may arise in the decision-making process due to imbalance of power between partners, lack of trust or perhaps lack of clarity of definition of responsibilities.

In competitor relationships such issues would need to be resolved if effective strategic decision-making is to take place.

Exam question 1.3

Identify a particular company that has successfully managed the changing dimensions of the competitive landscape of the markets in which they operate. Examine the reasons why they have succeeded in their objective to achieve a sustainable competitive marketing advantage.

Answer

The candidate in this question needs to show an appreciation of the changing dimensions of global competition and the impact this has had on the way firms achieve a competitive advantage. Discussion will include such issues as the growing complexity of world markets, the faster pace of change, the drive to globalization, the rising global wealth in emerging markets, increasing sophistication of consumers, the impact of the speedier communications across the globe and so on. This has all led to a competitive advantage being harder to sustain. Therefore companies have to ensure strategic marketing decisions enable a company:

- To develop innovative and creative strategies.
- Leverage learning across markets.
- Embrace the concept of hard-edged marketing. That is to ensure they make decisions that create superior value for all stakeholders, especially customers and shareholders and prove the value of marketing's contribution to business by the use of meaningful marketing metrics.

In a question where the candidate is asked to identify a specific company then it is important that the candidate follows the brief and specifies the company they are to discuss and identify the reasons why in the light of the above discussion they believe they were successful in sustaining their competitive advantage. The factors identified will obviously vary depending on the context of the company identified but may well incorporate such factors as:

1. How they responded to a major environmental challenge and so made changes in their targeting.
2. How they responded to a particular competitive threat and realigned their strategic focus.
3. How they engendered innovative thinking in the organization and responded with an effective marketing programme.
4. How they were able to deliver superior customer value.
5. How they built an effective knowledge management system and so respond to new environmental conditions.
6. How the firms used data analysis in their decision-making.

Unit 2

Exam question 2.1

Identify the principal challenges that strategic marketing decision makers are likely to face over the next decade and comment on the possible implications for the making of effective strategic marketing decisions.

Answer

This has been a common type of question in the CIM Diploma in the past and it is likely that such questions will be asked in some form in the new syllabus. The question is in two parts and it is important that the candidate considers both parts of the question.

The first part requires you to identify the key strategic challenges, such challenges may be specific to particular industries. In the new syllabus it is likely that such a question will be related to a case study or scenario and so it is important that you ensure your answer is applicable to the scenario provided. Such questions are used to test your awareness of the global marketing environment and gives good students the opportunity to show they have read widely and can draw upon resources from outside the confines of the Coursebook or a specific programme of study. Given there is limited choice in the new CIM examination, building such a knowledge is imperative. However, there are some general aspects covered in this unit that will be applicable to such a question. They are factors such as:

- Shrinking communications
- Impact of the Internet and World Wide Web
- Increased globalization
- Demographic changes globally
- Rise of new emerging markets and new global competitors and so on.

The second part of the question asks you to comment on the implications for strategic marketing decision-making. For each of the challenges you have identified, you need to consider the implications for the strategic marketing decision maker attempting to develop a strategy to build a sustainable competitive advantage in such a future time horizon.

Exam question 2.2

The principles of hard edge marketing assert that marketing managers should be evaluated by the economic returns they generate for shareholders and owners. Using examples fully evaluate this statement.

Answer

In tackling questions of this nature, it is important that the candidate does not simply agree or disagree with the statement but shows they understand both sides of the argument. It is therefore necessary to discuss the arguments in favour of the statements, the arguments against the statement and then show you can formulate a robust conclusion as a result of your analysis. The question also asks the candidate to use examples. The easiest way to do this is to illustrate each of the points discussed by applying them to a specific situation or company.

The arguments in favour of such a statement would incorporate such factors as:

- The need for marketing managers to have a voice at board level and so marketing decisions have to be transparent and accountable.
- In deciding amongst potential strategic options the potential added value to the company has to be a key decision criterion for managers.
- The effectiveness of marketing managers can be assessed only by the application of robust and relevant marketing metrics.

Arguments against the statement will centre on such issues as:

- ○ Shareholders/owners are only one stakeholder amongst many and it is important all stakeholders are satisfied to sustain a long-term competitive advantage.
- ○ It is not always possible to directly link isolated marketing decisions to specific financial criteria.
- ○ It could mean managers are less willing to take risks and be innovative if they are required to prove financial gains prior to a decision being made.
- ○ In innovative new ventures the projected economic added value may be difficult to ascertain.

Exam question 2.3

The emergent school of strategy formulation is very distinct from the rational planning approach. Using examples discuss the advantages and disadvantages of both approaches.

Answer

This question asks the candidate to discuss the major differences between the emergent school of strategy formulation and the rational model planning approach. Then using examples discuss the advantages and disadvantages of both approaches. As we said in the previous question, it is important that the candidate answers all parts of the question.

The key component of the rational planning approach is that it is a highly formal linear sequence which requires a highly formalized approach to strategic marketing decision-making and a mechanical programming approach to its implementation. Underlying the rational approach is the assumption that the process of strategy development is like a machine, if each of the component parts are executed as specified then the end product, that is the resultant strategy, will be effective and efficient.

The emergent school of strategy development on the other hand believes strategies are formed and not necessarily formulated. In other words, strategies are built from a number of little actions and decisions made by different managers in an organization sometimes with little thought to the strategic consequences. Taken together over time these small changes produced a major shift in direction.

In answering this question the candidate needs to consider the advantages and disadvantages of both these approaches in specific situations.

Unit 3

Exam question 3.1

What type of information should be collected as part of an industry/market analysis? How might you analyse such information?

Answer

The information collected as part of an industry/market analysis would incorporate such factors as: what is the size and value of the sector/industry? Who are the major players? What are the levels of concentration or fragmentation in the sector/industry? Is the industry growing or declining and what are the growth/decline rates, the pace of technological change within the industry? What is the power balance among suppliers, buyers and competitors in the sector/industry? What are the future trends in the sector/industry? In analysing the information you could use the Porter 5 Competitive Forces model.

Exam question 3.2

For a service organization of your choice, evaluate the problems and opportunities in developing an Internet-based global marketing strategy.

Answer

The question is couched in a service context, so the answers must be suitably tailored to this context. The opportunities could include such factors as:

- The opportunity to develop a global strategy rather than simply selling services.
- The possibilities for developing a global communications strategy.
- The possibility of building online service capabilities relatively cheaply.
- The opportunity to form relationships with other suppliers and so offer a virtual integrated package.
- The capability to manage customers interactively online.
- The ability to offer services 24/7.

The problems could be related to security issues, data protection, dissatisfaction of customers if the service breakdowns are slow for any reason, the problems in dealing with services that are complex and need personal interaction.

Exam question 3.3

Write a report advising a company on what they need to do to become an effective learning organization with a fully integrated knowledge management capability.

Answer

In answering this question you first need to define what is meant by an effective learning organization and why it is important in competing in today's marketing environment. You then need to examine the capabilities of a learning organization, in terms of the organizational values, the linkages between learning and knowledge management, the inclusion of persons contributing to the marketing process and the importance of building a knowledge management system which can be accessed and understood by all. However, to be effective the company need to be able to access past learning through an organizational memory which is built upon and used in making strategic marketing decisions.

Unit 4

Exam question 4.1

Explain the reasons, giving examples, why smaller firms are often more successful in exploiting industry breakpoints and technology discontinuities? What do you consider to be their greatest limitations in growing an innovative business?

Answer

The answer to this question first requires an explanation of the concepts of breakpoints and discontinuities and an explanation of what differentiates proactive businesses from reactive ones. It is necessary to discuss the nature of larger firms and their greater tendency to be more driven by administrative management rather than entrepreneurial management as is the case of many small firms. A contrast should be drawn between the characteristics of the two styles of management.

It is then possible to explain that to exploit these situations requires speed to market and fast decision-making, focus on the opportunity (not just a particular product), risk-taking and management risk and a willingness to quickly adapt the business as more is learned about the new market situation.

The lack of resources of smaller firms can make it difficult to pursue simultaneous penetration of the existing market, development of new markets and new product development (for the next generation product) and they can be more vulnerable to more powerful competitors.

Exam question 4.2

As a consultant to a company, that until now has been successful but is now experiencing slow growth in sales and declining profits in a mature market, explain the main characteristics of a marketing strategy that would be needed to achieve fast growth.

Answer

To be a pioneer in an industry an organization must be capable of achieving both step changes and continuous incremental marketing innovation. The organization must seek to develop breakthrough ideas based on new technology, such as Internet marketing or other major innovations, such as a new route to market that will offer a quantum leap in customer value. At the same time, it is necessary to explain how opportunities for marketing innovation occur at each point in the marketing strategy development process. For a product in the mature phase of the life cycle, customer service enhancement is a major factor in building exceptional customer value and loyalty.

Exam question 4.3

Choose an industry that has been affected significantly by Internet marketing (e.g. travel or purchase of books and CDs). Explain how the drivers of Internet marketing have affected customer purchasing and the strategies of the firms in the industry.

Answer

You should first outline the nature of innovation and change in the industry that you select and then explain in some detail the drivers of Internet marketing and particularly how they add value for the customers and organization. It is necessary to provide detail about exactly how customers will benefit and emphasize the importance of Internet marketing strategies that are customer (and marketing)-led and are not technology-led. You should use the industry to provide examples of companies that have been successful and unsuccessful and explain the reasons for this. You may wish to complete the answer by drawing some lessons of good practice.

Unit 5

Exam question 5.1

Many global airlines have found it difficult to cope with market changes and unexpected events in the environment over the last decade. Define the factors that have made it necessary to change their strategy, explain the strategic options they now have and how they might make the decision on which strategy to pursue.

Answer

You should carry out an environmental analysis to highlight the external factors before carrying out an internal analysis of their strategy and assumptions on which it is based. From through their management approach, you will be able to assess their capability to cope with unexpected events, ability to learn and take action.

Exam question 5.2

Develop a segmentation strategy for a city or country tourist destination of your choice. How would the segmentation strategy help in making marketing mix decisions?

Answer

You should first explain the importance of marketing the diversity of attractions in the city or country and avoiding simply mass marketing one attraction to one customer segment. You should then explain the segmentation approach based on developing a hierarchy of segmentation and a number of crtiteria. The destination will offer experiences and benefits that will appeal to different global tourist segments (adventure, sightseeing, sun etc.). The visitors will have different characteristics (e.g. backpackers with little money to spend, older affluent tourists and business visitors) and they will come from different countries and the marketing mix includes the products (e.g. attractions, accommodation facilities and infrastructure), pricing (packages and individual elements of the holiday) and communications (targeted at the specific segments).

Exam question 5.3

Increasing globalization is stretching the resources of all but the very largest firms. In response many are focusing on core activities and effectively becoming niche marketers. Using examples explain the criteria for success in adopting a niche market.

Answer

From the recommended reading you should identify the criteria for success for a market niche: its size and purchasing power, growth potential and being of no interest to major competitors. Effective market nichers have the skills and resources to effectively service the niche and defend the organization from potential competitor attack by raising market entry barriers. You should explain how this might be achieved.

You should give examples of how nichers have focused on the nature of their specialization, for example geographically, type of end user, product or product line, specification, service levels, size of customer and a particular product feature.

You should also discuss the growth options and the dangers of overfocus on a too-limited niche and straying into associated areas that are served by major competitors, thus provoking an attack on the original niche.

Unit 6

Exam question 6.1

As the brand manager of an international organization of your choice, write a report highlighting the difficulties in global marketing planning and how these may be addressed.

Answer

In listing the difficulties you should include issues such as:

- Clarity of communications (two-way)
- Clarity of organizational structures and reporting responsibilities
- Cultural issues and the problems of self-reference criteria
- Differences in working practices and reward structures
- Operational difficulties
- Clarity of planning and the lack of a planning culture
- Risk assessment in different market environments.

The difficulties might be addressed by:

- Using local expertise.
- Establishing clear communication lines and checking that messages are being received correctly.
- The use of risk assessment models.
- Training in all aspects of the business and recognizing that staff must recognize their country and regional/global management responsibilities.
- Appropriate planning models.

Exam question 6.2

What is culture? Why is it important for international marketing managers to take account of culture and do you consider increasing globalization means that it will become less important in the future?

Answer

You should define culture and explain the elements of culture including the beliefs, values and customs. You should then explain how it includes elements such as language, religion, aesthetics, education, values and attitudes, law and politics, technology and material culture and social organizations.

Earlier we have discussed the drivers of globalization and you should include a discussion of the relevant elements, such as increasing homogeneity of demand before presenting your arguments as to whether you believe it will be less important in future.

Exam question 6.3

You have changed your job from being a marketing manager in a large global business to marketing manager in a small firm, selling to eight European countries. What differences in organizational form, resources and operations would you expect to see and what might the implications be for your marketing strategy?

Answer

The introduction should recognize the two parts to the question (1) differences (2) implications for the marketing strategy and then the three areas of consideration: organizational form, resource and operations.

The answer should start by providing a conceptual underpinning – domestic, international, multinational and global before considering the changes in organizational form, resources and operations.

Organizational form
- ○ Size of firm and business
- ○ Number of foreign countries in which it operates and level of involvement
- ○ Organization's overseas objectives for its foreign business
- ○ Experience in international business
- ○ Value and variety of products, the nature of the marketing task and resources available
- ○ Differences between export department/subsidiary with headquarters/subsidiary arrangement (centralization-decentralization) and matrix, product or brand structure.

Differences in resources
- ○ Staff issues, recruitment, training
- ○ Sources of finance – local to international banks
- ○ Physical resources – local and global manufacturing and marketing.

Operations may involve a consideration of:
- ○ Management of local and global operations
- ○ Partnerships and alliances and the distribution channels
- ○ Marketing development.

Unit 7

Exam question 7.1

The biggest challenge for businesses is managing through difficult periods that affect their business prospects, such as a recession, war or a new competitor entering the market. Explain the problems organizations face in such periods and explain how entrepreneurial management can help to overcome such problems.

Answer

The answer requires an explanation of some of the generic problems that might result but it would also be useful to give some examples of some specific, and often unexpected problems that result. The problems include:

- Declining sales
- Less predictability in customer behaviour
- Customers losing confidence in certain products and services
- Customers making different choices about what they are willing and not willing to do
- Competitors cutting price to very low levels in order to try to survive and maintain customer loyalty
- Overcapacity (unused staff, machinery, facilities etc.).

The strategies that might be used to overcome the problems fall into two categories: first, maintaining a flexible strategic approach to the business, which makes it easier to deal with problems as they arise, and second, build in the key characteristics of an entrepreneurial business of flexibility, adaptability and responsiveness. Your answer should include:

- Maintaining a low cost base (fixed costs particularly) and being willing to cut costs quickly where necessary
- Managing cash flow (inventory control and chasing debtors, etc.)
- Maintaining flexibility in the use of resources – following opportunities and areas of activity where there is more demand
- Avoiding expensive and inflexible assets, such as manufacturing operations
- Willing to take decisions quickly to innovate and invest in areas of future potential that will help the business survive
- Develop strategies to quickly maximize the opportunities when the market starts to grow
- Reduce overcapacity – chance to use staff to pursue new markets/products and so on.

Exam question 7.2

'Innovation in itself is not the key to generating fast growth in large businesses – other factors are crucial too.' Justify your view of this statement using examples to illustrate your case.

Answer

In answering this question there is a need to explain:

- The need to be customer oriented, not product oriented
- The need to exploit the ideas commercially quickly, and cost effectively, moving fast into the market
- Clearly identifying and satisfying customer intangible needs, through brand imagery, as well as 'selling' the new product or service
- To follow this by building the business by taking away unnecessary resources from routine products and activities, and refocusing them on new areas
- Balancing the organization's need for control of resources with the customer need for responsiveness and products and services that meet their needs
- The need for a culture that encourages innovation throughout
- The need to achieve a balance between administrative and entrepreneurial management (Unit 4)
- The need to build a team with the right competencies and a company with the right assets for future competitiveness.

Exam question 7.3

Choose an industry sector that is already globalized. Explain the role of the Internet in the evolution and restructuring of the sector and suggest ways in which the Internet might facilitate the use of competencies and assets to create competitive advantage for organizations in the future.

Answer

After describing the current role of the Internet in the industry and explaining the business models and website approaches that are being used, you should explain how value is currently being added for customers and organizations. You should particularly focus on the issues covered in Unit 6 relating to global business and explain the advantages and disadvantages of e-business in this context.

You should apply some of the concepts and good practice lessons including:

- The benefits of interactivity
- The speed of research and information collection
- The ability to customize offers
- The opportunity for integration (including physical exchanges)
- Improving ease of market entry
- Changing the way business is transacted
- Improving relationship management.

You should then go on to discuss the basis of competitiveness in the industry in the future and decide what the critical success factors will be. You could use the checklist under the heading 'knowledge management' (as well as other factors) above to highlight some key criteria.

Unit 8

Exam question 8.1

What factors do you consider to be important in creating a valuable global brand. How do the factors differ when creating a consumer service brand, such as in fast food, a consumer 'high involvement purchase' product brand, such as a car, and a B2B brand, such as in large computer systems.

Answer

The introduction should include an outline of global branding and make reference to different sectors.

The success of global branding is affected by both external (uncontrollable) and internal (controllable) factors.

Some critical success factors in global branding are:

- ○ The consistency of the customer perception of the brand despite cultural differences.
- ○ The consistency and clarity of positioning in different countries and avoiding potential positioning problems such as different price positioning due to the stage of development.
- ○ Effectively integrated communications (see Unit 9).
- ○ Consistency of corporate identity/logo/design (see Unit 9).
- ○ Standardization of the marketing mix.
- ○ Effective PR management, for example ethical issues and crises.
- ○ Appropriate band stretching.
- ○ Reinvigorating the portfolio with innovations that have global appeal.

In the second part of the question, it is important to contrast between: service and product brands; high involvement and low involvement purchases and B2B as well as B2C brands. This should prompt a discussion of the difficulty of delivering services consistently around the world, the importance of managing the customer experience through from information search to post-purchase reassurance in high involvement purchases and what the actual benefits of B2B brands are.

Exam question 8.2

Many products and services have reached the mature phase of the life cycle and have effectively become commodities. Using appropriate examples explain what options are available to firms to manage the situation.

Answer

The introduction requires an explanation of the life cycle concept and the strategies that are needed to manage a product in the mature phase of the cycle. An explanation of commoditization and its causes is required. You might refer to not only portfolio analysis, international market development and branding issues but also other mix factors, such as lazy management, lack of investment and poor promotion that might have contributed to this. A number of strategies might be considered including rationalization in order to release investment for more profitable products, new product development and repositioning or service enhancement.

Exam question 8.3

Explain the difficulties and benefits of marketing a standardized product across the countries of the EU. Use examples to illustrate you answer.

Answer

The introduction should include an explanation of standardization and adaptation and some comment should be made on the fact that certain products and services are culturally sensitive, such as food and others are promoted strongly through imagery, which is often also culturally sensitive. Although technology, such as computing is usually not culturally sensitive, some adjustments must be made, for example the language of the manual.

The benefits for standardization include economies of scale, learning effect and standardized processes, and the marketing benefits from projecting a consistent image and identity because of the convergence of global tastes and the development of international communications. The arguments for differentiation include cultural differences, differing physical conditions, stage of development and life cycle stages.

The difficulties include differences in consumer purchasing behaviour because of culture, religion and language, in the perception of marketing communications, in different levels of ability to pay high prices and differences in levels of service.

Unit 9

Exam question 9.1

Frequently a firm's international communications fail to convey to customers the messages that are intended. Using examples, explain how factors within and outside the firm's control contribute to this.

Answer

The introduction should include an explanation of the issues in international marketing communications and the areas where problems can arise, including internal, interactive and external communications and the reasons why the communications might fail with an external audience. You should then consider the factors within the organization's control including:

- o Inconsistency of messages (e.g. the Internet allows comparison)
- o Different styles of presentation of corporate identity, brand, product image
- o Lack of co-ordination of messages
- o Differences in fields of perception of sender and receiver.

And those outside the organization's control

- o The importance of culture
- o Having to change the media used
- o Counterfeiting (negative images may stick to the firm/brand)
- o Grey marketing, leading to customer confusion and annoyance
- o Competitors, governments and pressure groups.

Exam question 9.2

A supplier of office equipment to businesses that currently uses traditional promotion methods, including small distributors, is considering moving to a Web-only communication strategy to improve efficiency. As a consultant appointed to help the company, make the right decision, explain the advantages and disadvantages of the suggestion.

Answer

The introduction to the answer should include an explanation of disintermediation and the possible benefits but also explain that companies can disappear on the Internet and so reintermediation might be necessary.

Then the advantages of a Web-based strategy can be explained, including:

- ○ Low transaction and administration costs
- ○ Targeted and more responsive marketing to a wider audience supported by a database
- ○ An explanation of the benefits and use of Internet advertising.

You should then explain some disadvantages including:

- ○ High set up costs
- ○ Fulfilment is still needed
- ○ Payment and Internet security issues.

The alternative traditional promotion should be considered in terms of the effectiveness and added value to customers and the organization, including sales force, exhibitions, press advertising, direct mail and so on.

Exam question 9.3

Worldwide tourism has suffered because of fears of SARS, Chicken flu and terrorism, and a number of tourist attractions have suffered falling revenues. As the marketing manager of a tourist attraction of your choice, what steps would you take to increase the number and spend of international visitors?

Answer

You should start by acknowledging whether the attraction you have chosen would be a destination itself or part of a number of attractions that visitors might visit, in which case you need to explain how you would work in partnership with others.

Then an understanding of the market environment, customer choices and decisions is needed, so that communications decisions can be taken. You should particularly recognize the different segment needs and develop a segmentation hierarchy, before indicating a targeting strategy. The decision made about tools, messages and media to use will be affected by the available budget and joint promotion activity with partners and suggestions.

In each of these areas, you should highlight the decisions that you would take and explain the rationale for taking them.

Unit 10

Exam question 10.1

What pricing problems might a multinational company face in marketing to less-developed countries. Outline some ways in which they might be overcome?

Answer

The introduction would outline the challenges posed by less stable LDC economies, and the need to trade in different currencies.

The problems encountered would include:

- Inflation
- Weak currency, variable exchange rates
- Political and legal restrictions
- Market issues
- Customers with less purchasing power and their ability to pay (and perceived value)
- Smaller potential market due to unemployment
- Local competition – undercutting and counterfeiting and so on.

Outline ways to overcome

- Managing currency forward purchasing
- Counter trade
- Market entry methods to manage risk.

Exam question 10.2

The arrival of the global village has had a major impact on companies' distribution methods. Identify four factors involved and explain how each has influenced distribution.

Answer

The factors could include:

- Integration of markets
- Global branding
- Global product positioning
- Global corporations
- Development of trading blocs
- Lowering of tariff barriers
- The growth of alliances
- Internet marketing
- Datamining
- Mass customization.

The discussion covering four areas could include:

- Integrated supply chain management
- Global supplier intranets
- Integrated multimodal transportation
- Concentration/internationalization of retailing chains
- Direct marketing
- JIT/flexible supply management
- Joint marketing operations.

Exam question 10.3

As a marketing manager of a global manufacturer of air conditioning equipment contributing to the board debate on the value chain, explain the criteria that should be used to make the decisions about whether to outsource products and services.

Answer

Your introduction should include an explanation of the concepts of the value chain, customer requirements, tangible and intangible assets. You should also explain the quality and type of inputs (especially management resources), outputs and comparative advantage that might influence the decision including:

- ○ Technology, procurement, marketing, logistics and operations
- ○ Quality of people, skills, competencies
- ○ Gaps, underperformance and areas of excellence.

The criteria should include:

- ○ Cost R&D, marketing, operations
- ○ Specialization and expertise of service providers and manufacturers
- ○ Lack of 'leading edge' expertise of the organization.

Risks should also be considered, including:

- ○ Loss of intellectual property.

Unit 11

Exam question 11.1

You are a product manager for a soft drinks company with profit responsibility for a range of canned drinks sold through vending machines. Fully explain the type of financial analysis you will require and how you would use such information to manage the brands for which you are responsible.

Answer

Financial information is primarily required to:

- ○ compile a position audit for a company to assess its marketing strengths and weaknesses from a financial viewpoint
- ○ appraise any investment proposal in long-term decision-making
- ○ assess the financial outcomes in short-term decision-making
- ○ monitor and control the implementation of marketing programmes.

Thus the results of the financial analysis will be used to make both tactical and strategic decisions. In the development of new products, and new channel strategies, an investment appraisal will be necessary. In making tactical decisions with regard to pricing and changes in the marketing programmes, it will be necessary in assessing the possible alternative solutions. It will of course be used in identifying profitable/unprofitable products and distribution venues.

Exam question 11.2

The advertising agency for which you work is considering the launch of a new range of services for its clients. Identify the marketing and financial criteria you would use to evaluate the proposal for the new services.

Answer

In this question the candidates need to take care in applying their answer to the specific situation identified in the question. A way of answering the question is to take the process of new service development and launch, and consider the marketing and financial criteria that would be needed at each stage to evaluate the proposal.

Possible *financial* criteria that could be considered would be factors such as:

- Expected ROI
- Expected return on capital required
- Break-even analysis/pricing analysis
- Cost/volume/profit analysis
- Cross subsidy from other operations
- Cost-benefit analysis.

Possible *marketing* criteria to consider

- Forecasted sales volume
- Market attractiveness/competitor strength analysis
- Trends/growth potential and size of market
- Positioning/pricing issues
- Support required/compatibility with existing services
- Consumer behaviour considerations
- Organizational implications.

Exam question 11.3

Scrumptious Cakes PLC supply a range of pastries and cakes to supermarkets, delicatessens and tea shops. In search of further growth they are trying to decide whether they should:

(a) adopt a programme of product development and expand their range of products, or
(b) consolidate their position with their current products but further develop their sales through new distribution outlets.

Advise them as to how they should evaluate the two options?

Answer

In evaluating the two options the Scrumptious Cakes need to review each one in line with the objectives they are hoping to achieve. One way would be to establish a ratings scale set against the particular objectives the company hope the two options will achieve, and then rate them on a number of financial criteria. The financial criteria used to assess the options could incorporate such things as:

- initial investment required
- continuing investment required over a period of time
- discounted cash flow projections
- long-term profitability expectations
- cost/volume/profit analysis and so on.

With regard to the rating scale, both options may well score relatively low in terms of the initial investment required but option (a) may be viewed as scoring higher on profitability expectations. However the company would need to ask if option (a) can be supported by the cash flow throughout the period it will be required to do so.

Unit 12

Exam question 12.1

In developing a mechanism for evaluating and controlling the implementation of strategic marketing decisions, what factors would you take into account? How might you use the information generated? Use examples to illustrate your answer.

Answer

In this question consider that any mechanism must have the capability to set standards for strategy implementation, measure performance, assess areas of strengths and weaknesses and to establish mechanisms for taking corrective action. Thus in answering the question the candidate needs to consider how these might be achieved and give examples from companies on the way these have or have not been achieved. In establishing the mechanisms the candidate would need to consider such factors as the type of information required, the metrics to be used for performance measurement, the methods to be used to carry out the monitoring and the resources required to do it. The candidate would then need to show how such information can be used for compiling a position appraisal, assessing performance and identifying any problem areas in the implementation programme.

Exam question 12.2

Critically evaluate the use of a profit measurement approach to the measurement of performance. Use examples to explain your answer.

Answer

The candidate needs to ensure they fully discuss both the advantages and disadvantages of using a profit measurement approach. To gain good marks the use of examples will be essential. The arguments for the use of profit measurements would incorporate such arguments as:

o Profit is a universally recognized parameter on which to evaluate business.
o In small businesses the strategic focus is often solely geared towards profitability measures.
o It is consistent with the principle of shareholder add value, in that the profit is what is distributed each year.
o Profit is an important criterion in investment appraisal and a measure of the success of the policies pursued by company directors.
o Profitability is a major determinant of the employee reward system in organizations.

However equally the candidate would be expected to discuss that there are clear limitations to the use of profit as measure and the figures that can be manipulated, it ignores the importance of cash flow management which is vital for short-term survival and it is a short-term measure and so puts undue focus on the income statement rather than the long-term viability of the marketing programmes.

Exam question 12.3

Discuss to what extent the pursuit of a policy of corporate social responsibility conflicts with contributing to the economic added value of a company.

Answer

It is argued by many commentators that it is only through the pursuit of a policy of social responsibility that a long-term competitive advantage can be sustained. Without it the long-term corporate reputation and image would suffer if the company did not respond to the concerns of their consumers. In the long term, therefore, there is no conflict between such a policy and the principle of shareholder/owner added value. However, from the perceptions of the shareholder/owner, programmes resulting from such a policy could reduce profits in the short term and so conflict may arise. Part of the problem arises in situations where profit maximization or economic added value is the sole objective. In such companies it could be difficult for managers to appreciate the importance of other objectives. The candidate needs to discuss the wider stakeholder implications of the question, perhaps suggest ways in which the conflict can be resolved and use examples to support the arguments made.

Specimen Examination Paper 2: Strategic Marketing Decisions

Section A

Case study: The telecommunication market

Since the late 1990s, things have changed dramatically in the global telecommunications market.

The start of this period was driven by Internet mania and the assumption of astronomic rates of global telephone traffic growth. This was spurred on by Bullish investors and led to the creation of a number of start up firms who splurged on vast infrastructure investments. The former national monopolies in Europe, AT&T in America and NTT in Japan all tried to transform themselves into global operators. They built new networks and bought stakes in foreign operators. European companies gambled that the supposed surge in demand for fixed communications capacity would be followed by a similar leap in demand for mobile capacity, and they paid over €100 billion ($90 billion) for licences to run 'third-generation' (3G) mobile networks. In the process, they ran up huge debts.

We can now see that many of the global alliances have collapsed – like the BT and AT&T venture – Concert communications. Many – like BT – have largely re-trenched to their home markets. There has been a huge amount of casualties and consolidation among the surviving start-ups. The trouble was, this construction boom and the creation of global alliances was founded on a number of fallacies.

The first was the mythical growth rate expected. Between 1998 and 2003 total transmission capacity increased 500-fold. But over the same period, demand merely quadrupled.

When it became clear that the industry had bet on an increase in demand that was not likely to materialize in the near future, ferocious competition and frantic price-cutting ensued.

There certainly has been growth in the market. Internet traffic is said to be doubling every year, and voice traffic on both fixed and mobile networks is rising. But as the industry has found to its cost, traffic growth does not translate into revenue growth. Moreover, in the rich world at least, markets are saturated.

Moreover the two most successful new telecommunications technologies of the past decade – Internet access on fixed networks, and text messaging on mobile networks – were both unexpected breakthroughs that emerged in spite of, rather than because of, the industry's best efforts.

Source: Simon Kelly, Sheffield Hallam University, July 2003.

Compulsory: Both questions MUST be answered

Question 1

1. Critically evaluate the changing base of competitive advantage in the telecommunications market and explain why companies have met with the apparent difficulties outlined in the case study.

(25 marks)

2. How would the development of an effective learning strategy help companies in this industry make more effective strategic marketing decisions.

(25 marks)

Section B

Answer TWO questions only. All questions carry 25 marks each.

Questions

1. Identify a particular company that operates in the global market. Examine the reasons why they have either failed or succeeded in their objective to achieve a global competitive marketing advantage.
2. Small and medium sized enterprises appear to follow the informal emergent school of strategy formulation in making strategic marketing decisions as distinct from the more formal rational linear approach. Discuss the benefits that such an opportunistic approach may bring an SME and comment on any problems they may experience in using such an approach to their strategic marketing decision-making.
3. Evaluate the impact of e-business developments on the strategic marketing decisions of a small company that designs and produces high quality silver jewellery.
4. As a management consultant writing a report for the management of a global engineering business, suggest ways in which an evaluation and control strategy can help ensure the effective implementation of the strategic marketing decisions taken.

Debriefing 1

Candidates would need to give a good indication as to the competitive challenges facing the company chosen. To do this they would need to examine the challenges in the macro environment, within the industry and the challenges facing them with regard to the changing consumer demands.

They should then identify the reasons for the company either being successful or failing and discuss how the company dealt with the issues faced.

The discussion may encompass a range of factors such as:

○ How they dealt with consumer/cultural challenges
○ The issues of competing across a global market
○ How they reacted to particular competitive threats
○ The ethical dilemmas they faced
○ How the firm built a knowledge management system and incorporated learning into decision-making.

They would then need to evaluate the implications of these on the changing nature of the strategic marketing decision-making.

○ Changes in segmentation targeting and positioning
○ Strategic focus
○ Changes in the development and implementation of marketing programmes.

Debriefing 2

The decision-making in SMEs may often rest with one person who neither had time nor the resources to instigate the formal mechanisms inherent in rational model planning approach to strategic marketing decision-making. Consequently, they take a much more emergent approach.

Many commentators would argue this is a much healthier approach as strategic marketing decisions give the company an inbuilt flexibility to respond to challenges in the marketing environment. The strategy development processes need to be an iterative process allowing a company to reflect and respond to challenges and so the company has to be proactive in seeking knowledge to anticipate future developments but also have the ability to react and change the strategic basis should the market demand it.

However, strategic decisions do need to be based on an effective knowledge management system and it is important they are effectively controlled and that performance is monitored. A good candidate would discuss the problems inherent in ensuring that if an emergent approach is taken to decision-making and the problems in sustaining a long-term perspective to strategy development.

Debriefing 3

The specific context given is important in tackling this question in that it is a small firm, probably with limited resources, that is in a specialist niche market. To achieve a pass grade the candidate would have to show they have the ability to asses the impact of e-business developments with reference to this context.

The introduction should identify the key developments of e-business in a global marketing context and then make an assessment of the impact by examining the opportunities and threats to such a firm of e-business.

For a small firm, e-business has the ability to break down country barriers and so gives them access to global markets. For a silver designer, it gives the opportunity to offer an interactive design service, capabilities, build online communication capabilities as well as access to highly fragmented markets.

However, for a firm where their design capability is the basis of their competitive advantage issues of data security, competitor access, system failure and corruption could all be potential problems.

Debriefing 4

Strategic marketing decisions can only be effective if they result in marketing programmes that offer superior value to the customer and deliver added value to the shareholder. Any control and evaluation system therefore needs to assess marketing programmes in this light. It is only by carrying out rigorous control and evaluation programmes that marketing managers can show how the decisions made add to the value of the company and ensure their voice is heard at a strategic level. The candidate could discuss the importance of taking a balanced and integrative view to performance measurement and the need to incorporate non-financial as well as financial measures and how they would approach developing an effective evaluation and control system.

appendix 4

past examination paper and examiner's report

The Chartered
Institute of Marketing

Professional Postgraduate Diploma in Marketing

Strategic Marketing Decisions

62:     **Strategic Marketing Decisions**

Time: **14.00 – 17.00**

Date: **8th December, 2004**

3 Hours Duration

This examination is in two sections.

PART A – Is compulsory and worth 50% of total marks.

PART B – Has **FOUR** questions; select **TWO**. Each answer will be worth 25% of the total marks.

DO NOT repeat the question in your answer, but show clearly the number of the question attempted on the appropriate pages of the answer book.

Rough workings should be included in the answer book and ruled through after use.

© The Chartered Institute of Marketing

Professional Postgraduate Diploma in Marketing

PART A

Case Study: Lego

Lego is one of the world's best-known toy brands and yet things have not being going well. In 1998 it reported its first loss in the history of the company and in 2003 Lego announced its third and biggest ever loss of £125 million. Hundreds of jobs have been cut and the company is now rethinking its strategy.

Lego bricks, devised by a carpenter in Denmark in the 1930s, has grown from a small family company to a global concern. However, it is now having difficulty competing in a world where children are growing up more quickly. Fifty years ago the plastic bricks faced little competition; these days children are wooed by electronic toys such as computer games.

Lego, which has become used to decades of unbroken sales growth, is seen by commentators as having lost its way in a market that is more competitive, faster moving and more fad-driven than ever.

After the company posted its first losses in 1998, the company negotiated lucrative product tie-ins with the Harry Potter and Star Wars movies, as well as with Disney. More than one million Hogwarts Castle Lego sets were sold when the first two Harry Potter films came out, helping the company back into profit in 2001 and 2002. But with no film about the boy wizard last year and constant fears about an impending recession, sales slumped. Lego now believe that too much of their growth was generated by licensed products which only offered short-term sales.

Other brand extension strategies also failed to deliver the expected growth. Galidor, the cartoon-related series of Lego action figures recently withdrawn from the market, was criticised for the lack of open-ended imaginative play for which the Lego brand is known, and for stretching the brand too far. The Lego music builder aimed at pre-school children also failed. Lego themselves feel they placed too much emphasis on chasing the fashion of the day and failed to focus on their core brand. They became over-dependent on licences and forgot their core market segment, small children.

They made a decision to phase out the pre-school Duplo brand (which Lego had used since 1969) and replace it with Lego Explore. Too many parents thought Lego had simply stopped making the larger-sized Duplo bricks for children aged 18 months to five years. Lego's revenues in the pre-school market halved in a year. The Duplo brand is now being reactivated and a new brand, Quatro, with even bigger bricks for children up to two years old, is being launched.

In the US, Lego failed to predict what its best-sellers would be, particularly among its popular Bionicle, figures and so ended up overstocked in some products and under stocked in the key successful ones. Worldwide there have been complaints from adults that new colours introduced for the bricks did not match the old colours!

Jon Salisbury, an editorial consultant on the UK's *Toy News*, comments. "Lego were so successful for so long, they didn't have to question their marketing or product development ability. Every retailer in Europe wanted to sell Lego. Now they are having to compete with the rest of the toy industry on toy industry terms."

In the past five years other construction toys have been eroding Lego's market share, particularly in the US, which accounts for 40 per cent of sales. Two of Lego's biggest rivals, Hasbro and Mattel, have much broader product ranges and are therefore better able to ride out a disappointing performance by one product. The market is now much more crowded and many more brands are competing for the same market. CLICs, knex, Magic Blocks, and the German brand Ploy-M have all successfully built a market presence. Magnetic construction toys such as geoMag, Imag and Magnetix (to name but three) are threatening Lego's performance in their traditional heartlands.

Despite its problems, Lego is still the fourth biggest toy retailer and sixth most recognised brand in the world. It was named toy of the century by *Fortune* magazine and the British Association of Toy Retailers last year, and the Bionicle range was named toy of the year in 2003.

(Source: Adapted from *The Independent*; Jan. 3, 2004; *Financial Times* April 2; 2004)

SECTION A

Question One
(a) Critically evaluate the branding strategy that Lego has pursued in its quest to reverse its fortunes in the period since 1998.

(25 marks)

(b) In the light of your answer to Question a, advise Lego on the decisions they should take in order to develop a branding strategy to build a sustainable global competitive position.
(25 marks)
(Total 50 Marks)

SECTION B

Question Two
You are the managing director of a company supplying leading edge accounting software in the global B2B market. Critically appraise the major factors and difficulties you will need to consider when making strategic marketing decisions in a global market.
(Total 25 Marks)

Question Three
You have changed your job from being a regional brand manager in a large global business to marketing director of a small firm operating in a global niche market.

(a) What differences in organisational form, resources and operations would you expect to see?

(10 marks)

(b) What are the implications for the strategic marketing decisions you will be making.
(15 marks)
(Total 25 Marks)

Question Four
A small firm operating in the B2B market is trying to decide whether it should follow the emergent approach of strategy formulation as opposed to a rational linear planning approach.

(a) Discuss the advantages and disadvantages of both approaches.

(15 marks)

(b) Explain which approach you consider most appropriate for strategic marketing decision-making of the small firm operating in the B2B market.
(10 marks)
(Total 25 Marks)

Question Five

   (a)   The advertising agency for which you work is considering the launch of a new range of services for its clients. Identify the financial decision-making tools and financial criteria you would use to evaluate the proposal for a new service.

(10 marks)

   (b)   One of the new services that the agency is considering introducing, markets will involve the following additional costs.

Cost	£
Marketing Executive monthly salary plus additional costs*	4000
Support Staff monthly salary plus additional costs*	2000
Fixed Expense per month	3000
Variable cost per billed Hour	10

*The additional costs cover national insurance, pensions and holiday pay.

The firm is planning to charge clients £100 per hour (the billing rate) for this new service. The Marketing executive will work a standard 38 hour week.

Required

   1.   Calculate the numbers of hours the firms needs to charge clients per month if it is to breakeven.

(2 marks)

   2.   Calculate the numbers of hours the firms needs to charge clients if it is to make a profit of £4500 per month on this service.

(3 marks)

   3.   Calculate the number of hours the firm needs to charge clients per month to produce a profit margin of 20% of the billing rate (work to the nearest whole hour).

(5 marks)

   4.   Comment on the viability of this proposed new service.

(5 marks)
(Total 25 Marks)

The Chartered
Institute of Marketing

Professional Postgraduate Diploma in Marketing

Strategic Marketing Decisions

62:   Strategic Marketing Decisions

SENIOR EXAMINER'S REPORT FOR DECEMBER 2004 EXAMINATION PAPER

© The Chartered Institute of Marketing, 2004

SENIOR EXAMINER'S REPORT FOR
DECEMBER 2005 EXAMINATION PAPER

MODULE NAME: STRATEGIC MARKETING DECISIONS

AWARD NAME: PROFESSIONAL POSTGRADUATE DIPLOMA
IN MARKETING

DATE: DECEMBER 2004

1. General strengths and weaknesses of candidates

There was a huge variation in the standard of scripts not only between students but also between centres. Given this is a post graduate and professional diploma the examiner is looking for an understanding of the conceptual underpinning of the module content and an ability to contextualise the answers within the remit of the brief given in the questions. A huge variation in understanding the theory and the ability to apply knowledge came through in the papers. Some scripts were very immaturely written considering the level of the examination and the fact that at this stage candidates should all be showing a level of professionalism in their answers. However the time management of candidates seemed to be far better with four questions than in the old syllabus where there were five.

Strengths

The stronger answers were given in the more descriptive questions that required the candidates to show their knowledge. Good candidates clearly offered a good level of knowledge, but there was an overall general weakness in applying and contextualising this knowledge. This was particularly apparent in question 1 and question 2. In other questions the application of knowledge was much better.

Having said that, the stronger candidates did well in that they were able to show an underpinning of appropriate theory, evidence of strategic thinking, and an incisive level of critical evaluation. There was also good use of examples to demonstrate relevant points in the stronger papers.

Weaknesses

Inherent in all the CIM professional PG diploma papers is the ability to think strategically on a global scale. The weaker candidates showed a lack of international/global perspective even when the question specifically asked for this. The use of theory was sometimes indiscriminate for weaker candidates and there was inappropriate application on occasions with a limited use of examples.

Some weaker candidates also viewed this paper as a marketing planning paper and inherent in their answers was a focus on showing they knew planning process. These skills are tested at the professional diploma level. In this module it is more important for the candidate to show they have the ability to consider the issues behind key strategic marketing decisions and are able to critically evaluate these issues as a professional manager making strategic marketing decisions.

2. Strengths and Weaknesses by Question

Question 1a

In this question it is important that the candidate focuses on the evaluation of the branding strategy and not evaluate Lego on a general basis. Furthermore it is important to critically evaluate and not just summarise the information in the case study. You need to show the examiner that you understand the strategic implications of the branding strategy to date. It could perhaps be a good idea to identify the characteristics of a successful global brand and then evaluate how far Lego meet the criteria identified in the decisions they have made in the last six years. Your discussion would incorporate an analysis of brand stretching and brand extension strategies, the nature of innovation – breakthrough and incremental change – and an appreciation of marketing to young consumers and how this affects the company's strategic decisions.

To gain higher marks the examiner would expect the candidate to show they have an appreciation of how the changing competitive landscape will influence the branding strategy Lego. It is also important to consider the Jikely future strategies pursued by their competitors as well as the potential implication for Lego of the changing characteristics in consumer behaviour on their branding strategy.

Question 1b

In 1b you will be expected to give specific strategic advice which relates back to the analysis you have given in Q1a. A good idea may be to briefly summarise the key strategic issues facing Lego and recommend to Lego possible global branding strategies they could pursue in the light of the answer to 1a. You need to show the examiner you have the ability to evaluate the branding options open to Lego and the implications these have for the capabilities that Lego need to build if they are to make effective strategic marketing decisions.

In doing this the candidate must appreciate the need for Lego to address changing customer needs, competitive pressures and an appreciation that if Lego has lost focus it needs to address its strategic objectives, re-orientate its branding strategy and reassess its relationships with its customers in terms of their potential life time value. Important aspects will be the basis on which Lego can build its global brand values through relationships, its communications strategy as well as its distribution channels. Remember the question specifically mentions the branding strategy you recommend should help build a global sustainable competitive position. Thus it is important to consider the global dimensions in formulating your answer.

Question 2

In this question you could perhaps start by giving a brief synopsis of the issues facing a company offering professional services to the B2B global market which is characterised by high levels of technical change, market structure changes, customer uncertainty and intense competition. In this question it is important that you contextualise your answers rather than give just a general discussion about strategic marketing decisions in global markets. You then should go onto appraise the nature of the competitive landscape in this market and the requirements of effective decision-making in the global B2B market. Good answers would incorporate an evaluation of perhaps the difficulty of making decision where there is uncertainty in the technological, competitive and customer environments the different competitive strengths the company may have in different markets and the difficulties presented by the variations in the product life cycle of accounting software and the varying infrastructures to support the markets across the globe.

Question 3

In this question it is important to recognise the two parts to the Question (1) differences (2) implications for the marketing strategy and then evaluate the three areas of consideration: organizational form, resource and operations in each part of the question. Do bear in mind the marks allocated to each part and ensure your answer is structured accordingly.

The discussion should include an analysis of the differences in the three areas such as *Organisational form*: Size of firm and business. Number of foreign countries in which it operates and level of involvement organisation's overseas objectives for its foreign business experience in international business value and variety of products, the nature of the marketing task and resources available differences between Export department/subsidiary with headquarters/ subsidiary arrangement (centralisation-decentralisation) and matrix, product or brand.

Differences in resources staff issues, recruitment, training sources of finance physical resources.

Operations may involve a consideration of management of local and global operations partnerships and alliances and the distribution channels marketing development

Question 4

In this you have to show an appreciation of the two forms of strategy development, *The Rational planning approach* is a highly formal linear sequence which requires a high formalised to strategic marketing decisions-making and a mechanical programming approach to its implementation. *The Emergent* school of strategy development on the other hand believes strategies are formed and not necessarily formulated. Strategies are built from a number of little actions and decisions made by different managers in an organisation sometime with little thought to the strategic consequences. Taken together over time these small changes produced a major shift in direction. The question asks you to make a specific decision as to which approach you consider most appropriate so it is important to do so in answering Part b.

Question 5a

The important thing in this question is to make sure you differentiate between the tools for making a short term or long term assessment.

- o The short term financial decision tools you could discuss are such things as CVP analysis, Cost/Volume/Profit analysis, cost benefit analysis, cash flow, break even analysis/pricing analysis.
- o The long term financial decisions tools would include ROI- return on investment, expected return on capital required, NPV-net present value Payback.

It is important in considering the tools to apply your answer to the specific situation identified in the question. Good answers could take the process of new service development and launch and consider the financial criteria that would be needed at each stage to evaluate the proposal. Examples of possible new service areas could be given and you could perhaps highlight some practical financial assessment issues and identify the circumstances that would lead to go/no go decisions.

Question 5b

CVP – service business	£	
Billing Rate per hour	100	
Variable Cost per hour	10	
Fixed Expenses per month	3000	
Wages: Marketing exec	4000	
Support Staff	2000	
Profit Target as % of Fixed expenses	0.5	
Profit Target as a % of Billing rate	0.2	

Q1

Breakeven in hours	Fixed Costs	9000
	Contribution	90
	BE	100

Q2

BE with Fixed Expense profit target	Profit	4500
	Fixed Cost + profit	13500
	BE	150

Q3

BE with Billing rate profit target	Fixed Costs	9000
	Profit	20
	Contribution	70
	BE	128.5714

Q4 – Viability

Work hours 38 × 4 = 152 hours !

To breakeven % of billed hours = 100/152 = 66%

Profit of £4500% of billed hours = 150/152 = 99%

20% profit % billed hours = 129/152 = 85%

May breakeven but perhaps you need to consider the profit targets and whether these are infact achievable.

3. Future Themes

This examination will continue to use a variety of contexts in which the issues and challenges of strategic marketing decision making can be considered. The need to critically evaluate the issues and make strategic marketing recommendations will always be prevalent in the papers. However equally important is to ensure such strategic decisions are financially viable and accountable, thus the financial considerations in strategic marketing decisions will always be an important theme in examination papers.

The Chartered
Institute of Marketing

Professional Postgraduate Diploma in Marketing

Strategic Marketing Decisions

62:      Strategic Marketing Decisions
Time: 14.00 - 17.00
Date: 8 June 2005

3 Hours Duration

This examination is in **TWO** sections.

PART A - Is compulsory and worth **50%** of total marks.

PART B - Has **FOUR** questions; select **TWO**. Each answer will be worth **25%** of the total marks.

DO NOT repeat the question in your answer, but show clearly the number of the question attempted on the appropriate pages of the answer book.

Rough workings should be included in the answer book and ruled through after use.

© The Chartered Institute of Marketing, 2005

Professional Postgraduate
Diploma in Marketing

Strategic Marketing Decisions

PART A

Case Study: Dyson

James Dyson is the sole owner of Dyson, the domestic appliance company that he set up in the UK in 1993 and is the inventor of the high suction vacuum cleaner[1] that revolutionised the vacuum cleaner market by dispensing with the need for a bag to collect dust. He invented the machine in 1978. After five years and 5,127 prototypes he had a working model, but it took a further ten years before it reached the market. The cleaners are also a change from convention in other ways. They have a highly functional, innovative design and incorporate bright colours - blue, yellow and purple alongside grey. The dirt that has been collected is clearly visible and not hidden, so demonstrating the machine's effectiveness. They are priced much higher than the competition, typically around US$350 whereas their main competitors are priced between US$175-200.

Dyson's management style is based on the principles of James Dyson, the owner, and this is also different from many competitors. Dyson bans smoking and ties, has little time for memos and emails, which he considers to be a way of avoiding responsibility. The majority of staff are young, often straight from university. The company emphasises quality throughout and it operates the Dyson Overnight Courier Service (DOCS), which collects cleaners from customers' homes free-of-charge, repairs them and returns them the next day. James Dyson is very much the high profile face of the company, featuring prominently on the website, in comparison to the chief executive, who is not mentioned.

Dyson concentrates on design-led marketing and produces special edition models at a premium price. Somewhat surprisingly the cleaners became a fashion item in the late 1990s. Dyson places a strong emphasis on research and development, and introduced in 2000 a quality washing machine selling for nearly US$1200 compared to an average price of between US$500-600. It is large, equally brightly coloured and again different from other kitchen appliance. Unlike the vacuum cleaner the washing machine is always 'on show' and is not put in a cupboard.

The company grew rapidly during the 1990s reaching over 40% of the vacuum cleaner market by volume in the UK. However, the competitors, such as Hoover, Electrolux of Sweden and Glen Dimplex (the Morphy Richards brand) are fighting back with their own version of the bagless vacuum cleaners and low priced competitors from China and South East Asia, such as LG and Samsung of South Korea and Hitachi are offering products for less than US$150. The influx of cheaper models from China and South East Asia is leading to greater fragmentation in the vacuum cleaner market. Dyson is concerned that the sector in general will risk devaluation from poor quality, cheap products.

In response to this Dyson moved production to Malaysia in order to save 25% on production costs, despite promising never to separate production from research and development. Some critics have suggested that the move, which resulted in

600 manufacturing job losses, has affected their sales in the UK. In 2003 the company was still the UK market leader in vacuum cleaners, but volume had dropped 5 percentage points over the previous year to 15% and value dropped 6 percentage points to 38%. Of its sales of US$ 400 million, only 10% come from washing machines. 35% of sales come from outside the UK. Market research company, GFK, claimed that only 35% of Dyson owners would buy another one compared with 50% five years earlier.

CEO of Dyson, Martin McCourt responded to the criticism by saying the company was still growing in the UK despite Chinese made cylinder cleaners being marketed for less than US$75. He believed these cheap cleaners were being purchased as second or third cleaners in the house and he believed that this had expanded the market by 1 million units. The company was growing fast in 32 countries and in the first year of trading in the US the company had sold 188,400 units from more than 4,000 outlets.

[1] an electrical device that collects dust by means of suction

The above data has been based on a fictitious situation drawing on a variety of events and do not reflect the management practices of any particular organisation.

Section A

Question One
(a) Critically evaluate the long term sustainability of Dyson's global competitive advantage in view changing competitive landscape outlined in the case study.

(25 marks)

(b) In the light of your answer to (Question 1a) advise Dyson on the strategic marketing decisions they should take in order to secure a sustainable global competitive position.

(25 marks)
(Total 50 marks)

Section B

Question Two
It is said that market leaders exhibit the value disciplines of either operational excellence, product leadership or customer intimacy. Using examples, fully evaluate how each of these can be developed to achieve a sustainable competitive advantage. Examine the implications of your assessment for the strategic marketing decisions of the companies you discuss.

(Total 25 marks)

Question Three
Concepta Ltd has been successfully selling contemporary jewellery in several countries through small specialist retailers. However the company is now experiencing slow growth in sales and declining profits and fears their current markets have reached maturity. Advice the managing director on the opportunities for innovation in the marketing process the company can seek to rebuild their competitive advantage.

(Total 25 marks)

Question Four
A supplier of office equipment that currently uses traditional promotion and distribution methods is considering moving to a Web-only strategy to improve efficiency. As a consultant appointed to help the company, make the appropriate decision, explain the advantages and disadvantages of the options the company has and recommend a course of action to them.

(Total 25 marks)

Question Five
Pelican drinks supply a range of soft drinks to supermarkets, vending suppliers and a range of smaller retailers. In search of further growth they are trying to decide whether they should:

(a) Adopt a programme of product development and expand their range of products, or
(b) Consolidate their position with their current products but further develop their sales through new distribution outlets.

(Total 25 marks)

Advise the company on how they should financially appraise the two options.

The Chartered
Institute of Marketing

Moor Hall, Cookham
Maidenhead
Berkshire, SL6 9QH, UK
Telephone: 01628 427120
Facsimile: 01628 427158
Website: http://www.cim.co.uk

The Chartered
Institute of Marketing

Professional Postgraduate Diploma in Marketing

Strategic Marketing Decisions

62:   STRATEGIC MARKETING DECISIONS

SENIOR EXAMINER'S REPORT FOR JUNE 2005 EXAMINATION PAPER

SENIOR EXAMINERS REPORT FOR
JUNE 2005 EXAMINATION PAPER

MODULE NAME: STRATEGIC MARKETING DECISIONS

AWARD NAME: PROFESSIONAL POSTGRADUATE DIPLOMA IN MARKETING

DATE: JULY 2005

1. General Strengths and Weaknesses of Candidates

Strengths

The good candidates in this examination showed evidence of strategic thinking and were able to give answers that were underpinned with some appropriate theory. It is important in this examination for candidates to be able to show they are able to contextualise their thinking and apply the syllabus content and the underlying concepts in a variety of different problem situations where strategic decision making is required. The stronger candidates had clearly been helped to perform in the situation by studying marketing decision problems in many different contexts rather than being simply trained in the mechanics of marketing planning. It was in the ability to apply marketing principles to the various situations presented where there was the more clear differentiation between candidates.

Weaknesses

In the weaker papers the candidates presented very general answers which were not specific to the scenario and so they did not contextualise their answers. There was a tendency in some papers to make a lot of statements as to 'what' strategic decisions need to be made, but generally there was a lack of evaluation of the options and frequently no real consideration of the implications of the decisions made. There was also a lack of the international/global perspective especially in the case study.

A number of answers were very immaturely written, simply presenting bullet point lists and regurgitating the fail safe models eg. Porter's competitive strategy, Ansoff etc where sometimes they were either inappropriate or as was often the case, not applied to the answer. At this level little credit is given for simply presenting models, they have to be used appropriately and applied to the problem being discussed.

Given this is a professional paper there is an expectation that the examination scripts will be presented in a professional manner. In the weaker papers there was a general lack of business language, writing in report style and the third person etc.

2. Strengths and Weaknesses by Question

Question 1a

In this question to gain a good grade you would have to show the examiner that you have a strong appreciation of the changing dimensions of the global market in which Dyson operate. You perhaps could evaluate how the changing competitive landscape has influenced the market position of Dyson, their competitors and the new entrants to the market from China and then critically evaluate Dyson's attempts to sustain their global competitive advantage in light of this. Further discussion could centre on the importance of Value Based Marketing and the characteristics of developing a sustainable competitive advantage throughout the supply chain followed by an evaluation of how far Dyson meet the criteria identified. Some discussion of the nature of innovation breakthrough and incremental change would be good, together with a demonstration of how this can be achieved by Dyson.

Question 1b

It is important in this question to make sure you link your answer directly back to your previous discussion and build on your previous answer. The best way to do this is to briefly summarise the key strategic issues facing Dyson from your discussion in Question 1a and then go onto to outline and critically evaluate the relevant strategic and assess the implications of each for Dyson if they have build the necessary capabilities and make effective strategic marketing decisions. You should then go on to make recommendations as to strategic marketing decisions Dyson should make. Your answer of course should reflect the need for Dyson to address customer needs, competitive pressures and to achieve its own strategic objectives in relation to the development of global competitive positioning. Good answers would demonstrate an understanding of the requirements of building a competitive capability and would consider the potential for Dyson to pursue a strategy that could add value for customers and to shareholders when margins and their innovative lead are both being eroded.

Question 2

If you tackle a question such as this, you need to ensure you can demonstrate an understanding of the three value disciplines and cite examples of companies achieving a competitive advantage following one these disciplines. However your examples must be used in the context of your discussion on the three value disciplines and not merely anecdotal stories without any conceptual underpinning. Thus you need to show the ability to critically evaluate the three value disciplines in the light of the changing basis of competitive advantage in today's markets and show how these disciplines can be applied to varying stages of the market life cycles. The candidate should be able to give best practice examples of sustained commitment over many years to these disciplines as well as innovative approaches. In each area you may want to consider some of the following issues:

Operational excellence:

About efficiency not necessarily about effectiveness. The competitive advantage has to be built on being cheaper, faster and more efficient. However it can only be a basis of obtaining customer preference if it is geared to a strategy which delivers superior value to the customer. The problem for companies is how to sustain such an advantage over time. However there are a number of good examples, for example Dell, Direct Line, easy Jet.

Customer Intimacy:

Can be extremely effective not only in the service sector but in industries that have the capability to build detailed individual profiles on customers through data mining as it allows for a mass customisation strategy and a one-to-one targeted personalised strategy. Good examples are supermarket retailers and online retailers such as Amazon are examples of companies that have such a capability.

Product leadership:

Companies using this either build brand leadership or have to maintain a consistent innovative edge. The problem is how to deliver an extra value proposition, which is valued by the customer in order to sustain product leadership over a period of time. Other problems are concerned with how to maintain a premium price in an era of Internet marketing and price transparency. Grey marketing has led in some markets to the deteriorating perception of the value of some brands.

Question 3

To do well in this question you need to explain how opportunities for marketing innovation occur at each point in the marketing strategy development process and make relevant applications to the context set in the question. It is important you do not simply identify the points in the process but also give an indication of the criteria that would determine their success. In doing this, you will need to:

- o Discuss the different levels of innovation, *incremental* and *radical* and evaluate how each may be used in the context given.
- o Evaluate the need for the company to build the capability to achieve both radical and continuous incremental marketing innovations.
- o The various ways in which the company can seek to develop breakthrough ideas based on new technology such as Internet marketing or other major innovations, such as a new route to market that will offer a quantum leap in customer value.
- o The implication of the company being in the mature phase of the life cycle and the importance of such things as customer service enhancement and the importance of building exceptional customer value and loyalty.

Question 4

In questions such as this you need to follow the instructions in the question. Thus you need to discuss the advantages and disadvantages of moving to a Web-based strategy and make specific recommendations. Your discussion should involve such advantages as low transaction and administration costs targeted and more responsive marketing to a wider audience based on a database together with an explanation of the benefits and use of Internet advertising.

Some disadvantages would include such things as high set up costs fulfilment of customer needs is still needed, payment and Internet security issues.

You might also discuss alternative traditional promotions that perhaps could be considered in terms of the effectiveness and added value to customers and the organisation.

Question 5

In order to answer this question, you will need to show knowledge of the financial criteria used to assess the options. Criteria could incorporate such factors as initial investment required, continuing investment required over a period of time discounted cash flow projections long term profitability expectations cost/volume/profit analysis and so on. You would then have to show how Pelican Drinks could review each option in line with the objectives they are hoping to achieve.

One way Pelican could evaluate the options would be to establish a ratings scale set against the particular objectives the company hope the two options will achieve and then rate them financial criteria specified. You then might discuss, however, how in using a rating scale both options may well score relatively low in terms of the initial investment required but option 'a' may be viewed as scoring higher on profitability expectations. However the company would need to ask if option 'a' can be supported by the cash flow throughout the period it will be required to do so.

3. Future Themes

In order to gain good grades in the Strategic Marketing Decisions paper it is important for tutors and candidates to not simply focus on the knowledge, content and concepts of the syllabus but to add depth to the decision making skills of candidates, increase the level of their thinking in different problem situations, and to learn how to challenge assumptions and so create solutions to problems in a complex competitive environment. SMD is about how to make decisions in a changing competitive environment, it is not about how to go through the marketing planning process and so it is important that tutors therefore prepare candidates for the complexities of this paper by dealing with the strategic issues facing companies today. For instance; how are customers and competitors and environment changing and what can the firm do about it. How can a firm second guess what competitors will do, how can firms respond? How do firms deal with marketing problems; e.g. how should they counter commoditization, deal with price transparency, integrate communications, work the value chain and decide where they can contribute value best. If you are a small firm, what can you do to stand out (with limited resources), how do you compete against the giants. If you are a large firm how can you become more responsive?

In articulating the future themes in this paper perhaps in conclusion it is important to say that the paper will invariably be problem based and the candidates that perform well will be those that can contextualize their thinking, identify the key issues in a complex problem scenario, critically evaluate strategic options and make strategic marketing decisions in a multi-dimensional competitive environment.

appendix 5

curriculum information and reading list

Aim

The Strategic Marketing Decisions module covers the second part of strategic marketing in a global context by building on the skills and knowledge gained from the study of the Analysis and Evaluation module. The focus of this module is on the nature of competitive strategy in a global context. It examines how, in such a dynamic environment, competitive advantage might be developed through strongly differentiated positioning and exploited in a cost-effective manner. Its emphasis is on where and how the organization competes and, in doing this, highlights the strategic marketing significance of brands, innovation, alliances and relationships and e-marketing. An important theme running through the module is the development of the capability to develop innovative solutions that enhance an organization's competitive position in its chosen markets.

Related statements of practice

Bd.1   Promote a strong market orientation and influence/contribute to strategy formulation and investment decisions.
Bd.2   Specify and direct the strategic marketing planning process.
Cd.1   Promote organization-wide innovation and cooperation in the development of brands.
Dd.1   Develop and direct an integrated marketing communications strategy.
Ed.1   Promote corporate-wide innovation and cooperation in the development of products and services.
Fd.1   Promote the strategic and creative use of pricing.
Gd.1   Select and monitor channel criteria to meet the organization's needs in a changing environment.

Learning outcomes

Participants will be able to:

- Appraise a range of corporate and business visions, missions and objectives and the processes by which they are formulated, in light of the changing bases of competitive advantage across geographically diverse markets.
- Identify, compare and contrast strategic options and critically evaluate the implications of strategic marketing decisions in relation to the concept of 'shareholder value'.

295

- o Evaluate the role of brands, innovation, integrated marketing communications, alliances, customer relationships and service in decisions for developing a differentiated positioning to create exceptional value for the customer.
- o Demonstrate the ability to develop innovative and creative marketing solutions to enhance an organization's global competitive position in the context of changing product, market, and brand and customer life cycles.
- o Define and contribute to investment decisions concerning the marketing assets of an organization.
- o Demonstrate the ability to re-orientate the formulation and control of cost-effective competitive strategies, appropriate for the objectives and context of an organization operating in a dynamic global environment.

Knowledge and skill requirements

Element 1: The changing dimensions of competitive advantage (10 per cent)

1.1 Examine the role of life cycles in strategic decisions to manage competitive advantage across global, international and domestic markets.

1.2 Examine the influence of market position on strategy and performance.

1.3 Critically appraise the changing dimensions of strategic decisions made to sustain competitive advantage in today's global markets.

1.4 Assess how product/market/brand/customer life cycles can be managed strategically across markets.

1.5 Examine the role of competitive relationships and how organizations compete to achieve customer preference.

1.6 Apply the concepts of project management to limited-life products and technologies.

Element 2: Challenging traditional strategic thinking: innovation and the re-orientation and reformulation of competitive marketing strategies (25 per cent)

2.1 Examine the significance and application of new marketing thinking to strategic decisions.

2.2 Explain the nature of innovation in marketing and the factors affecting its development in decisions to create competitive advantage and customer preference.

2.3 Evaluate the role of innovation management and risk-taking in achieving competitive advantage.

2.4 Examine the issues in creating an innovative marketing culture within an organization.

2.5 Determine drivers for realignment in strategic thinking.

2.6 Explore the alternative approaches to strategic marketing decisions (e.g. formal/analytical approach v transformation approaches).

2.7 Explore competitive marketing strategy as an emergent/learning process.

2.8 Examine the role of knowledge management in sustaining competitive advantage.

2.9 Evaluate the incorporation of customer-led Internet marketing into marketing strategies.

2.10 Examine issues in strategic marketing decision-making in SMEs.

Element 3: Strategic marketing decisions for the global marketplace (25 per cent)

3.1   Examine the issues of decisions to build competitive capability and approaches to leveraging capability to create advantage across geographically diverse markets.

3.2   Evaluate Porter's three generic strategies in the context of today's competitive environment.

3.3   Critically appraise strategic marketing decisions for pioneers, challengers, followers and niche players.

3.4   Identify and critically evaluate strategic options in relation to shareholder value, using appropriate decision tools.

3.5   Describe the formulation and evaluation of competitive strategies.

3.6   Determine the lessons of best practice from strategic decisions made by successful global companies.

3.7   Evaluate the use of e-technology to build and exploit competitive advantage.

3.8   Critically appraise innovative marketing strategies in small and large companies operating on global markets.

3.9   Appreciate the value of effective knowledge management in creating competitive advantage.

3.10   Leverage individual and corporate learning across geographically diverse markets for competitive advantage.

Element 4: Strategic marketing decisions in the management of the portfolio (25 per cent)

4.1   Explain and evaluate the contribution of value-based marketing.

4.2   Assess the nature and dimensions of branding/brand decisions, their role in the development of advantage and their significance in global markets.

4.3   Examine product strategies and the role of new product development in competitive strategy.

4.4   Evaluate the role of integrated marketing communications in competitive global strategy.

4.5   Understand the concept of relationship marketing and the role of long-term customer relationships in creating and delivering value.

4.6   Determine the importance of managing marketing relationships in generating customer commitment.

4.7   Examine the role of alliances and the creation of competitive advantage through supply-chain development and marketing partnerships.

4.8   Examine how pricing policies and strategies can be used to build competitive advantage.

4.9   Explain the strategic management of the global portfolio and the expanded marketing mix.

4.10   Assess the issues of corporate and social responsibility (CSR), sustainability and ethics in achieving competitive advantage, enhancing corporate reputation and creating stakeholder value.

Element 5: Investment decisions and control (15 per cent)

5.1   Examine the implications of strategic marketing decisions for implementation and control.

5.2   Explain the concept of, and evaluate methods such as Balanced Scorecard for, stakeholder value measurement.

5.3   Apply investment appraisal techniques to marketing investment decisions.

5.4 Examine alternative approaches to modelling potential investment decisions in the deployment of marketing resources.

5.5 Define performance measurement systems for the deployment of marketing assets and the implementation of marketing plans.

5.6 Define budgetary and planning control techniques for use in the control of marketing plans and explain the pitfalls of control systems and how they may be overcome.

Assessment

CIM will offer a single form of assessment based on the learning outcomes for this module. It will take the form of an invigilated, time-constrained assessment throughout the delivery network. Candidates' assessments will be marked centrally by CIM.

Recommended support materials

Core texts

Doole, I. and Lowe, R. (2005) *Strategic Marketing Decisions in Global Markets*, London, Thomson Learning.

McDonald, M., Smith, B. and Ward, K. (2005) *Marketing Due Diligence*, Oxford, Butterworth-Heinemann/Elsevier.

Syllabus guides/Workbooks

Doole, I. and Lowe, R. (2005) *Strategic Marketing Decisions*, Oxford, Butterworth-Heinemann/Elsevier.

BPP (2005) *Strategic Marketing Decisions*, London, BPP Publishing.

Supplementary readings

BH (2006) *CIM Revision Cards: Strategic Marketing Decisions*, Oxford, Butterworth-Heinemann/Elsevier.

BPP (2006) *Strategic Marketing Decisions: Practice and Revision Kit*, London, BPP Publishing.

Collier, P.M. (2003) *Accounting for Managers: Interpreting Accounting Information for Decision-making*, Chichester, John Wiley & Sons.

De Wit, B. and Meyer, R. (2004) *Strategy: Process, Contents, Context*, London, Thomson.

Doole, I. and Lowe, R. (2004) *International Marketing Strategy: Analysis, Development and Implementation*, 4th edition, London, Thomson Learning.

Fill, C. (2005) *Marketing Communications: Contexts, Strategies and Applications*, 4th edition, Harlow, Pearson.

Gilligan, C. and Wilson, R. (2004) *Strategic Marketing Management: Planning, Implementation and Control*, 3rd edition, Butterworth-Heinemann.

Johnson, G. and Scholes, K. (2004) *Exploring Corporate Strategy: Text and Cases*, 7th edition, Harlow, Prentice Hall.

Kapferer, J.-N. (2004) *The New Strategic Brand Management*, London, Kogan Page.

Lee, K. and Carter, S. (2005) *Global Marketing Management*, Oxford, Oxford University Press.

Mintzberg, H. and Quinn, J.B. (2003) *The Strategy Process*, 4th global edition, Harlow, Prentice Hall.

Walker, O.C., Harper, B.B. and Mullins, J. (2005) *Marketing Strategy: A Decision Focused Approach*, 5th edition, Maidenhead, McGraw-Hill.

Overview and rationale

The development of strategies that build upon and leverage an organization's competitive position globally is fundamental to strategic marketing decisions made in organizations. However, in a fast changing and dynamic environment, senior marketing managers need not only the ability to develop problem solving strategies but also the mindset that enables them to reinvent periodically the basis on which an organization can compete. The challenges of doing this across a spectrum of fast moving, geographically and culturally varied markets in an effective manner represent a significant intellectual challenge and requires the development and refinement of decision-making skills.

This module builds on the Marketing Planning module at Professional Diploma in Marketing and the Analysis and Evaluation module. It introduces the knowledge and skills needed by aspiring senior marketing managers if they are to contribute to the strategic marketing decisions to build a sustainable competitive advantage. It places strong emphasis on developing the insights needed to rethink and re-orientate the marketing direction of an organization at a strategic level and therefore provides a valuable foundation for both the Managing Marketing Performance module and the final module, Strategic Marketing in Practice.

Approach

This module provides the knowledge and skills for the contributing to strategic marketing decisions in the formulation of a competitive strategy. The end point of the module is a set of strategic decisions for the organization that may be built into a corporate or business plan. This is taken forward into implementation in the Managing Marketing Performance module. It incorporates the relevant knowledge and understanding of strategic decisions within domestic, international and global contexts. The knowledge and skills acquired are applied in the Strategic Marketing in Practice module.

This module focuses on the decisions needed to develop a more innovative approach to the strategic development of the organization that will build competitive advantage by creating added value for customers and other stakeholders. In doing this it is necessary for participants to study in an integrated way the complete strategic decision process to identify new marketing opportunities, areas for innovation and value creation in an organization. They will need to learn the lessons of good practice of other organizations from different contexts from their own. Participants will have the opportunity to build concentrated experience that comes from studying the management of a series of critical incidents and emerging trends that have led to leading edge developments in marketing.

Finally, the module recognizes that there is no 'right' strategic marketing decision for an organization. It encourages participants to explore and propose approaches that require the re-evaluation and re-formulation of the strategies of organizations to survive and grow in today's global competitive environment.

Syllabus content

Element 1: The changing dimensions of competitive advantage (10 per cent)

This element develops an understanding of the dynamics of the changing dimensions of competitive advantage and how, in order to sustain competitiveness, organizations must make strategic marketing decisions effectively to manage brand, product and market life cycles across fragmented and complex global markets. It then goes on to examine the role of competitive relationships and how organizations compete globally. The influence of an organization's market position is also explored in the formation of these alliances and relationships as well as the possible implications on their strategic positioning and performance.

Element 2: Challenging traditional strategic thinking: innovation and the re-orientation and re-formulation of competitive marketing strategies (25 per cent)

This is a key element to this module in that it provides an understanding of how senior managers, in making successful strategic marketing decisions, need continuously to reflect and challenge the assumptions on which previous strategies have been built, both in their own organizations and elsewhere. Central to this element is the examination and application of new marketing thinking. In doing this, the element explores the alternative approaches to strategic decisions (e.g. formal/analytical approach v transformation approaches) and develops the knowledge and skills managers need to determine drivers for realignment in strategic thinking. The element then goes on to evaluate the role of innovation management and risk-taking in organizations in achieving competitive advantage and what organizations need to do to create an innovative marketing culture. The conclusion of this element examines the innovative strategy making process as an emergent learning process and how organizations can encourage such a process within their organizations.

Element 3: Strategic marketing decisions for the global marketplace (25 per cent)

This element aims to provide an understanding of the concepts that underpin strategic marketing decisions for the global marketplace. It addresses the factors that determine which strategic options firms might decide on to make an appropriate response to their competitive situation, whilst at the same time creating customer and stakeholder value. In doing so it examines the issues of competitive capability and decision approaches that can be used to leverage capability and create advantage. The element then goes on to examine different patterns of development and different ways of building relationships in the supply chain as well as giving consideration to the use of more innovative approaches to the development of competitive strategies that will be successful in the future. As such the leveraging of individual and organizational learning, knowledge management and the use of e-technology to exploit competitive advantage should be discussed.

Element 4: Strategic marketing decisions in the management of the portfolio (25 per cent)

This element encourages participants to consider the practical application of the competitive strategy by addressing the management of the elements of the global portfolio of products and services. In doing this, strategic decisions are explored for branding, communications, pricing and distribution, which are both innovative and integrated. The challenge is to add value and remove costs within the firm and from the supply-chain, and there are a number of enabling technologies that support this goal. The role of integrated marketing communications in a competitive strategy, the concept of relationship marketing and its role in the creation of global competitive advantage through supply-chain development are all explored.

Element 5: Investment decisions and control (15 per cent)

The final element develops the structure for the evaluation and appraisal of the strategic options. Techniques are discussed for making decisions on investment to support new strategies and the risks involved. Assessment of the increase in stakeholder value and cost reduction of the new strategies key performance indicators that will indicate future success are examined. The application of capital investment appraisal techniques to marketing investment decisions and the use of performance measurement systems in relation to the deployment of marketing-based assets and the implementation of marketing plans are central to this element as well as the use of budgetary and planning control techniques in the control of marketing plans.

Delivery approach

Tutors will need to demonstrate the lessons of good practice of organizations from different sector contexts. Case study drawn from successful global companies as well as small organizations lends themselves to this task.

Additional resources (Syllabus – Stage 3)

Introduction

Texts to support the individual modules are listed in the syllabus for each module. This Appendix shows a list of marketing journals, press and websites that tutors and participants may find useful in supporting their studies at Professional Postgraduate Diploma in Marketing.

Note: These resources are yet to be confirmed.

Marketing journals

Participants can keep abreast of developments in the academic field of marketing by reference to the main marketing journals.

- *Corporate Reputation Review* – Henry Stewart
- *European Journal of Marketing* – Emerald
- *Harvard Business Review* – Harvard
- *International Journal of Advertising* – WARC
- *International Journal of Consumer Behaviour* – Henry Stewart
- *International Journal of Corporate Communications* – Emerald
- *International Journal of Market Research* – WARC
- *Journal of the Academy of Marketing Science* – Sage Publications
- *Journal of Marketing* – American Marketing Assoc. Pubs Group
- *Journal of Marketing Communications* – Routledge
- *Journal of Marketing Management* – Westburn Pubs Ltd.
- *Journal of Market Research Society* – NTC Pubs
- *Journal of Product and Brand Management* – Emerald
- *Journal of Services Marketing* – Emerald
- *Marketing Review* – Westburn Pubs Ltd.

Press

Participants will be expected to have access to current examples of marketing campaigns and so should be sure to keep up to date with the appropriate marketing and quality daily press, including:

- *Campaign* – Haymarket
- *Internet Business* – Haymarket
- *Marketing* – Haymarket
- *Marketing Business* – Chartered Institute of Marketing
- *Marketing Week* – Centaur
- *Revolution* – Haymarket.

Websites

The Chartered Institute of Marketing

www.cim.co.uk	The CIM site with information and access to learning support for participants
www.connectedinmarketing.com	A CIM site providing information on current marketing issues and applications
www.cim.co.uk/learning zone	Website for CIM students and tutors containing study information, past exam papers and case study examples. Also, access to 'the marketer' articles online.
www.cimeducator.com	The CIM site for tutors only

Publications online

www.revolution.haynet.com	*Revolution* magazine
www.brandrepublic.com	*Marketing* magazine
www.FT.com	A wealth of information for cases (now charging)
www.IPA.co.uk	Need to register – communication resources
www.booksites.net	*Financial Times*/Prentice Hall Text websites

Sources of useful information

www.acnielsen.co.uk	AC Nielsen – excellent for research
http://advertising.utexas.edu/world/	Resources for advertising and marketing professionals, participants and tutors
www.bized.com	Case studies
www.esomar.nl	European Body representing Research organizations – useful for guidelines on research ethics and approaches
www.dma.org.uk	The Direct Marketing Association
www.eiu.com	The Economist Intelligence Unit
www.euromonitor.com	Euromonitor consumer markets
www.europa.eu.int	The European Commission extensive range of statistics and reports relating to EU and member countries.
www.managementhelp.org/research/research.htm	Part of the 'Free Management Library' – explaining research methods
www.marketresearch.org.uk	The MRS site with information and access to learning support for participants – useful links on ethics and code of conduct

www.oecd.org	OECD statistics and other information relating to member nations including main economic indicators
www.quirks.com	An American source of information on marketing research issues and projects
www.un.org	United Nations publish statistics on member nations
www.worldbank.org	World bank economic, social and natural resource indicators for over 200 countries. Includes over 600 indicators covering GNP per capita, growth, economic statistics, and so on.

Case sites

www.bluelagoon.co.uk	Case – SME website address
www.ebay.com	Online auction – buyer behaviour
www.glenfiddich.com	Interesting site for case and branding
www.interflora.co.uk	e-commerce direct ordering
www.moorcroft.co.uk	Good for relationship marketing
www.ribena.co.uk	Excellent targeting and history of comms

Index